Judi Strauss'
Big Red Cookbook

Judi Strauss'
Big Red Cookbook
by Judi Strauss

The Charmed Kitchen
http://www.TheCharmedKitchen.com

All Rights Reserved.

ISBN 9781626132382
LCCN 2020943698

Copyright 2020

Published by ATBOSH Media ltd.

Cleveland, Ohio, USA
http://www.ATBOSH.com

Introduction   24

Chapter 1:   27
Appetizers
- The Big Cheese
- Cheese and Bread Ladder
- Cheese Tower
- Cheese Carrot and Parsnips
- Cheese Kebobs
- Chunky Cheese
- Cheese Balls and Beyond
- Brie Bundle
- Olive Spread (Tapenade)
- Easy Pâté
- Zakooskas
- Fondue Bread
- Quick Herb Spread
- Lola's Smoky Crescent Rolls
- Herbed Nuts
- Brie with Pesto and Sun-Dried Tomatoes
- Sweet Potato Chips
- Rueben Dip
- Prosciutto Wraps
- Appetizer Cheesecake
- Salmon Ball
- Seafood Appetizer Cheesecake
- Crab Mousse
- Mini Turkey Burgers
- Aunt Marcie's Taco Dip
- Ginger Drums
- Pastrami Bites
- Peppered Pecans
- Squash Dip
- Fast and Easy
- Zucchini Bites
- Holiday Ham Balls
- Spinach Puffs
- Italian Sausage Snacks
- Mushroom Appetizer

- Almond Pinecones
- Island Meatballs
- Guacamole
- Bean Dip
- Flat Bread
- Caviar Berries
- Caviar Stars
- Caviar on Celery
- Classic Caviar Presentation
- Herbed Fried Pasta
- Bruschetta
- Marinated Vegetables

Chapter 2: 58
Sunday Brunch

- Basic Brunch Dishes
- Brunch Egg Casserole
- Sausage and Onion Quiche
- Stewed Tomatoes
- Crepes
- Green Herb Crepes
- Dessert Crepes
- Chocolate Crepes
- Salmon and Sour Cream Crepes
- Taco Crepes
- Seafood Crepes
- Purple Passion Crepes
- Strawberry Crepes
- Crepes Suzette
- Chocolate Crepes
- Breakfast Pizza
- Herbed Cream Cheese Spread
- English Muffin Bran Bread
- Orange Upside Down Biscuits
- Overnight Coffee Cake
- Praline Biscuits
- Scotch Eggs
- Pepper Puffed Eggs
- Brunch Scrambled Eggs

- Stuffed French Toast
- Mimosa
- Kirsten's Overnight French Toast
- Easy Danish
- Salad Bowl Puff
- Ham Salad Filling
- Chicken Waldorf Salad Filling
- Swiss and Bacon Squares
- Chili-Cheese Rounds
- Apples with Bacon

Chapter 3:   79
Tea Time
Celebrating Tea and Tea Parties

- A Brief History of Tea
- Brewing a Proper Cup of Tea
- Is it Tea?
- Section 1: The Savory
- Minted Cucumber Sandwiches
- Curried Egg Sandwiches
- Cheshire Cheese Tart
- Cheese Plate
- English Garden Salad
- Cheddar Walnut Tea Sandwiches
- Smoked Turkey Finger Sandwiches
- Pepper Tea Sandwiches
- Chicken Salad Sandwiches
- Deviled Ham Toasts
- Blueberry Chef Salad
- Section 2: The Sweet
- Mrs. Pettigrew's Lemon Tea Bread
- Scones
- Mock Clotted Cream
- Angel Shortcakes
- Strawberries in Raspberry Sauce
- Crumpets
- Sherried Ladyfinger Toasts
- Strawberry Cheese
- Jam Stacks

- Cranberry-Buttermilk Scones
- Pineapple Spice Scones
- Raisin Scones
- Blueberry Scones
- Cream Scones
- Almond Poppy Seed Scones
- Oatmeal Scones
- Cinnamon Scones
- Fruitful Oat Scones
- Section 3: Take You Child to Tea
- Peachy Shake
- "Peanutty" Patties
- Gorp
- Cheese on a Stick
- Raspberry Punch
- Sparkling Fruit Juice
- Whole Wheat Roll-ups
- Ants on a Log
- Honey Bears
- Blossom Punch
- Fruit Kabobs
- Munchkins
- Peter Cotton Tails
- Tiger Paws
- Pretzel Cabins

Chapter 4:   113
My Mother's Polish Kitchen

- Busha's Coffeecake
- Spinach and Sorrel Roulade
- Creamed Herring
- Creamed Spinach
- Aunt Tillie's Crock Pickles
- Duck Soup / Czarnina
- Sorrel Soup
- Polish Mushroom Soup
- Oxtail Soup
- Split Pea Soup
- Sweet and Sour Cabbage

- Jellied Pigs' Feet
- Red Cabbage Salad
- Pierogi
- Lazy Day Pierogi
- Polish Sausage/Kielbasa
- Angel Wings
- Potato Pancakes
- Goldenrod
- Stuffed Cabbage
- Stuffed Peppers
- Noodles and Eggs
- Pork Chops Florentine
- Kolachky
- Beet Soup
- Iced Mazurek
- Zakooskas
- Spaetzels
- Polish Butter Cookies

Chapter 5: Cooking With Tortillas   140

- Wraps
- Cinnamon Crisps
- Turkey and Swiss Wrap
- Pizza Rolls
- Grilled Vegetable Wraps
- Tortilla Spring Rolls
- Layered Enchilada Casserole
- Mini Texas Style Burritos
- Asian Burritos
- Vegetable Tortilla Lasagna
- Mexican Pizza
- Nutty Olive Quesadillas
- Tortilla Blintzes
- Tortillas with Eggs
- Vegetable Quesadillas
- Corn and Bean Wraps
- Bean and Cheese Quesadillas
- Flour Tortillas

- Chimichangas
- Chicken and Cheese Enchiladas
- Bean Enchiladas
- Tuna Roll Ups
- Brunch Enchiladas

Chapter 6: 159
Chicken
Fun and Easy Recipes

- Chicken Facts and Figures
- Q's and A's about Chicken
- Chicken Breasts in Hot Tomato Vinaigrette
- Southwest Chicken
- Baked Chicken Salad
- Chicken Sate
- Szechwan Chicken
- Chicken Florentine
- Chicken Cordon Bleu Stir Fry
- Chicken Diane
- Lemon Chicken
- Creamy Oven Baked Chicken
- Pacific Rim Stir Fry
- Minnesota Wild Rice Stuffed Chicken
- Easy Chicken Marinade
- Northwestern Chicken Salad
- Country Captain
- Chicken Cacciatore
- Sweet and Sour Chicken
- Chicken Marsala
- Sesame Chicken Salad
- Crispy Chicken Bites
- Buffalo Wings
- Chicken Salad California
- Chicken Marengo
- Chicken Curry
- Chicken with Mangoes
- Luxury Baked Chicken
- Orange Rosemary Chicken

Chapter 7:   188
Seafood Made Easy
- Preparing Fish
- Creole Seafood Seasoning
- Parchment Fish
- Smelts
- Creole Jambalaya
- Fish Chowder
- Salmon Bake with Pecan Crunch Coating
- Salmon Quiche
- Linguine with Clam Sauce
- Surimi Salad
- Stuffed Baked Bass
- Paella Salad
- Fish Parmesan
- Flounder Florentine
- Maryland Clams Casino
- Greek Seafood Salad
- Asian Steamed Tuna with Vegetables
- Mussels in White Wine
- Lime Garlic Broiled Shrimp
- Surimi with Melon
- Basic Seafood Seasoning
- Crab Cakes
- Shrimp and Asparagus Pizza
- Cooking Scallops
- Scallop Stir-Fry
- Crab Puffs

Chapter 8:   213
Saucy Sauces
- Sweet and Sour Sauce
- Plum Dipping Sauce
- Cranberry Barbecue Sauce
- Chicken Sauces
- Orange Barbecue Sauce
- Cherry Dipping Sauce
- Raspberry Sauce
- Rhubarb Glaze

- Cranberry Mayo
- Mango Chutney
- British Mint Sauce
- Vidalia Onion Relish
- Sweet and Sour Peach Salsa
- Cilantro Sauce
- Easy Cranberry Glaze
- Easy Barbecue Sauce
- Sofrito
- Chili Con Queso
- Mango Salsa
- Herb Dipping Sauce
- Dill Gravy
- Green Sauce
- Onion Relish
- Tomato Chutney
- India Sauce
- Dill Marinade
- Salsa Verde
- Salsa
- Favorite Barbecue Sauce
- Seafood Marinade
- Meat Marinade
- Marinade for Lamb or Pork
- Basic White Sauce (Béchamel)

Chapter 9:   241
Pasta Sauces

- Broccoli Pesto
- Creamy Tomato Sauce with Cheese
- Walnut Cheese Sauce
- Orange Beef Sauce
- Spinach Sauce
- Carrot Sauce
- Pesto Sauce
- Parsley Pesto
- Ratatouille Sauce
- Chicken Cacciatore Sauce
- Asian Pasta Sauce

- Red Wine Sauce with Chicken
- White Clam Sauce
- Marinara Sauce
- Mushroom and Tomato Sauce
- Zucchini, Tomato and Basil Sauce
- Sun-Dried Tomato Pesto
- Chick Pea and Rosemary
- Herbed Fish Sauce
- Indonesian Peanut Sauce
- Almost Alfredo Sauce
- Mushroom Sauce
- Ethiopian Vegetable Sauce
- Artichoke Sauce
- Fresh Tomato Sauce
- Beef and Mushroom Sauce

Chapter 10: 261
One Pot Meals
- Cooking in a Crock Pot
- Easy Rice Casserole
- Chicken and Asparagus Casserole
- Sage and Rosemary Pork Stew
- New England Corn Chowder
- Boston Boiled Dinner
- Ham with Fruit Chutney
- Joe's Special
- Ham and Cheese Strata
- Chicken and Dumplings
- Ethiopian Chicken
- Tuna Noodle Combo
- Tortilla Soup
- Parmesan Chicken
- Whole Wheat Baking Mix
- Garden Skillet
- Slow Cooker Stew
- Brown Rice Casserole
- Beef Stew Milanese
- Hearty Cassoulet
- Versatile Vegetable Soup

- Turkey and Wild Rice Casserole
- Skillet Pork and Rice
- Cheesy Italian Tortellini
- Spring Vegetable Stew with Pesto
- Fiesta Chicken Chili
- Cream of Wild Rice Soup
- Two Grain Vegetable Casserole
- Quick Veggie Chill with Cheese
- Barley and Cheese Strata
- Crab Potage
- Lentil and Barley Soup

Chapter 11: Vegetarian Cooking   290

- Definitions
- Protein Pairing
- How much do I need to eat to get enough protein?
- Basic Bean Burgers
- Mexican Bean Dip
- Mexican Bean Salad
- Chili Bean Spoon Bread
- Hummus
- Black-eyed Pea Salad
- Almond Tabbouleh
- Spinach Lasagna
- Eggplant Parmesan
- Curried Black Bean Soup
- Easy Frittata
- Quinoa with Mushrooms
- Basque Soup
- Vegetarian Tacos
- Pecan Cheese Balls
- Scrambled Egg Casserole

Chapter 12:   310
Great Grains

- Grain Terminology
- Types of Grains
- Basic Quinoa
- Quinoa Vegetable Soup
- Storing Grains
- Quinoa Pilaf
- Quinoa and Garbanzo Salad
- Quinoa and Chicken Salad
- Quinoa Paella
- Wild Rice Salad with Basil and Tomatoes
- California Stir Fry
- Three Rice Stir Fry
- Red Beans with Rice
- Italian Rice
- Cream of Rice
- Dirty Rice
- Brown Rice Salad with Mint
- Spanish Rice
- Tropical Rice Salad
- Barley with Zucchini and Peanuts
- Fried Rice
- Rice Stuffed Peppers
- Kasha Pilaf
- Tabbouleh
- Whole Grain Vegetable Pilaf
- Amaranth Date Nut Bread
- Mandarin Millet
- Amaranth Hot Cereal
- Three Grain Salad with Pesto Vinaigrette
- Super Salad
- Granola
- Wheat Berry Salad
- Couscous Salad
- Couscous Salad with Shrimp and Dill
- Herbed Couscous with Vegetables
- Barleycorn Salad
- Venetian Cornmeal Cookies

Chapter 13: 343
It's Soy Wonderful
Cooking with Soy and Soy Products

- Soy Products
- Some easy ways to get more soy in your diet
- Using Tofu
- Soy "No Milk" Shake
- Soy Orange Smoothie
- Berry Good Tofu Smoothie
- Soy Tortoni
- Stir-Fried Vegetables with Tofu
- Hot and Sour Soup
- Types of Tofu
- Nutty Coleslaw Spring Rolls
- Soy Chili
- Easy Tofu Dip
- Tofu Italiano
- Squash and Tofu Balls
- Tempeh Stir Fry
- Miso Soup
- Miso Vinaigrette
- Lentil and Tofu Soup
- Rice and Tofu Salad
- Fried Tofu Bites
- Orange Oat Muffins
- Portobello Mushroom Pizza
- Soybean and Cabbage Salad
- Sweet and Sour Tofu
- Easy Vegetarian Lasagna
- Szechwan Spicy Tofu

Chapter 14: 370
Soup's On

- Homemade Soup Stock
- Stock Options
- Mock Wonton Soup
- Acorn Squash Soup
- Broccoli Soup
- Cream of Chicken Soup

- Crab Bisque
- Leftover Turkey Soup
- Sweet Potato and Leek Soup
- Zucchini Soup
- White Gazpacho
- Easy Corn and Chicken Chowder
- Avocado Soup
- Bean and Barley Soup
- Pumpkin Soup
- Hot and Sour Soup
- Aunt Josie's Clam Chowder
- Yellow Split Pea Soup
- Aunt Josie's Cabbage Soup
- Turkey Soup with Herbs
- Tomato Bisque Soup
- Rita's Vegetable Soup

Chapter 15: 388
Totally Terrific Tomatoes
Cooking & Canning Tomatoes

- Tomato Relish
- Stuffed Tomatoes
- Cream of Fresh Tomato Soup
- Chicken Tomato Sauce
- Ratatouille
- Chopped Arabic Salad
- Tomato and Herb Dressing
- Cornbread Salad
- Vegetables in Lemon-Herb Dressing
- Marinated Tomato Salad
- Tomato Baby Bites
- Italian Bread Salad
- Pizza Zucchini
- Warm Pasta Salad
- Caponata
- Greek Salad
- Zucchini and Tomato Casserole
- Canning Basics
- Green Tomato Sweet Pickles

- Acidity and Tomatoes
- Tomato Sauce
- Freezer Tomato Catsup
- Salsa
- Freezing Tomatoes

Chapter 16: 411
Awash in Squash
Cooking with Summer & Winter Squash

- About Squash
- Zucchini Bake
- Fried Squash Blossoms
- Summer Squash Strata
- Zucchini Bread
- Zucchini Carrot Cake
- Quick Corn and Zucchini Sauté
- Zucchini Potato Pancakes
- Easy Zucchini Pie
- Baked Zucchini with Mushrooms
- Fresh Summer Squash Relish
- Vegetable Pizza
- Zucchini Drop Cookies
- Orange Zucchini Cake
- Multi-Grain Squash Bread
- Pumpkin Chiffon
- Zucchini Wraps
- Curried Pumpkin Soup
- Pumpkin Crunch
- Pumpkin Bread
- Pumpkin Squares
- Cooking Winter Squash
- Pizza Butternut Squash Sauté
- Pumpkin Cheesecake
- Pumpkin Roll
- Chocolate Zucchini Cake
- Zucchini Rice Casserole

Chapter 17:   435
Cooking With Apples & Pears
- Cooking With Apples and Pears
- Helpful Hints
- Autumn Chicken Salad
- Apple and Cheese Salad
- Ham and Apple Salad
- Spirited Applesauce
- Pear Sauce
- Pork with Pear Sauce
- Open-Faced Turkey and Apple Sandwiches
- Cider Rice Pilaf
- Smoked Turkey and Pear Salad
- "Pearadise" Pork Tenderloin
- Beef in Cider Sauce
- Apple Crumb Cake
- Classic Apple Cake
- Apple Oatcakes
- Easy Fruit Cobbler
- Easy Apple Granola Bake
- Autumn Sweet and Sour Cabbage
- No-Bake Apple Cranberry Relish
- Waldorf Pita Sandwiches
- Oat Bran Apple Muffins
- Pear Oatmeal Muffins

Chapter 18:   456
Bread Baking
- Choosing Yeast
- Butter Coffeecake Braids
- Whole Wheat Bread
- Challah
- Judi's Herb Braids
- The Upper Crust
- Rich Squash Rolls
- Pumpernickel Bread
- Rueben Loaf
- Philadelphia Sticky Buns
- Seeds

- Oatmeal Bread
- Rich Hot Rolls
- Whole Wheat Swiss Bread
- Whole Wheat Sugar Bears
- Croissants
- Hot Cross Buns

Chapter 19:   475
Holiday Baking

- Some tips to make holiday baking easier
- Holiday Pound Cake
- Hearth Loaf
- Cheese Puffs
- Holiday Cranberry Bread
- Herbed Sweet Potato Biscuits
- Dog Biscuits
- Honey Date Nut Bread
- Hawaiian Wedding Cake
- Warm Cranberry Cake
- White Chocolate Cheesecake with Cranberry Swirl
- Coconut Cake Squares
- Christmas Tree Coffee Cake
- Chef Pastry Mix/Biscuit Mix
- Polish Poppy Seed Bread
- Cranberry Bounce
- Maple Cookies
- Yule Log
- Meringue Mushrooms
- Garlic Batter Bread
- Nisu
- Holiday Wreath Bread
- Ribbon Cake

Chapter 20:   500
Coffee House Treats

- Tiramisu Cheesecake
- Rich Brownies
- Black and White Cookies
- Chocolate Apple Bread

- Caramel Scones
- Russian Tea Biscuits
- Classic Babka
- Poppy Seed Tea Cake
- Pumpkin Maple Scones
- Oatmeal Orange Scones
- Lemon Poppy Seed Muffins
- White Chocolate and Ginger Biscotti
- Easy Bear Claws
- Tiramisu
- Citrus Topped Cake
- Blueberry Crumb Cake
- Marble Pound Cake
- Chocolate Lovers' Biscotti
- Fruit Filled Ladder Loaf
- Almond Biscotti
- Hazelnut Biscotti
- Easter Egg Biscotti

Chapter 21:   525
Cookies, Cookies and More Cookies
- Cookie Baking Know How
- Snow People
- Roscoe Village Gingerbread Cookies
- Puppy Kibble
- Thumbprint Cookies
- Jan Hagel
- Buckeyes
- Sugar Cookies
- Royal Icing
- Holiday Chocolate Fans
- Cream Wafers
- Russian Teacakes
- Snickerdoodles
- Pecan Tassels
- Foldovers
- Versatile Butter Cookies
- Chocolate Peanut Clusters
- Cookie-Candies

- Martha Merrick's Shortbread
- Chinese Almond Cookies
- Hazelnut Ovals
- Santa Claus Cookies
- Oatmeal Chocolate Chip Cookies
- Chocolate Sparkles
- Lemon Squares
- Viennese Shortbread
- Candy Cane Cookies
- Sandbakelser (Sand Tarts)
- Butterscotch Lace Cookies
- Death by Chocolate Cookies
- Craisin Nut Cookies
- Lemon Meltaways

Chapter 22:   553
Chocolate Lover's Cookbook

- Chocolate Know-How
- Chocolate Pecan Pie
- Flourless Chocolate Mousse Cake
- Princess Brownies
- Extra Extra Fudgy Brownies
- Frozen Mocha Cheesecake
- Fudge Cheesecake
- Hot Fudge Cinnamon Sauce
- Chocolate Chip Cake Mix Cookies
- Chocolate Sorbet
- Hot Fudge Sauce
- Chocolate Chip Oatmeal Cherry Cookies
- Chocolate Coconut Bowls
- No-Cook Fudge
- Easy Chocolate Glaze
- Chocolate Cabbage Cake
- Aunt Josie's Ho Ho Cake

Chapter 23: Cupcakes
Little Cakes, Big Flavor

- Chocolate Pecan Cupcakes
- Black and White Cupcakes
- Chip and Cream Filled Cupcakes
- Peanut Butter Cupcakes
- Spicy Chocolate Zucchini Cupcakes
- "Twinkle" Cupcakes
- S'Mores Cupcakes
- Ice Cream Cone Cupcakes
- Apple Banana Cupcakes
- Black Forest Cupcakes
- No-Bake Strawberry Cupcakes
- Spicy Carrot Cupcakes
- Gingerbread Cupcakes
- Molten Chocolate Cupcakes
- Mint Surprise Cupcakes
- Chessman Cupcakes
- Classic White Cupcakes
- Sour Cream Lemon Cupcakes
- Coconut Orange Cupcakes
- Banana Cupcakes
- Spicy Pumpkin Cupcakes
- Rich Chocolate Sour Cream Cupcakes
- Mocha Cupcakes
- Strawberry Cupcakes
- Favorite Creamy Icing
- Cream Cheese Frosting
- Mocha Frosting
- Easy Chocolate Butter Cream
- Creamy Chocolate Frosting
- Chocolate Silk Frosting
- Crunchy Chocolate Peanut Butter Frosting
- Caramel Frosting
- Cooked Custard Frosting
- Easy Chocolate-Peanut Butter Frosting
- Easy Vanilla Frosting
- Classic Butter Cream

- Chocolate Cream Cheese Frosting
- Super Fluffy Frosting
- Pink Lemonade Frosting
- Strawberry Frosting
- Finishing Touches
- Chocolate Covered Goodies
- Pretzel Kisses
- Fudgy Buttons
- Chocolate Dipping Sauce
- Cocoa Mint Hearts
- Whoopie Pies
- Chocolate Pound Cake
- Chocolate Angel Food Cake
- Chocolate Shortbread
- Chocolate-Orange Scones
- Chocolate Shortcakes
- English Toffee Crunch
- Chocolate Peanut Butter Pie
- Chocolate Pecan Bars
- Chocolate Turtles
- Mocha Brownies

Chapter 24: 617
Gifts from the Kitchen
- Multi Bean Soup Mix
- Horseradish Mustard
- Bavarian Mustard
- Spicy Mustard
- French Herb Mustard
- Sugared Nuts
- Candied Cashews
- Seasoned Almonds
- Sweet and Savory Nuts
- Citrus Sugar
- Sesame Salt
- Caramel-Coated Pears
- Italian Seasoning
- Salad Herbs
- Creole Spice

- Pizza Seasoning
- Poultry Seasoning
- Curry Powder
- Hot Cocoa Mix
- Coffee Liqueur
- Herb Vinegars
- Orange and Rosemary Jelly
- Grape and Thyme Jelly
- Wine Jelly

About the Author   635

Introduction

Let me tell you about Judi Strauss. She's the reason I'm fat. No, not really but you certainly don't starve around Judi. In Cleveland, Judi is a legend, she teaches workshops on cooking, gardening, and food to all ages – children and adults. She knows food and she knows how to communicate about food. She frequently shows up on the local news doing awesome demos and is sincerely one of the nicest and friendliest people I know.

I met Judi many years ago (long before I started a publishing company) and helped her setup her website TheCharmedKitchen.com – it is intense. Every day (and I mean EVERY day) she brings you recipes and pictures and stories about food. All by herself. And it's been years! She later expanded to Facebook and even has a monthly newsletter you can subscribe to on her website.

My two favorite "food stories" about Judi. The first is when she created for me the "Ruben Calzone" (I call it the "Irish" Calzone – which is not in this book – you need to go to her website for it. She put corned beef and Swiss cheese in a rye dough bread pocket and filled it with a homemade (of course) Thousand Island dressing. And in fine Judi fashion she didn't make me one or two but dropped off 2 dozen at my house and told me to freeze them for later.

My other favorite food memory of Judi is when I came over to her house and she handed be a baggie with a pound of maple bacon she had made for me. And then a moment later another baggie of regular bacon she made in the maple bacon grease. With Judi everything is on the table – health food – not health food – old world and old school cooking and modern tips and tricks.

After I started my publishing company my first order of business was to republish her Charmed Garden and Charmed Kitchen books. With all the thousands of recipes she has – those books have been at her core for years.

But Judi has another series of books she sells, her "Little Red Cookbooks". Short one off booklets on a wide variety of subjects. It wouldn't have been cost effective to publish the individual booklets, so instead we worked on publishing eBooks of 24 of these on Amazon.

But editing Judi's recipes is a hungry proposition. And having gone through the hundreds and hundreds and recipes I told Judi that we needed to take it to the next level. So here we are, 24 "Little Red Cookbooks" have now been assembled for the first time as one "Big Red Cookbook".

There is so much in this cookbook. I did have to make some edits. Where do I put this frosting or this sauce or this rice dish? They could easily have gone in so many places. So make sure you browse through the table of contents. This book is a feast for the eyes and if you follow Judi's very clear directions it will be a feast for your tummy as well.

Don't forget to go to TheCharmedKitchen.com and subscribe to her mailing list and follow her on Facebook. The food never ends!

Jared Bendis
Publisher (and Friend)
ATBOSH Media Ltd.
September 2020

Chapter 1: Appetizers

The Big Cheese

Cheese is such a versatile staple of the appetizer spread you will probably use it, too. Display is everything. Here are some ways to serve cheese.

Cheese and Bread Ladder

In a long, narrow basket or on a long plate alternate slices of party rye and thins slices of cheese. They should be about the same size and turn the cheese so little points stick out between bread slices. Lay on an angle

Cheese Tower

Cut cheese into ½ x ½ x 4-inch pieces. Stack them by placing 2 parallel pieces a few inches apart on your serving tray. Place 2 more pieces crosswise on top of the first two. Sort of like a little log cabin. Stack as high as you dare and fill the little towers with olives, tiny pickles etc. You can also alternate colors for more variety or make several towers of different heights on the same tray.

Cheese Carrot and Parsnips

Take a small amount of white or yellow cheddar cheese, grated and combine with a little butter in a processor, mixing until smooth I use about 1 T. of butter for every 1-2 cups of cheese. Form this mixture by tablespoons into tiny "carrots" or "parsnips". Garnish with a little sprig of parsley or dill.

Cheese Kebobs

On a skewer place a cube of cheese. Add a piece of salami folded into quarters and then add a strawberry or melon cube. Simple and pretty.

Chunky Cheese

Don't cube cheese, but rather get big hunks and leave out with knives and a cheese slicer. Let guests serve themselves.

Cheese Balls and Beyond

Since we all have favorite recipes for cheese balls you can present them in different ways. Try rolling the cheese ball in chopped nuts, fresh herbs, seeds (sesame, sunflower, flax, pumpkin, poppy, fennel, etc., alone or in combination) or even paprika. One of my favorite ways to decorate a cheese ball is to shape it like an apple and dust with paprika. Finish off with a bay leaf and voila!

You can also form the cheese ball into mini versions and roll in assorted ingredients. Now they can be served on skewers or on a platter with smoked meats, pickled vegetables or fruit.

Brie Bundle

Wrap a piece of Brie in puff pastry. Tuck dough underneath and trim off excess. Bake in a 400 degree oven until golden and serve with crackers. You can cut a design in the pastry before you bake it or brush with beaten egg for a shiny surface. Serve with breads and crackers. Always impressive.

Olive Spread (Tapenade)

1 can ripe, pitted olives, drained and chopped fine
1 T. chopped anchovies
1 t. salad oil
2 t. lemon juice
small lettuce leaves
¼ c. sour cream
Chopped green onions

Combine olives with anchovies, oil, and juice. Cover and chill. When ready to serve line a serving dish with lettuce leaves. Top with olive mixture and then spoon over sour cream and green onions. Serve with crackers.

Easy Pâté

8 oz. liverwurst
2 T. softened butter or margarine
¼ t. Worcestershire sauce
1 T. very thinly sliced green onion
2 T. crumbled bacon or turkey bacon
4 oz. softened cream cheese

Mash liverwurst in mixing bowl. Stir in next four ingredients and mix until smooth. Place on wax paper and from into a 3x5-inch rectangle. Chill at least thirty minutes. Frost chilled pâté with cream cheese and chill at least 30 more minutes before serving. Serve with crackers, rye or pumpernickel bread.

Zakooskas

½ medium onion, diced
2 t. butter or margarine
1 T. flour
1 c. chicken or vegetable stock
½ c. sour cream
1 t. Worcestershire sauce
2 drops Tabasco
2 cooked potatoes
2 t. butter
2 c. ham or turkey ham cut into strips 2 x 1/2-inch
2 small dill pickles
1 c. grated cheese

Sauté onion in butter or margarine until tender, but not browned. Stir in flour and cook 5 minutes. Add stock, sour cream, Worcestershire sauce and Tabasco and simmer 10 minutes over low heat. Slice potatoes very thin and sauté in remaining butter 5 minutes. Slice pickles very thin. Combine all ingredients together in casserole and cover with cheese. Cook in a preheated 350 degree oven until cheese has melted and dish is bubbly. Serve with crackers or bread.

Fondue Bread

1 T. sugar
2 t. yeast
2 packages active dry yeast
about 4 c. flour, preferably bread flour
½ c. butter or margarine
1 c. milk
2 eggs
1 lb. Muenster cheese, shredded, or use any cheese that you like

Combine sugar, salt and yeast with 1 c. of the flour. Heat together butter or margarine and milk until very warm (120-130 degrees). Beat milk mixture into flour mixture with an electric mixer and beat 3 minutes. Beat in 1 c. flour and mix 2 minutes longer. With spoon, start to stir in enough flour to make a soft dough. Turn onto lightly floured surface and knead, adding more flour until dough is smooth and elastic. Kneading will take about 10 minutes. Shape dough into a ball, cover with bowl and let rest 15 minutes. Meanwhile, reserve 1 egg white and combine remaining eggs with the cheese. Grease 9-inch round cake pan.

On lightly floured surface with a rolling pin roll dough into a rectangle about 24x6-inch. Shape cheese into a tube lengthwise along the center of the dough. Fold sides of dough over cheese making about a 1½-inch overlap. Pinch seams to seal. Place roll, seam side down in prepared pan to form a ring. Ends should overlap. Pinch ends together. Cover with a towel and let rest 15 minutes. Preheat oven to 375 degrees. Brush top of ring with reserved egg whites and bake about 1 hour. Loaf will be golden brown and sound hollow when tapped. Remove from pan right away and let stand 15 minutes for easier cutting. Makes 1 large loaf. To serve cut into wedges. Makes 8 main dish or 16 appetizer servings. To reheat, wrap breads in foil and heat in a

350 degree oven for 30 minutes or until bread has warmed and cheese is melted.

Quick Herb Spread

1 (8 oz. package) cream cheese, softened
1 T. balsamic vinegar
2 T. chopped fresh parsley, chervil or cilantro
1 T. finely chopped chives or green onions
1T. finely chopped dates
1 T. finely chopped walnuts

Combine all ingredients and serve as a spread on crackers or bread. Also good on bagels and quick breads.

Lola's Smoky Crescent Rolls

2 packages refrigerated crescent rolls, 8-count size
1 (16 oz. package) smokies, 8 count package, we use Kahn's

Open crescent rolls and divide into 4 pieces, pressing edges together to form 4 rectangles of dough. Roll a sausage up in each piece of dough and repeat with remaining ingredients. You will have 4 rolls. Slice rolls in ¾-inch pieces and place on ungreased baking sheet. Leave about ½-inch between pieces. Open second package of crescent rolls and repeat procedure with remaining sausages. You will need 2 baking sheets to hold all the rolls. Bake in a preheated 375 degree oven for 15 minutes, or until golden brown. Remove from sheet immediately and place on serving dish, preferably heated. Serve with dipping sauce, if desired. We like to use horseradish sauce, barbecue sauce, honey mustard, sweet and sour sauce or even ketchup.

Herbed Nuts

2 T. oil
1 T. fresh rosemary, minced or 1 t. dried, crumbled
1T. fresh chopped parsley or 1 t. dried, crumbled
1 t. Tabasco, optional
2 c. nuts (walnuts, pecans, almonds, cashews or mixed)

Toss all ingredients together and bake on a cookie sheet for 10-15 minutes in a 350 degree oven. Store in an airtight container and keep cool. Makes 2 cup.

Keeps longer if frozen.

Brie
with Pesto and Sun-Dried Tomatoes

2 c. basil leaves
3 T. pine nuts
2 T. olive oil
2 cloves garlic
3 T. Parmesan cheese
salt and pepper to taste
½ c. sun-dried tomatoes, soaked in water and chilled overnight
1 T. oil
1 t. oregano
small wheel of Brie 1-2 lbs.

Combine first five ingredients in a blender or processor until smooth. Add salt and pepper to taste. Drain tomatoes and chop coarsely. Combine with remaining oil and oregano and season to taste. Split Brie horizontally into 3 pieces. Spread one layer with pesto and top with a piece of Brie. Spread with tomato mixture and top with remaining Brie. Wrap and chill overnight. Serve at room temperature or warm slightly. Goes best with crusty breads.

Sweet Potato Chips

3-4 large sweet potatoes
oil
salt
garlic powder

Slice potatoes as thin as possible. Heat oil to 375 degrees and fry potatoes a few at a time. They will shrink and get darker. Drain and season to taste. Store in an airtight container.

Rueben Dip

8 oz. cream cheese, chopped
½ c. sour cream
½ lb. lean corned beef, chopped
2 T. fine chopped onions
1 T. ketchup
2 t. spicy mustard
1 c. chopped Swiss cheese

Mix all ingredients and place in a covered casserole dish. Bake in a 375 degree oven for 30 minutes, stirring about 15 minutes into the cooking. Uncover casserole and bake 5 minutes more. Serve warm with crackers or bread, preferably rye.

Note: You can also heat this dish up in a microwave oven for 7-10 minutes, or until bubbly. If you want it browned on the top just place under broiler (in broiler-safe dish), for a minute or 2.

Prosciutto Wraps

1 whole honeydew or cantaloupe, peeled and seeded
8 oz. very thinly sliced prosciutto or smoked ham
1 bunch green onion tops, cut into 6-inch slices

Cut melon into 2 x ½-inch slices. Wrap a small piece of meat around each and tie with a piece of the onion. Makes about 4 dozen.

Appetizer Cheesecake

1 c. plain crouton crumbs
3 T. melted margarine
1 envelope unflavored gelatin
½ c. cold water
2 (8 oz. packages), each, cream cheese
8 oz. liverwurst
¼ c. mayonnaise
3 T. chopped pimento
2 T. grated onion
1 T. mustard
½ t. lemon juice

Combine crumbs and margarine and press into bottom of 9-inch spring form pan. Bake in a 350 degree oven for 10 minutes. Soften gelatin in cold water Cook over low heat until dissolved. Combine cheese and liverwurst in medium bowl and mix until well blended. Beat in gelatin mixture and add remaining ingredients. Mix well and pour in prepared crust. Chill until firm. Remove from pan and serve garnished with green onion and pimento, if desired.

Salmon Ball

1 (15 oz. can) salmon, drained, boned and flaked
1 (8 oz. package) cream cheese, softened
1 T. lemon juice
2 t. dried minced onion
2 t. horseradish
salt and pepper to taste

Combine all ingredients and form into a ball. Roll in chopped nuts and chopped parsley and chill until ready to serve. Serve with crackers or bread.

Seafood Appetizer Cheesecake

1 c. crushed buttery crackers
3 T. melted margarine
2 (8 oz. package) each, cream cheese
3 eggs
¾ c. sour cream
1 (7¾ oz. can) salmon, drained, flaked
1 t. lemon juice
1 t. dried minced onion
1/8 t. pepper

Combine crumbs and margarine and press into the bottom of a 9-inch spring form pan. Bake at 350 degrees for 10 minutes. Combine cheese, eggs and ¼ c. of the sour cream and mix until well blended. Add remaining ingredients and mix well. Pour into prepared crust and bake in a 325 degree oven for 45 minutes. Loosen rim of pan while still warm. Cool and chill. Remove rim and spread top with remaining sour cream.

Crab Mousse

1 envelope unflavored gelatin
3 T. cold water
1 can cream of mushroom soup
1 (8 oz. package) cream cheese, softened
1 (6 oz. can) crab meat, drained
1 c. minced celery
¾ c. mayonnaise
¼ c. minced onion
1 T. lemon juice

Dissolve gelatin in cold water and set aside. In microwave safe dish heat soup until hot. Stir in gelatin mixture and blend thoroughly. Stir in remaining ingredients and pour into an oiled mold. Cover and chill at least several hours, or until set. Unmold on plate and serve with crackers or bread. This looks nice served on dark-colored plates or on a bed of lettuce leaves.

Mini Turkey Burgers

1 lb. ground turkey
1 egg
½ c., or more, bread crumbs
¼ c. chopped onion
2 cloves minced garlic
2 T. ketchup
1 t. salt
2 t. basil
2 t. oregano
2 t. parsley flakes
½ t. red pepper flakes, or to taste

Combine all ingredients, adding more bread crumbs if mixture is too wet. Chill. Shape into 10-inch balls and flatten into burgers. Pan-broil, bake or grill until thoroughly cooked. Serve on prepared refrigerated biscuits with assorted condiments. Makes 25-30.

Aunt Marcie's Taco Dip

2 (8 oz. package) each, cream cheese, softened
2 T. milk
1 small can diced green chilies, drained
1 (8 oz. jar) taco sauce
12 oz. shredded taco or Mexican style cheese
1 head iceberg lettuce. shredded
tortilla chips
sliced ripe, pitted olives, optional

Combine cream cheese, milk and chilies and spread in a mound on large serving platter. Sprinkle with about 1 c. of the shredded cheese and pour over the entire bottle of taco sauce. Cover with remaining cheese and surround with shredded lettuce. Serve with tortilla chips and top with a few olives for decoration, if desired.

Note: You can cut the recipe in half for smaller groups, or divide the ingredients on 2 or 3 smaller plates so you can set them around at a party. Always a hit.

Ginger Drums

24 chicken wings cut into thirds (discard tips)
½ c. pineapple juice
2 T. ketchup
2 T. honey
2 T. soy sauce
2 cloves minced garlic
1 T. fresh grated ginger

Place chicken in a dish and mix remaining ingredients in a separate bowl. Pour marinade over the chicken, cover and refrigerate overnight or for at least 3 hours. Place chicken pieces in a baking dish and cook in a 375 degree oven until browned and until juices run clear when pierced with a fork, about 30 minutes. Brush with marinade a few times during cooking and discard any unused marinade. Serve with dipping sauce or honey mustard

Honey Mustard
Combine equal parts honey and mustard and if desired, mayonnaise.

Pastrami Bites

2 T. butter or margarine
8 oz. mushrooms, chopped fine
2 T. chives or green onions, chopped fine
¼ c. bread crumbs
¼ c. minced celery
½ c. shredded mozzarella cheese
2 T. mayonnaise
12 slices pastrami
brown sugar

Sauté mushrooms and chives or onions in butter until tender and most of the liquid is gone. Add remaining ingredients, except pastrami and sugar and mix well. Spread mixture on meat and roll up. Cut into thirds and secure with toothpicks. Roll in sugar and broil until heated through. Makes 3 dozen. Note: You can also use slices of ham if you prefer.

Peppered Pecans

2 c. pecans
¼ c. butter or margarine
salt and coarse ground pepper to taste

Place nuts and butter in skillet and cook over medium heat until nuts are lightly toasted. Place nuts in heat proof bowl and sprinkle with salt and pepper to taste, tossing to coat. I like to use multi-color peppercorns in this recipe. Makes 2 cups.

Can be stored in an airtight container for up to a month or frozen for up to 6 months.

Squash Dip

2 acorn squash or 1 butternut, halved and seeded
1 c. sour cream or strained yogurt
½ c. diced sweet onion
¼ c. mayonnaise
2 T. honey
1 T. chopped fresh parsley or 1 t. dried
2 t. oregano
1 t. chili powder
1 t. cumin
1 t. dried minced garlic
½ t. paprika
dash hot pepper sauce
salt to taste
crusty breads and smoked sausage

Bake acorn squash, cut side down in a shallow baking dish with ½-inch of water in pan. Bake at 350 degree for 45 minutes, or until squash is tender. Cool enough to handle and spoon out pulp. Mash until smooth. Add all ingredients, except bread and meat and stir until blended. Heat before serving. Serve with breads and sausage (heated). Makes about 4 cups.

Fast and Easy

The following are some quick appetizers you can mix and match for any occasion

Tiny Antipasto
Spread cracker with mustard and top with a ¼ slice of salami, cheese and garnish with slice of pimento.

Taco Bites
Top a large cracker with bean dip and a few kidney beans, chopped olives and minced sweet pepper. Add a dollop of sour cream or salsa.

Cucumber Cools
Mash cream cheese with a little dill weed and spread some on a cracker. Top with a slice of cucumber (sliced thin and patted dry). With a decorating tip pipe a little more cream cheese on top and garnish with chopped chives, green onion or paprika.

Deli Delight
Spread rye cracker with mustard and top with fine shreds of red cabbage, pepperoni slice and pickle slice.

Mini Pizza
Spread mini bagels (split) with a little pizza sauce, slice of mozzarella and diced sweet pepper. Place under broiler until cheese has melted.

Ruebenettes
On rye cracker or min bagel, split spread with Thousand Island dressing. Place a piece of corned beef, sauerkraut and Swiss cheese. Broil until cheese melts.

French Favorite
Spread toasted slices of French bread (halved) with a little French dressing and top with a slice of hard-cooked egg and a sliced, stuffed olive.

Pilgrim's Delight
Combine cranberry sauce with mayo until smooth. Place a slice of turkey on a cracker and top with the cranberry mixture and a few toasted (hulled) pumpkin seeds.

Bacon and Eggs
On a cracker or mini bagel, split and toasted spread egg salad and top with crumbled bacon.

Onion Crisps
Spread sour cream on a cracker and top with French fried onions. Broil until toasted.

Zucchini Bites

2-3 T. chopped onion
1 clove minced garlic
1 T. butter or margarine
1½ c. shredded zucchini
1½ c. shredded Monterey Jack cheese
3 T. cornmeal
½ t. oregano
¼ t. cumin
3 eggs, beaten

Sauté onion and garlic until tender. Add zucchini and cook 3 minutes longer. Place in bowl and combine with remaining ingredients. Pour into greased 8x8-inch baking pan. Bake in 350 degree oven for 20 minutes, or until set. Cut into squares and serve hot. Makes 16-25 depending on how big you cut them.

Holiday Ham Balls

3 c. biscuit mix (Bisquick or Jiffy Mix)
1½ c. fully cooked ham or turkey ham, chopped
4 c. shredded cheddar cheese
½ c. grated Parmesan cheese
2 T. parsley flakes
2 t. spicy mustard
2/3 c. milk

Mix all ingredients and form into 1-inch balls. Place 2-inches apart on lightly greased baking sheet and bake in a 350 degree oven for 20-25 minutes. Serve warm with honey-mustard dip or sweet and sour salad dressing. Makes 80.

Spinach Puffs

1 (10 oz. package) frozen spinach, cooked and drained well
2 T. dried minced onion
2 eggs
½ c. shredded cheddar cheese
½ c. grated Parmesan cheese
½ c. ranch dressing
2 T. oil
¼ t. garlic powder
2 c. biscuit mix (Bisquick or Jiffy Mix)

Mix all ingredients and chill several hours or overnight. Roll into 10inch balls and place 2-inches apart on a greased baking sheet. Bake in a 350 degree oven for 10-12 minutes. Makes about 60.

Italian Sausage Snacks

3 c. biscuit mix
1 lb. cooked Italian sausage, crumbled
1 lb. shredded mozzarella cheese
2/3 c. milk

Combine all ingredients and form into 1-inch balls. Place 2-inches apart on lightly greased baking sheet and bake in a 400 degree oven for 15-20 minutes. Makes about 7 dozen. Serve with marinara sauce or barbecue sauce.

Mushroom Appetizer

2 lbs. fresh mushrooms, washed and stems trimmed
1 stick butter or margarine
2 T. balsamic vinegar
1 package dried Italian salad dressing mix

Cook butter and mushrooms together in skillet for about 30 minutes or until most of the liquid is gone. Add vinegar and seasoning packet and cook 30 minutes longer. Serve warm or at room temperature. Makes 3 cups.

Almond Pinecones

1¼ c. whole un-blanched almonds
8 oz. cream cheese, softened
½ c. mayonnaise
5 slices crisp bacon or turkey bacon, crumbled
1 T. chopped green onion
½ t. dill weed
1/8 t. pepper

Place almonds on baking sheet and toast in a 300 degree oven for 15 minutes. Cool and set aside. Combine remaining ingredients and form into an oval (sort of almond shaped) on a serving dish. Starting at the bottom of the oval start laying down almonds at an angle to make the cheese mixture look like a pinecone. Decorate with a sprig of greenery (real or fake) if you like. Serve with crackers.

Island Meatballs

1 lb. lean ground beef or turkey
1 egg
1/3 c. bread crumbs
1 small onion, diced
2 t. grated ginger
1 t. salt
½ t. allspice
¼ t. red pepper flakes
1 (20 oz. can) pineapple chunks, in juice, drained (reserve juice for sweet and sour sauce – see recipe for sauce in Saucy Sauces)

Combine meat with egg, crumbs, onion and seasonings and chill. Formed chilled mixture into 1½-inch balls and bake in a 350 degree oven for 45 minutes. Place 1 meatball on a skewer with a chunk of pineapple and brush with a little sweet and sour sauce. Return to oven for 10 minutes or broil for 3-5 minutes. Serve with extra sauce. Makes about 30.

Guacamole

3 ripe avocados, peeled, seeded and diced
¼ c. minced onions
2 T. lemon juice
½ t. salt
2 cloves minced garlic
1 medium tomato, seeded and diced
chili powder to taste

Place avocados in a bowl and mash until no big lumps remain. Stir in remaining ingredients and adjust seasonings. Cover and chill until ready to use. Serve with tortilla chips, pita toasts or assorted vegetables. Note: Work quickly with avocados as they turn brown quickly once cut. You can use the lemon juice in the recipe to keep them from discoloring by tossing the avocado chunks with the juice as you cut them.

Bean Dip

2 c. cooked beans (kidney, black beans, etc.), drain if canned
½ c. chopped cilantro
3 cloves garlic
2 T. dried minced onions
2 T. oil
juice of 1 lime
1 t. cumin
1 t. chili powder
1 t. oregano
½ t. paprika
½ t. red pepper flakes, or to taste
salt to taste
1 T. red or cider vinegar, optional

Place beans in food processor and start to run adding remaining ingredients and blending until smooth. If dip is too stiff add a little more vinegar or oil. Makes 2½ cups. Serve with tortillas or pita toasts.

Flat Bread

½ c. warm water
1 packet yeast
2 T. flour
1 t. sugar
2 c. warm water
1 T. salt
about 6 c. flour
¼ c. chopped rosemary
½ c. cornmeal
flour

Decorations: Sage leaves, parsley leaves, strips of green onions or chives, onion, tomatillos, cherry tomatoes

Combine first 4 ingredients and let sit in a warm place for 30 minutes. Stir in remaining ingredients and enough flour to make a soft dough. Knead until smooth, cover and let rise 45-60 minutes. Pull off small knobs of dough and roll out real thin. I make 2 big ones that fill a cookie sheet. Think of them as oversized crackers. Brush with oil and press in herb leaves, thin slices of onions, fanned out, sliced tomatillos and sliced cherry tomatoes, whatever you like and have. Bake 400 degrees 12 minutes. Serve standing up in a basket and use with cheeses and cheese balls or other spreads and dips.

Caviar Berries

4 oz. softened cream cheese
about 30 pine nuts, toasted
2 oz. jar red caviar
2 oz. jar black caviar
parsley sprigs for garnish, optional

Place ½ t. of cream cheese around each pine nut. Drain caviar and roll the cream cheese covered nuts in one color or the other, pressing very lightly to help them stick. Place "berries" on paper towel lined dish and chill until ready to serve. Decorate them with a sprig of parsley, if desired. Makes about 30.

Caviar Stars

8 oz. frozen puff pastry, thawed
1/3 c. sour cream
1 oz. red or black caviar
3 T. minced chives or green onions

On floured board roll pastry to 1/8-inch thickness. Cut out with 3-inch star cookie cutter. You should get 8 stars. Place on a greased baking sheet and cook in a 400 degree oven for 12-15 minutes. Cool on rack then split to make 16 stars. Place starts on a platter cut side up. When ready to serve place a dab of sour cream on each star than add a little caviar and a sprinkling of chives or onions. Makes 16.

Caviar on Celery

2 oz. red caviar
4-6 oz. cream cheese
1 t. garlic powder
½ t. dill weed
½ t. paprika
1/8 t. pepper
celery sticks

Drain caviar and set aside. Combine cheese and seasonings and pipe onto celery sticks. Sprinkle with caviar and chill until ready to serve.

Classic Caviar Presentation

caviar
hard-cooked eggs, peeled and chopped
minced green onions
sour cream

Drain caviar and set aside. On small serving plate place chopped eggs, surround with sour cream and sprinkle with caviar and onions. Serve with crackers. You can also place caviar in its own tiny bowl on the platter with everything else.

Herbed Fried Pasta

1 lb. pasta like shells or bow ties, cooked, drained, patted dry
oil
1/3 c. Parmesan cheese
1 t. each dried basil and parsley
1 t. salt
½ t. chili powder
½ t. garlic powder
½ t. onion powder
½ t. dried marjoram
¼ t. cayenne pepper

Heat 1-2-inches of oil in a skillet and fry pasta a few handfuls at a time until golden brown. Drain and set aside. Combine remaining ingredients in a large plastic bag and add pasta, shaking to coat. Makes about 6 cups. Very crunchy.

Bruschetta

1 loaf Italian or French bread
¼ c. olive oil
3 cloves minced garlic
1 T. oil
1 medium onion, chopped
salt and pepper to taste
12 oz. mushrooms, washed, trimmed and chopped
2 c. shredded provolone cheese
2 medium tomatoes, sliced thin
1-2 T. Italian or Pizza Seasoning
1 c. ripe pitted olives, sliced

Slice bread on the diagonal 1-2-inches thick. You can cut big slices in half. Combine olive oil and garlic and brush on bread slices. Grill or bake bread until toasted. This will take about 10-15 minutes in a 350 degree oven. Cook onion and mushrooms in remaining oil until tender, season and divide among bread slices. Divide remaining ingredients among bread and bake in a 400 degree oven until heated through. You can broil them instead, if you like. Makes 24.

Note: Variations are almost limitless for these. Use seasonal vegetables when possible. Some of my favorites include grilled eggplant, diced sweet peppers, artichoke hearts, pepperoni pesto sauce and more.

Marinated Vegetables

Marinade
½ c. olive oil or canola oil
1 c. vinegar, cider or red wine vinegar preferred
1/3 c. sugar, or to taste
¼ c. water
1 t. salt
1 t. dried minced garlic
2 T. dried mixed herbs, your own mixture or say Mrs. Dash

Vegetables
Choose from the following list: broccoli, cauliflower, zucchini, mushrooms, cherry tomatoes, peppers, baby carrots (parboiled), canned baby corn and pearl onions (parboiled).

Mix marinade and set aside. Wash and trim vegetables as needed and cut into bite-sized pieces, if needed. Place vegetables in a bowl and pour over the marinade. The marinade does not have to cover the vegetables completely as the marinade will draw moisture out of them. Still, for a large batch of vegetables you may want to make a double batch of the marinade. Cover and refrigerate for at least a few days for best flavor. Some vegetables like tomatoes and peppers will be better if marinated for a day or two. Carrots, cauliflower and broccoli are best with three days or more so don't be afraid to start the vegetables on one day and add more vegetables later.

To serve: Drain vegetables and serve as is or add olives, artichoke hearts, cheese cubes and smoked meats for an antipasto. I've also known people to serve them with crusty bread.

Chapter 2:
Sunday Brunch

Basic Brunch Dishes

Along with an assortment of quiches, crepes etc. other dishes you might include are:

Assorted meats like bacon, Canadian bacon, ham (regular or turkey), sausages, etc.

Fruits, in salads, on skewers, in compotes or on plates with assorted cheeses.

Baked goods such as muffins, quick breads, coffeecakes, scones, biscuits, breads, croissant strudels, etc.

Bagels with assorted toppings like cream cheese (regular or flavored with herbs or fruit), smoked salmon (lox) with thin slices of onions, ham, chicken or seafood salads or sliced meats (ham, corned beef, smoked turkey with condiments) You might even prefer to use mini bagels so folks can try more combinations.

Beverages should include coffee and tea, of course but also include juices, punch, mineral waters or mimosa. Make sure that alcohol laced beverages are marked clearly so no one drinks without intending to.

Since brunches generally last a couple of hours you don't need to serve everything at once. Change dishes a few times. This is especially helpful if you are trying to keep several dishes hot and don't have warming trays or chafing dishes. Bring out a hot dish, let it stay for 20-30 minutes, then replace it with a different hot dish or more of the original dish.

Plan for at least one dish for guests to construct like the crepes or bagels. It will be fun for them and less work for you. Also have several dishes that can be done ahead so you won't be frantically cooking five things at once as guests walk in the door.

Bacon can be cooked the night before and just reheated before serving.

Combine tastes, textures, colors and temperatures on your table. Have something sweet and something savory. Have some crunchy foods to complement the softer foods. Decorate with bright colored fruits or maybe sweet peppers. Use edible flowers when you can get them to add interest to the table.

If space allows, place beverages away from food to keep traffic flowing.

If it helps you, make a time line to remind yourself about when to throw stuff in the oven and when to replace foods.

Brunch Egg Casserole
Make 2 days in advance

8 eggs
4 c. milk
10 slices bread, well-buttered and cubed
½ lb. cheddar cheese, grated 1 t. dry mustard
1 T. curry powder, or to taste
salt and pepper to taste

Lightly beat together eggs and milk. In an ungreased casserole alternate layers of bread cubes and cheese. Add seasoning to milk mixture and pour over bread and cheese. Cover and refrigerate for 48 hours, although I've done it on 24 hours and it was fine. Remove from fridge ½ hour before baking. Bake at 350 degrees for 35-40 minutes. Serves 8.

Note: For variation you can add diced cooked ham, cooked crumbled bacon or cooked sausage to this dish, layering after bread and before cheese.

Sausage and Onion Quiche

½ lb. breakfast sausage
1 T. butter
3 c. chopped onions
3 eggs
1 c. whipping cream (or evaporated skim milk)
2 T. Dijon mustard
nutmeg, salt and pepper to taste
1 c. grated Swiss cheese
1 (9-inch) unbaked pie crust

In heavy skillet, cook sausage over medium heat, breaking up clumps as you go. When meat is cooked, remove and drain well. Leave 1 T. of sausage fat in the skillet and add butter. Cook the onions in skillet until golden. Drain onions. Place meat and onions in pie crust. Beat together remaining ingredients and pour in crust. Bake in a 350 degree oven for 35-45 minutes. Serves 6-8.

Stewed Tomatoes
A favorite in England

1 (28 oz. can) whole tomatoes, broken up slightly
pepper, basil and parsley to taste

Heat all together and serve on the side with scrambles eggs. Serves 6.

Crepes

¾ c. flour
1/8 t. salt
3 eggs, beaten
2 T. melted butter
¾ c. milk, approximately
butter or oil for pan

Beat together flour, salt and eggs until smooth. Stir in melted butter and then stir in milk until batter consistency is that of cream. Let stand for 30 minutes before using, or can be refrigerated, covered, overnight. Beat again, just before using.

Heat 6 or 7-inch skillet. Brush with butter or oil and pour in about 2 t. of batter, tipping pan to cover bottom of pan completely with batter. Cook until edges start to brown, turn over and cook until lightly browned (about 2 minutes per side.)

Crepes can be made day ahead or even frozen between sheets of waxed paper and frozen. Makes 12.

Crepes can be filled ahead or guests can fill their own. Fillings can be served warm and cold, and can be used as a main dish or a dessert.

Green Herb Crepes

Add 1/3 c. chopped fresh parsley, dill, chives scallions or a combination to basic crepe batter. Mix in blender until batter is flecked with green and creamy.

Dessert Crepes

1 c. flour
4 eggs
1½ c. milk
1 T. sugar
2 T. orange-flavored liqueur or orange juice concentrate
¼ c. butter, melted and cooled

Mix all ingredients in blender (except butter) until smooth, scraping sides often. Add butter and blend well. Prepare as basic crepes, Makes 20.

Chocolate Crepes

Use Dessert Crepe recipe but add 2-3 T. cocoa to flour and mix well before blending. You will probably need to add 1-2 T. extra milk, but mix first to check.

Salmon and Sour Cream Crepes

2 c. sour cream
½ c. chopped green onions
1 (15 oz. can) pink or red salmon, drained and flaked
Fresh lemon juice
8 crepes (green herb crepes are great in this)

Combine sour cream and green onions. Place some salmon and a dollop of sour cream mixture in a crepe. Roll up and add another dollop of sour cream to the top. Makes 8.

Taco Crepes

¾-1 lb. lean ground meat (beef, turkey or chicken)
1 onion, chopped fine
1 package taco seasoning
1 c. shredded cheese
sour cream
chunky salsa
8 crepes

Brown meat in non-stick skillet until no pink is visible. Drain off most of the fat. Add onions, seasoning and ½ c. water and cook until onions are tender and most of the water is gone, about 10 minutes. To serve. Place some meat mixture on crepe. Add a sprinkling of cheese and roll up. Garnish with a dollop of sour cream and a spoonful of salsa. Makes 8.

Seafood Crepes

2 T. butter
½ c. minced onion
3 T. flour
1 c. milk
salt and pepper to taste
1 (6-oz. can) crabmeat, drained, or 1 c. cooked cocktail shrimp
1 c. shredded mild cheese, Muenster, mozzarella or Monterey Jack
6-8 crepes (herb work well here)
chopped green onions

Heat butter in skillet and cook onions until tender. Add flour and mix well. Stir in milk and seasonings and cook until sauce is thickened and bubbly. Stir in seafood and heat through. Spoon some of this mixture onto a crepe. Add some cheese and roll up. Garnish with chopped green onions. Makes 6-8.

Purple Passion Crepes

1 c. cranberry/blueberry pie filling or half blueberry half cherry
1 c. sour cream or yogurt
2 T. sugar
8-10 dessert crepes
powdered sugar

In bowl combine pie filling and sour cream. Stir in sugar and chill until ready to use. Mixture will be purple. Spoon filling onto crepe and roll up. Garnish with a dusting of powdered sugar. Makes 8-10.

Note: Other pie fillings work well, too. You can serve them mixed with the sour cream, or separately. You can also serve pie fillings with pudding on the side, too.

Strawberry Crepes

1 qt. strawberries, hulled and sliced
¼ c. sugar, or to taste
1 t. grated orange peel
vanilla pudding, or whipped cream
8-10 dessert crepes

Place berries in a bowl with the sugar and orange peel and let stand at least 30 minutes, or chilled for several hours. Spoon berries into crepes and add a dollop of pudding or whipped cream. Roll up and garnish with additional pudding, whipped cream or whole berries. Makes 8-10.

Crepes Suzette

½ c. orange juice
¼ c. butter or margarine
2 T. sugar
½ t. grated orange peel
¼ c. orange flavored liqueur
12 dessert crepes

Heat juice, butter, sugar and orange peel in skillet or chafing dish. Fold crepes into quarters and place in the sauce to warm. Pour in liqueur and flame, if desired. Makes 12.

Chocolate Crepes

1 c. chocolate chips
½ c. butter
2 c. prepared vanilla pudding
½ t. cinnamon
8-10 dessert crepes, chocolate preferred

In microwave-safe dish heat together chips and butter for about 30-45 seconds. Stir until smooth and allow to cool down. Combine cooled chocolate mixture with pudding and cinnamon but do not combine too much. There should be swirls of both vanilla and chocolate. Spoon mixture in crepes and roll up. Makes 8-10.

Breakfast Pizza

1 lb. bulk pork sausage
1 package crescent rolls (8)
1 c. frozen loose packed hash browns, thawed
1 c. shredded sharp cheddar cheese, 4 oz.
5 eggs
¼ c. milk
salt and pepper to taste
2 T. grated Parmesan cheese

Cook sausage in a skillet until cooked. Drain and set aside. Press crescent rolls into a 12-inch pizza pan, rolling points to center, pressing dough to make a rim and sealing perforations. Sprinkle sausage on dough. Sprinkle with potatoes and cheese. Combine eggs, milk and seasonings and beat well. Pour on crust and sprinkle with Parmesan cheese. Bake in a 375 degree oven for 25-30 minutes. Serves 6-8.

Herbed Cream Cheese Spread

1 (8 oz.) package cream cheese, softened
3 T. dry white wine
¼ c. fine chopped fresh herbs
¼ c. fine chopped dried fruit or nuts

Blend cream cheese and wine until smooth. Stir in remaining ingredients. Makes 1¼ cup.

English Muffin Bran Bread

2¼ c. flour
1 c. wheat bran (or oat bran)
2 packages active dry yeast
1 T. sugar
2 t. salt
¼ t. baking soda
2 c. milk
½ c. water
3 c. flour
cornmeal

Place 2¼ c. flour in large mixing bowl with next 5 ingredients. Heat together milk and water until very warm. Add to dry ingredients, beating well. Stir in enough of the remaining flour to make very soft dough. Grease 2 8x4-inch bread pans and sprinkle with cornmeal. Divide the dough between them. Sprinkle the tops with additional cornmeal, cover and let rise about 45 minutes. Bake in a 400 degree oven for 25 minutes or until done. Remove from pans immediately and cool on racks. To serve slice bread and toast, then serve with favorite toppings. Makes 2 loaves.

Orange Upside Down Biscuits

¼ c. butter
½ c. sugar
½ c. orange juice
2 t. grated orange rind
2 c. flour
1 T. baking powder
1 t. salt
¼ c. shortening
¾ c. milk
4 T. butter, melted
¼ c. sugar
1 t. cinnamon

Preheat oven to 425 degrees. Melt butter in 8-inch square pan in oven. Add sugar, orange juice and rind and stir. Stir together flour, powder and salt. Cut in shortening to resemble coarse crumbs. Stir in enough milk to make soft dough. Knead about 20 strokes and roll or pat dough into a 6-inch square (about ¼-inch thick). Brush with melted butter. Combine remaining sugar and cinnamon and sprinkle over the butter. Roll dough up jellyroll fashion and pinch seams to seal. Cut into 12 slices (½-inch thick) and place in pan. Bake for 20-25 minutes. Invert on plate to serve. Makes 12 rolls.

Overnight Coffee Cake

16-18 frozen dinner rolls (unbaked)
½ c. butter
1 (3 oz. package) butterscotch pudding
½ c. chopped nuts
½ c. brown sugar
½ c. raisins

Night before put frozen rolls in well-greased Bundt pan or 13x9-inch pan. Sprinkle with pudding mix. Melt butter and combine with nuts, brown sugar and raisins. Pour over rolls and let rise overnight on kitchen counter, covered. Allow 8-10 hours. Bake at 350 degrees for 30 minutes. Remove from pan while hot. Serves 12.

Praline Biscuits

½ c. butter
½ c. brown sugar
36 pecan or walnut halves
cinnamon, to sprinkle
2 c. biscuit mix
1/3 c. applesauce
1/3 c. milk

Preheat oven to 450 degrees. In each of 12 muffins cups place 2 t. butter, 2 t. sugar and 3 nut halves. Sprinkle cinnamon in each. Heat in oven until melted. Combine remaining ingredients and spoon over nut mixture. Bake 10 minutes, invert on heatproof serving platter. Makes 12.

Scotch Eggs

1¼ lbs. bulk country style or herb sausage
1 t. sage (optional)
½ t. thyme
¼ t. cayenne pepper
4 hard cooked eggs, peeled
½ c. flour
2 raw eggs, beaten
1 c. fresh bread crumbs
vegetable oil for deep frying

Combine sausage and flavorings and mix well. Divide into 4 equal portions and flatten. Place an egg on each flattened sausage piece and press sausage to completely cover each egg. Dredge eggs in the flour, then dip in the eggs. Roll in the breadcrumbs and fry in 2 ½-inches of oil heated to 350 degrees until well browned. This will take about 10 minutes. Drain. Keep warm until served. Makes 4.

Pepper Puffed Eggs

10 eggs
1 lb. shredded mild cheese
2 c. cottage cheese
½ c. flour
1 t. baking powder
¼ c. butter, melted
½ c. diced sweet red pepper
½ c. diced sweet green pepper

Lightly butter a 9x13-inch glass baking dish. Combine all but peppers and mix well. Stir in peppers and pour into prepared pan. Bake in 350 degree oven until light brown and tester inserted in middle comes out clean, about 35 minutes. Serves 10-12.

Brunch Scrambled Eggs

1 (10 oz. package) frozen chopped spinach, thawed
12 eggs
½ c. milk
salt and pepper to taste
2 T. butter or margarine
2 c. shredded cheddar or Colby cheese

Squeeze out excess moisture from spinach and set aside. Combine eggs with milk and seasonings and beat well. Heat butter in large skillet and pour in eggs. As eggs set, lift and fold eggs with a large spatula, allowing uncooked eggs to flow underneath. Stir in spinach and half of the cheese and continue cooking, stirring as needed to cook evenly. When eggs are just cooked, invert to serving plate and sprinkle with remaining cheese. Serves 6.

Stuffed French Toast

1 (8 oz. package) cream cheese, softened
1 t. vanilla
½ c. chopped nuts
1 (16-oz. loaf) French bread
4 eggs
1 c. whipping cream
½ t. vanilla
½ t. ground nutmeg
1 (12 oz. jar) apricot preserves
½ c. orange juice

Mix together cream cheese, vanilla and nuts. Set aside. Cut bread into 10-12 1½-inch slices. Cut pocket in each slice and fill with 1½ T. filling. Combine eggs and whipping cream with remaining vanilla and nutmeg. Use tongs to dip the bread, taking care not to squeeze out the filling. Cook toast on lightly greased griddle until browned on both sides. Meanwhile heat together preserves and juice. Keep toast warm in oven until ready to serve. Drizzle with hot preserve mixture when serving. Makes 10-12 slices.

Mimosa

1 bottle champagne, chilled
2 qts. orange juice, chilled

Combine in pitcher when ready to serve. Pour into stemmed glasses. Makes about 12 servings.

Kirsten's Overnight French Toast

1 c. brown sugar
½ c. butter or margarine
2 T. light corn syrup
12 slices sandwich bread
6 eggs
1½ c. milk
1 T. vanilla
cinnamon, optional

Heat together sugar, margarine and syrup. Cook until thickened slightly, but don't overcook. Pour into a glass 9x13-inch pan. Place six slices of bread in pan and place remaining slices on top. Combine the remaining ingredients and pour over the bread. Cover and refrigerate 8 hours. Bake, uncovered in a 350 degree oven for 40-45 minutes. Keep warm until ready to serve. Invert onto serving platter to put syrup on top. Serves 6.

Easy Danish

2 c. biscuit mix
2 T. sugar
½ c. butter or margarine
2/3 c. milk
assorted preserves or pie fillings or even sweetened cream cheese or ricotta
½ c. confectioner's sugar
milk

Combine biscuit mix and sugar. Cut in butter. Stir in milk. Drop rounded tablespoonsful on lightly greased baking sheet. Indent middle using spoon. Leave 2-3-inches in between as they grow. Spoon preserves, or pie filling into indents. Bake in 400 degree oven for 10-15 minutes or until lightly browned. Combine confectioner's sugar with enough milk to make a runny glaze. Drizzle over cooled Danish. Makes 12.

Salad Bowl Puff

2/3 c. water
¼ c. butter or margarine
1 c. biscuit mix
4 eggs
salad filling, **recipes follow**

Heat oven to 400 degrees. Generously grease a 9-inch pie plate. Heat water and butter to boiling in a 2-quart saucepan. Add baking mix all at once, stirring over low heat until mixture forms a ball. Remove from heat and beat in eggs one at a time. Continue beating until smooth. Spread in bottom of pie pan and bake until puffed and dry, about 35-40 minutes. Cool. Fill with salad just before serving. Cut into wedges. Serves 6-8.

Ham Salad Filling

1½ c. frozen peas, thawed
2 c. cubed fully cooked ham
1 c. cheddar cheese, shredded
2 T. chopped green onion
¾ c. mayo or salad dressing
1-2 t. prepared mustard

Combine all ingredients and keep chilled until ready to fill puff.

Chicken Waldorf Salad Filling

2 c. cooked chicken, diced
2 large tart apples, peeled, if desired, cored and chopped
1 c. chopped celery
1 c. halved grapes or ½ c. raisins
½ c. chopped celery
¾ c. mayo or salad dressing
salt and pepper to taste

Combine all ingredients and chill until ready to fill puff.

Swiss and Bacon Squares

2 c. biscuit mix
½ c. cold water
8 oz. Swiss cheese slices
1 lb. bacon, fried crisp and crumbled
4 eggs
½ c. milk
½ t. salt

Grease a 13x9-inch baking dish. Combine biscuit mix with water and knead into a soft dough. With floured hands, press dough into dish covering bottom and coming up the sides ½-inch. Cover the dough with the cheese slices then top with the bacon. Combine remaining ingredients and pour over the cheese and bacon. Bake in a preheated 425 degree oven for 20 minutes. Use a knife inserted in the center to test for doneness. 6-8 servings.

Chili-Cheese Rounds

1 (16 oz. can) refried beans
¼ c. finely chopped onion
1 t. red pepper sauce
2 c. biscuit mix
1 c. sour cream
1 (4 oz. can) whole green chilies, seeded and diced
1 c. shredded Monterey Jack cheese

Mix beans, onion and pepper sauce. Set aside. Combine mix and sour cream. Knead into soft dough. On floured board roll or pat to ¼-inch thickness. With 2-inch biscuit cutter cut out about 30 circles, rerolling as needed. Press 1½-inch indent in circles and spoon in rounded teaspoon of bean mix. Add chilies and cheese. Bake at 400 degrees on ungreased sheet 10-12 minutes. Makes 30.

Apples with Bacon

4 large Granny Smith apples, cored, cut in ½-inch thick slices
1/3 c. sugar
2 T. fresh lemon juice
½ t. each nutmeg and cinnamon
½ lb. bacon, chopped

Combine apples with all ingredients except bacon. Cook bacon until crisp. Remove with slotted spoon and drain. Add apples to skillet and cook until tender. Pour apples into serving dish with juices in pan and sprinkle with bacon. Serves 4.

Chapter 3: Tea Time - Celebrating Tea and Tea parties

A Brief History of Tea

The drinking of tea originated in China and its popularity there is credited to Emperor Shen Nong. The Chinese already boiled water to make it safer for drinking. Legend has it that in 2737 BC, while water was boiling, some tea leaves fell in and steeped in the hot liquid. Shen Nong tasted and found it good and tea drinking was born. In the year 800 AD Luyu wrote a definitive work on tea including cultivation and varieties. Zen Buddhists introduced tea and the idea of a formal tea service to the Japanese.

Tea ceremonies are meant to be a religious experience using meditation as a component. The Japanese tea ceremony inspired the creation of teahouses. To serve a proper tea one would have to be trained for two years. This also caused the creation of the geisha.

A Portuguese Jesuit named Father Jasper de Cruz in about 1560AD first introduced tea in Europe. From there it spread to the Netherlands, France and the Baltic countries. It was expensive, often costing $100 a pound and was largely consumed by the wealthy. Eventually the price went down and a wider audience enjoyed tea.

Tea arrived in England between 1652 and 1654 and replaced ale as the national beverage. King Charles II and his Portuguese wife, Infanta Catherine de Braganza, initially popularized it. Anna, the Duchess of Bedford is largely credited with the introduction of the European tea service. The tea included small pastries, cakes and sandwiches. The tea was served in silver pots and poured into fine Chinese porcelain. Often served were fish and shrimp pâtés and crumpets. The English took tea drinking to a whole new level. Drinking tea became more than a pleasant break in the day. Tea drinking became a ceremony, a tradition, and a symbol of the realm and civility itself. Afternoon tea became a chance to socialize.

High tea it is a tea party where the food served requires a knife and fork. For the lower classes it was the main meal of the day. Low tea would be consumed by the higher classes and included the little tidbits mentioned earlier. Tea for the upper classes was as much about socializing and conversation as for the drinking of tea. Tea gardens sprung up as places in which to take tea.

Women would have tea in different homes each day and invite others to their homes for a constant supply of social engagements. Tea parties became more ornate. More than a simple "cuppa" and a scone, tea parties could include hot and cold savory dishes, cheese, salad and quiche. Sweet included little biscuits, scones, crumpets and assorted pastries served with clotted cream and preserves. Of course, these were women whose servants did the actual work.

Tea came to America around 1690 and by 1720 tea was a favorite beverage among the colonists. High taxes on tea caused colonists to smuggle in tea and to use herbal substitutes. Eventually rebels staged the Boston Tea party in 1767.

Tea merchant Richard Blechynden at the St. Louis World's Fair invented iced tea in 1904. While trying to promote his product he was hindered by sweltering heat. He dumped ice into the tea to cool it down.

In 1908 Thomas Sullivan of New York invented the first tea bag. The first tea bags were larger and meant to be used in commercial establishments for making pots of tea.
In the late 1880's tea dances were staged at the finest hotels and they peaked in popularity somewhere around 1910.

Tea today is really out there for all, not just the upper classes. More than a mere coffee break, tea is a chance to sit down with friends and refresh one's spirit, share the news of the day and get rejuvenated.

Brewing a Proper Cup of Tea

The British are very particular about how a proper cup of tea should be prepared. A British friend, who lived here for a year used to cringe at not only tea bags but at co-workers who would heat up a cup of water in the microwave. So now that we know how not to do it how do we make a proper cup of tea, British style?

Always start with fresh cold tap water, not water already in the teakettle. Bring the water to a boil while getting the tea ready. You'll need a rounded tablespoon of loose tea per cup and 4-5 T. per pot. Place tea in a tea ball, cheesecloth or some sort of infuser, which will allow the water to flow easily through the tea and still stain out the leave for serving. Some teapots have their own filters, but some are not great at keeping out all the bits of tea leaves. Use whatever you can to strain the tea and keep your tea from having little bits floating in it.

While the water is coming to the boil it is best to fill the teapot with hot water to warm it. Pour out the hot water just before adding the freshly boiled water. Add the tea and steep for about 5 minutes. Remove the tea if in an infuser, or use a strainer for loose tea. Proper tea in normally served black (plain) or with milk and/or sugar. Milk should be poured into the cup before the tea is added and then the sugar. Adding the milk first is supposed to keep the cup from discoloring. Milk is also preferred over cream. Lemon is not traditional in English tea. Many also swear by never using soap to wash out one's teapot, but rather just hot water.

Is it Tea?

Today we often speak of a cup of herbal tea. Actually herbal "teas" are not really tea at all. Herbal teas are really called tisanes, an infusion of leaves in water to flavor it.

Tea is a specific family of plants from the genus Camellia sinensis. There are over 600 species of tea plants. They are evergreens with broad leaves that contain resins, which impart flavor.

How teas are preserved determines whether it is black or green tea, or something in between. Green tea is just tea that has been allowed to dry. Black teas are partially dried than allowed to ferment. A third category is tea that is partially dried, then steamed leaving them somewhere in between a green and black tea. Oolong is such a tea. Jasmine tea is just tea that is flavored with jasmine flowers during the drying process.

Section 1: The Savory

"There are few hours in my life more agreeable than the hour dedicated to the ceremony known as afternoon tea."

Henry James

Minted Cucumber Sandwiches

6-8 oz. cream cheese, softened
4 t. fresh chopped mint
16 very thin slices white bread, crusts removed
1 English cucumber, sliced very thin

Beat together the cream cheese and mint. Cut each slice of bread in half lengthwise, forming 2 rectangles. Spread a piece of bread with some of the cream cheese mixture, then with cucumber slices, top with another slice of bread. Makes 16 sandwiches.

Curried Egg Sandwiches

3 T. mayonnaise
½ t. curry powder, or to taste
½ t. salt
¼ t. fresh ground pepper
4 hard-cooked eggs
6 T. butter, softened
¼ c. chutney, chopped, or sweet pickle relish
16 very thin slices whole wheat or pumpernickel bread, crusts trimmed

Combine mayo with seasonings. Chop eggs and add to mayo mixture, stirring to blend. In small bowl combine butter with chutney. Spread a slice of bread with some of the butter mixture then top off with some of the egg mixture. Top with another slice of bread that has also been spread with the butter mixture. Cut sandwich into quarters, diagonally, making 4 sandwiches. Repeat with remaining ingredients. Makes 32 sandwiches.

Cheshire Cheese Tart

1 (9-inch) unbaked pie crust
¼ lb. ham, chopped fine
1 t. dry mustard
6 oz. cheddar cheese, shredded
2 T. butter
3 T. flour
1 c. milk
4 eggs, separated, at room temperature
1 egg, beaten with 1 T. milk

In pie crust place ham and mustard. Top with about 1/3 of the cheese. Melt butter in sauce pan; stir in flour until smooth. Add milk and bring to a boil. Reduce heat and cook about 10 minutes, stirring occasionally. Remove from heat and stir in egg yolks and remaining cheese. Set aside. Beat egg whites into stiff peaks. Fold into cheese mixture and pour into crust. Brush edges of crust with egg/milk mixture. Bake in a preheated 400 degree oven about 30 minutes. Serves 8.

Cheese Plate

assorted cheeses, cubed
small pickles and/or other pickled vegetables
olives
cherry tomatoes
assorted crackers

Arrange cheeses with vegetables attractively on platter. Arrange crackers in basket or on edge of platter, space permitting. Allow 1-2 oz. cheese per person.

English Garden Salad

2 heads Boston lettuce, torn
2 bunches watercress, torn
6 oz. radishes, sliced thin

Dressing
1/3 c. each chopped chives and parsley
¼ c. white wine vinegar
½ c. olive oil
2 T. minced shallots
1 T. Dijon mustard
1½ t. salt
¼ t. pepper

Mix salad ingredients in a large bowl. Toss with dressing just before serving. Makes 16 tea time size servings.

Combine dressing ingredients in a container with a tight fitting lid and shake well to combine.

Cheddar Walnut Tea Sandwiches

½ c. shredded cheddar cheese
2 oz. cream cheese, softened
2 t. minced onion, or minced chives
½ t. Worcestershire sauce
2 T. fine chopped walnuts
1 T. mayo
8 slices whole wheat bread, crusts trimmed, or 24 slices cocktail bread
paprika
parsley sprigs or minced chives

Combine first 6 ingredients and spread on the bread slices. If using regular size slices, cut them into quarters, leave the cocktail bread whole. Dust with paprika and a sprig of parsley or a pinch of chives. Makes 24.

Smoked Turkey Finger Sandwiches

½ lb. smoked turkey, cut into cubes
1 stick butter or margarine
1 T. Dijon mustard
2 t. Worcestershire sauce
2 t. fresh lemon juice
2/3 c. fresh parsley
3 T. chopped fresh chives or green onions
16 thin slices firm bread, crusts trimmed
½ stick butter, softened

In processor combine first 5 ingredients until smooth. Place in small bowl and stir in ¼ c. parsley and chives. Cover and chill until ready to use. Spread mixture on 8 slices of the bread and top with the remaining bread. Press lightly to compact. Slice sandwiches crosswise into thirds. Spread remaining butter along long edges of sandwiches and dip in remaining parsley. Makes 24 sandwiches.

Pepper Tea Sandwiches

¼ c. ricotta cheese
2 T. mayo
1 T. grated onion
1 T. minced fresh basil
1-2 sweet peppers, assorted colors
about 30 crackers, containing cracked pepper, if possible

Combine cheese with mayo, onion and basil. Chill mixture at least 30 minutes. Seed peppers and cut into thin strips. Spread crackers with a little of the cheese mixture and top with pepper strips. Makes 30.

Chicken Salad Sandwiches

2 whole boneless chicken breasts, baked or poached
1 c. mayonnaise
1/3 c. minced green onions
1 t. fresh parsley or dill
1 c. radishes, washed and sliced thin, optional
24 very thin slices home style white or wheat bread
½ c. fine chopped nuts

Dice cooked and cooled chicken and combine with ½ c. of the mayo, onions, herbs add salt and pepper to taste. Make 12 sandwiches with the 24 bread slices, topping chicken salad with the radish slices before adding the top slice of bread, if desired. Cut out the sandwiches with a 2-inch round or other shape biscuit or cookie cutter. Spread the cut edges of the sandwiches with the remaining mayonnaise and then roll the edges in the chopped nuts. Makes 12 sandwiches.

Deviled Ham Toasts

12 slices toast
1 c. fine diced lean ham
1 T. Worcestershire sauce
2 T. Dijon mustard
3 T. butter
1 T. chopped parsley

Cut 2-3-inch circle from the toast and set aside. Combine remaining ingredients, except butter and parsley. Melt butter and add ham mixture, stirring until heated through. Pile mixture on toasts and sprinkle with a little parsley. Serve warm, makes 12.

Blueberry Chef Salad

1/3 c. honey
1 t. paprika
1 t. dry mustard
¼ t. salt
¼ c. vinegar
½ c. oil
2 t. sesame seeds
3 c. blueberries
6 c. torn salad greens
12 oz. sliced meat, chicken, turkey or whatever cut into strips
1 c. cubed cheese

Combine first 5 ingredients in a blender. With machine running slowly drizzle in oil until mixture becomes thick and smooth. Pour into bowl and stir in seeds and berries. Cover and chill until ready to use. To serve, arrange greens on large platter and top with meat and cheese. Serve with dressing on the side or drizzle with dressing. You can also divide the greens, meat and cheese among 6 serving dishes and serve with dressing drizzled on top or served on the side. Serves 6.

Section 2: The Sweet

Mrs. Pettigrew's Lemon Tea Bread

2 lemons
3 T. sugar for topping
½ c. butter or margarine, softened
¾ c. sugar
2 eggs, beaten
¾ c. flour
6 T. milk

Preheat oven to 375 degrees. Grease an 8-inch loaf pan and line with wax or parchment paper. Grate the lemon rinds and set aside. Combine the juice of 1 of the lemons with the 3 T. of sugar, stirring to dissolve sugar. Set aside.

Cream together the butter with the rest of the sugar and beat until fluffy. Beat in the eggs, a little at a time until well mixed. Stir in the flour and lemon peel and beat well. Add the milk and beat well. Pour batter into prepared pan and bake at least an hour. The cake should spring back when touched lightly. As soon as you remove the cake from the oven pierce it all over with a long tined fork or a skewer. Pour over the reserved lemon juice mixture. Cool cake in pan before serving. Cake will be moist and tangy.

Scones

4 c. flour
2 T. sugar
1 T. baking powder
2 t. baking soda
1 t. salt
½ c. cold butter or margarine cut up
½ c. currants or raisins, optional
2 egg yolks
1 1/3 c. plus 1 T. half and half

Preheat oven to 400 degrees. Grease 2 cookie sheets. Combine dry ingredients in medium bowl. Cut in butter or margarine to resemble coarse crumbs. Stir in currants if desired. Combine egg yolks and 1 1/3 c. half-and-half. Stir egg mixture into flour mixture, tossing to moisten evenly. Knead dough on lightly floured board until it just hold together, about 8-10 strokes. Pat or roll dough ¾-inch thick and cut with 2-inch round cookie cutter. Place scones on cookie sheets, re-rolling and cutting scraps of dough. Brush scones with remaining cream before placing in oven. Bake 15 minutes, or until golden. Serve warm with mock clotted cream and jam. Makes about 30.

Mock Clotted Cream

1 c. whipping cream
¼ c. sour cream

For clotted cream beat together cream and sour cream until soft peaks form. Makes 2½ cups.

Angel Shortcakes

¼ c. slivered almonds
½ c. sifted powder sugar
¼ c. plus 2 T. cake flour
4 egg whites
½ t. cream of tartar
1/8 t. salt
1 t. each lemon juice and vanilla extract
½ t. almond extract
vegetable cooking spray

Grind almonds in a food processor until very fine. Combine with the sugar and cake flour and set aside. Beat egg whites in medium bowl until frothy. Add Cream of tartar and salt and beat until soft peaks form. Sprinkle in lemon juice and flavorings and beat until stiff peaks form. Fold in 1/3 of the reserved almond mixture. Add the remaining almond mixture and fold in. Spray muffin tins with the non-stick coating and fill 2/3 full. Bake in a 300 degree oven for 30 minutes. Cool in pan 5 minutes before removing to wire rack to cool completely. Serve with Strawberries in Raspberry sauce (recipe follows) or other fruit sauce or preserves. Makes 12.

Strawberries in Raspberry Sauce

1 pint strawberries, sliced
1 (10 oz. package) frozen raspberries, thawed
¼ c. strawberry or raspberry preserves
2 T. orange juice concentrate, thawed

Place strawberries in a bowl and keep chilled. Place remaining ingredients in a blender and mix until smooth. Press raspberry mixture through a sieve to remove seeds. Combine with strawberries in bowl and chill until ready to use. Makes 3 cups.

Crumpets

2 c. skim milk, scalded
3 c. flour
1 t. salt
1 package active dry yeast
¼ c. warm water
¼ c. margarine, melted

Cool milk to lukewarm, then stir in flour and salt, beating until smooth. In small bowl place water and sprinkle over with the yeast. Let stand 5 minutes until bubbly. Stir in margarine then add this to the flour mixture, beating well. Cover and let rise in a warm place until doubled in bulk, about 1 hour. Grease 2½-inch muffin rings, or use 3½ oz. tuna fish cans and place in a hot, lightly greased skillet. Spoon 2 T. of batter into each ring, reduce heat to low and cook crumpets 12 minutes per side. Remove from rings and set aside to cool. Repeat procedure with remaining batter. Makes about 32 crumpets.

Sherried Ladyfinger Toasts

12 ladyfingers, split
vegetable cooking spray
3 T. cream sherry
1 T. sugar
½ t. fresh grated nutmeg

Separate ladyfingers and arrange on baking sheet sprayed with vegetable spray. Brush with the sherry. Combine sugar and nutmeg and divide evenly over the ladyfingers. Bake in a 250 degree oven for 20 minutes. Turn off oven and leave the ladyfingers in oven 15 more minutes. Remove to wire rack to cool. Makes 24.

Strawberry Cheese

4 oz. cream cheese
1 T. orange flavored liqueur or brandy
1 T. sugar
¾ c. sliced fresh or frozen strawberries

Beat cheese until fluffy then beat in liqueur and sugar. Fold in berries and serve with crumpets, scones and biscuits. Makes about 1 cup.

Jam Stacks

2 eggs
½ c. sugar
1 c. flour
½ c. butter or margarine, melted and cooled
6 T. red currant jelly, red raspberry jelly or seedless jam

Heat oven to 350 degrees. Lightly flour and grease a jelly roll pan. Beat eggs and sugar for 5 minutes until light and lemon colored. With rubber spatula fold in the flour, then butter until blended. Spread in prepared pan and bake for 12-15 minutes until cakes springs back when lightly touched. Use a knife to loosen edges and invert cake onto board. Cut cake crosswise into thirds. Spread one with half the jelly. Top with another third and spread with remaining jelly. Top with last third of the cake and press lightly. Cut cake into 5 lengthwise strips and then cut each strip into ¼-inch slices. Cool completely. Make 2 days ahead and store in airtight container. Makes 200.

Cranberry-Buttermilk Scones

3 c. flour
¼ c. plus 2 T. sugar
2 t. baking powder
¼ t. salt
1¼ sticks, (10 T.) chilled butter, cubed
¾ c. dried cranberries
½ c. buttermilk
3 large eggs
1 t. water

Preheat oven to 375 degrees. Combine flour with ¼ c. sugar, baking powder, and salt. Rub in butter with finger tips until mixture resembles coarse meal. Stir in cranberries. Combine milk with 2 of the eggs and beat together. Stir egg mixture into flour mixture and stir until dough begins to form into a ball. Turn dough onto a lightly floured surface and knead about 10 stokes until dough holds together. Grease 2 nine-inch cake pans. divide dough in half and place one piece in each cake pan. Press dough out evenly. Combine remaining egg with 2 t. water and beat until well mixed. Score top of loaves with sharp knife into 8 wedges each. Brush with egg mixture and sprinkle with reserved sugar. Bake until golden, about 30 minutes. Cool 5 minutes, turn onto plates and cool right side up. Cut along score marks. Serve warm. Makes 16.

Pineapple Spice Scones

3 c. flour
1/3 c. sugar
2½ t. baking powder
½ t. salt
¾ c. cold butter
1 (8 oz. can) crushed pineapple in its own juice, undrained
milk
3 T. chopped nuts
1 T. sugar
½ t. cinnamon

Preheat oven to 400 degrees. In mixing bowl combine dry ingredients. Cut in butter until mixture resembles coarse crumbs. Add pineapple and stir until dough forms. It will be sticky. Turn dough onto floured surface and knead gently 10-12 strokes until dough holds together. Roll or pat dough to a ¼-inch thickness and cut with a 2½-inch biscuit cutter. Re-roll scraps. Place scones on ungreased baking sheet. Brush with milk. Combine nuts, sugar and cinnamon and sprinkle on scones. Bake about 15 minutes. Makes about 21.

Raisin Scones

2 c. flour
2 t. baking powder
½ t. baking soda
½ t. ground nutmeg
½ t. salt
½ c. cold butter
1 c. raisins
2 T. sugar
1 egg, separated
¾ c. buttermilk
additional sugar for sprinkling

Preheat oven to 375 degrees. In bowl combine dry ingredients. Cut in butter until mixture resembles coarse crumbs. Add raisins and sugar and toss to distribute evenly. Mix egg yolk with buttermilk and add to flour mixture, stirring to combine. Turn dough onto floured surface and knead gently 10-12 strokes. Cut dough in half and form each half into a six-inch circle. Cut each circle of dough into 6 wedges, but do not separate. Place on ungreased cookie sheet and brush with egg white. Sprinkle with extra sugar and bake 18-22 minutes. Makes 12.

Blueberry Scones

2 c. flour
3 T. sugar
1 T. baking powder
¾ salt
6 T. chilled butter
1½ c. blueberries
1 t. lemon zest
2 large eggs
1/3 c. heavy cream

Mix dry ingredients together in bowl and cut in butter to resemble coarse crumbs. Toss in blueberries and zest. Beat together eggs and cream and stir into flour mixture. Mix very gently to avoid bruising berries. Press into 6x6-inch square. Cut into 3x3-inch squares, then into triangles Place on baking sheet, brush with a little cream and sprinkle with a little extra sugar. Bake in a preheated 400 degree oven for 20-22 minutes. Makes 8.

Cream Scones

2 c. flour
1 T. sugar
½ t. salt
1 T. baking powder
1 c. heavy cream

Preheat oven to 425 degrees. Sift together dry ingredients and gradually add cream to form soft dough. Knead lightly on a floured board until dough sticks together. Roll to ½-¾-inch thickness and cut with 2-inch biscuit cutter. Re-roll scraps and continue cutting, handling dough as little as possible. Place on baking sheet and bake 10-12 minutes or until golden. Makes 8-10.

Almond Poppy Seed Scones

2 c. flour
1/3 c. sugar
1 T. poppy seeds
1 t. baking powder
½ t. salt
½ c. chilled shortening, cut into pieces
¼ c. (½ stick) chilled unsalted butter. Cut into pieces
1/3 c. sour cream
1 egg
2 t. almond extract

Preheat oven to 400 degrees. Mix dry ingredients in food processor. Add shortening and butter. Pulse until mixture resembles coarse crumbs. Combine remaining ingredients and pulse just until dough forms ball. Transfer dough to lightly floured surface. Press dough into 15x3-inch rectangle. Cut into six 3x2½-inch pieces and cut each rectangle in to triangles. Bake on ungreased sheet about 15 minutes. Makes 12.

Oatmeal Scones

1¾ c. flour
1½ t. baking powder
¾ t. baking soda
½ t. salt
1/3 c. sugar
1½ sticks (¾ c.) cold unsalted butter, cut into bits
1 1/3 c. old fashioned rolled oats
½ c. each dried currants and buttermilk
1 egg, beaten lightly for brushing scones

Mix together dry ingredients. Cut in butter to resemble coarse meal. Add oatmeal, currants and buttermilk and stir until sticky dough forms. Roll or pat lightly kneaded dough 1-inch thick on floured work surface. Cut into 3-inch rounds and place on baking sheet. Re-roll and cut out more scones from the scraps. Brush with egg and bake in 375 degree oven for about 20 minutes. Makes about 12.

Cinnamon Scones

4 c. flour
¼ c. sugar
4 t. baking powder
1 t. salt
½ t. cream of tartar
2/3 c. butter
1 1/3 c. light cream
1 large egg
milk
1 t. cinnamon and 1 t. sugar, mixed

Preheat oven to 425 degrees. Mix together dry ingredients and cut in butter to resemble coarse crumbs. In small bowl beat together cream and egg and add to flour mixture. Stir with fork until just mixed and turn onto floured surface. Knead 5-6 times. Roll or pat half of the dough to ¾-inch thickness and cut into 2-inch rounds. Place on baking sheet and brush with milk, and then sprinkle with some of the cinnamon sugar. Re-roll scraps and cut again. Repeat with remaining dough until finished. Bake 12-15 minutes. Makes 22.

Fruitful Oat Scones

1½ c. flour
1¼ c. oats, regular or old fashioned
¼ c. sugar
1 T. baking powder
¼ t. salt
1/3 c. margarine
6 oz. (1 1/3 c.) Diced dried mixed fruit
½ c. milk
1 egg, beaten
1 t. sugar
1/8 t. cinnamon

Heat oven to 375 degrees. Combine dry ingredients and cut in margarine until mixture resembles coarse crumbs. Stir in fruit. Combine milk and egg and add to flour mixture, stirring until just moistened. Knead dough on lightly floured surface 5-6 times or until dough just holds together. Place dough on lightly greased baking sheet and pat into an n 8-inch circle. Cut into 12 wedges and sprinkle with combined cinnamon and sugar. Bake 20-25 minutes, or until golden brown. Makes 12.

Section 3: Take You Child to Tea

Children often enjoy having tea parties and while they would love many of the recipes in the adult section here are some additional recipes that they should enjoy.

Peachy Shake

1 pint frozen vanilla yogurt
1 medium peach, peeled and pitted
1 T. honey
1 T. creamy peanut butter

Combine all ingredients in a blender and puree until smooth. Makes 2 servings.

"Peanutty" Patties

1 c. sugar
1 c. corn syrup
1 c. creamy peanut butter
2 c. peanuts, preferably roasted

Lightly grease cookie sheets. In large saucepan combine the sugar and syrup. Bring to a boil over medium heat and boil 1 minute. Remove from heat and stir in peanut butter, stirring until it is completely melted. Stir in peanuts and drop by tablespoonfuls onto prepared cookie sheets. Cool until firm, store in fridge. Makes about 32.

Gorp

Known in some circles as trail mix, gorp can be a combination of lots of different foods. Try to use at least 3 different ones. Choice for ingredients could include: nuts, sunflower seeds, toasted pumpkin seeds, pine nuts, raisins or other dried fruits including apricots, pineapple, dates, figs, bananas, mangoes, papayas and apples. You can also add yogurt covered raisins, chocolate, peanut butter or butterscotch chips, M&M's, mini-marshmallows, Goldfish crackers, other small crackers, Teddy Grahams, Animal Crackers, small pretzels. Anyway, you get the idea. Gorp can be served in one bowl or better yet, tie each persons up in a small plastic bag to keep it cleaner and neat.

Cheese on a Stick

Skewer cheese cubes with small pretzel sticks.

Raspberry Punch

5 tea bags
¼ c. orange juice
1 T. sugar
1½ c. fresh or frozen raspberries, thawed
1 (6 oz. can) frozen lemonade concentrate, thawed

Cover tea bags with 2 c. boiling water. Steep 5 minutes and remove tea bags. Add 2 c. ice water, orange juice and sugar. Puree and strain berries, to remove seeds. Add raspberry puree, lemonade and 2 more c. cold water to tea. Stir and chill until ready to serve. Makes 16 servings.

Sparkling Fruit Juice

Fill a glass 2/3 full with your favorite chilled juice, and then add chilled lemon-lime soda or ginger ale. Decorate with a fruit slice, if desired.

Whole Wheat Roll-ups

Place a thin slice of whole wheat bread on a counter top and roll flat with a rolling pin. Spread with a little peanut butter, and sprinkle on a few raisins. Roll up and cut into 4 pieces.

Ants on a Log

celery stalks
cream cheese or peanut butter
raisins

Cut celery into 3-4-inch pieces. Spread inside with cream cheese or peanut butter. Press raisins into filling about ½-inch apart. Chill until ready to serve.

Honey Bears

4-5 c. flour
2 packages yeast
1 t. salt
2/3 c. evaporated milk
½ each water, honey and butter or margarine
2 eggs
raisins

Honey Glaze
½ c. honey
¼ c. butter or margarine

In bowl combine 1 c. flour, yeast and salt. Heat together milk, water, honey and butter until very warm and beat into the flour mixture. Beat 2 minutes on high speed. Beat in 1 c. flour and eggs. Beat 2 more minutes, until batter thickens. Stir in enough flour to make a stiff batter and chill, cover with plastic wrap for 2-24 hours. Place dough on lightly floured surface and divide into 15 equal pieces. Roll each into a 19-inch rope. Cut rope into a 12-inch piece, a 5-inch piece and 2 one-inch pieces. Coil 12-inch piece to form body, 5-inch piece to form head and-inch pieces to form ears. Place on greased cookie sheet and let rise, covered until doubled, about 25 minutes. Bake in a 375 degree oven for 12-15 minutes. Remove the cooling rack and brush with honey glaze. Place raisins on each to make eyes. Brush with additional glaze before serving, if desired. Makes 15 bears.

Honey Glaze
½ c. honey and ¼ c. butter or margarine heated together until warm.

Blossom Punch

1 (6 oz. can) frozen orange juice
1 (6 oz. can) frozen lemonade
1 t. vanilla extract
½ t. almond extract
2 liters chilled lemon-lime, grapefruit or ginger ale soda

Combine first 4 ingredients in punch bowl or large pitcher. Add soda slowly. Serve with orange wedges if desired. Makes 8-10 servings.

Fruit Kabobs

Assorted fruits in season like, melon balls, whole strawberries, kiwi fruit, peeled and quartered, pineapple chunks, star fruits, sliced, peaches, plums or nectarines, pitted and cut into quarters or eighths.
Bamboo skewers

Try to avoid fruits that discolor too quickly like apples, pears and even bananas. Alternate fruits to make pretty combinations. These can be made that morning or even the day ahead. Chill until ready to serve. These are a nice change from fruit salad in that you don't need utensils to eat them, which can be a plus at a picnic, depending on what other foods you are serving. Also a healthy snack, side dish or even dessert.

Munchkins

1½ c. boiling water
1 c. dried apricots
¼ c. raisins
½ c. chopped pecans
2 T. orange juice

In boil pour boiling water over fruit and let stand 30 minutes. Drain well. Stir in remaining ingredients and shape into balls. Chill.

Peter Cotton Tails

4 oz. cream cheese
½ c. shredded cheddar cheese
1 c. fine shredded carrots
½ c. fine chopped nuts

Mix cheeses with carrots and chill. Shape into balls and roll in nuts. Chill until ready to serve. Makes about 16.

Tiger Paws

1 (10 count package) refrigerated biscuits
melted butter or margarine
cinnamon sugar
slivered almonds

Separate biscuits and place on work surface. Brush top of each biscuit with a little butter or margarine and dip in the cinnamon sugar. Make several small cuts on one side of the biscuit. These will be the toes. Stick an almond in each "toe" to make claws. Bake as directed on package. Serve warm or cold with butter and jam. Makes 10.

Pretzel Cabins

thin pretzel sticks
melting chocolate
graham crackers
decorations, if desired like marshmallows, gummi bear candies etc.

Sort out whole pretzel sticks and place on a sheet of wax paper. Melt chocolate over simmering water in a double boiler or in the microwave. Place 2 pretzels on wax paper parallel to each other and about 3-inches apart. Dip the ends of another pretzel in the chocolate and place on the edges of the two pretzels. Repeat with another pretzel and place on the other end of the 2 pretzels. You will have formed a square. Let the pretzels set up for thirty seconds or so and start with another pair of pretzels, setting them parallel to the first two pretzels. Repeat until your "cabin" is about 3-inches tall. Allow setting up for 2-3 minutes and then applying the roof. Break the graham crackers into individual sections. Dip long edges of 2 sections in chocolate and carefully place them on the top of your cabin being careful to place them between the last 2 pretzels. Dip another pretzel into the chocolate along an entire edge and place on the peak of your roof. Cabins can be decorated, if desired with small candies. They can be used as a party favor, or placed over a small cupcake or other treat.

Chapter 4:
My Mother's Polish Kitchen

Busha's Coffeecake

1 c. light brown sugar
6 T. butter, softened
2 t. cinnamon
1 c. chopped nuts
¾ c. sugar
½ c. shortening
1½ t. vanilla
3 eggs, room temperature
1 c. sour cream
2 c. flour
1 t. baking powder
1 t. baking soda

Mix first 4 ingredients together and set aside. Combine sugar and shortening until fluffy. Add vanilla and beat well. Beat in eggs one at a time. Stir in sour cream. Combine dry ingredients and add to egg mixture. Grease a tube pan or 9x9-inch square pan. Line bottom with wax paper. Pour half of batter in pan. Top with half of nut mixture, crumbling to spread evenly. Add remaining batter, spreading to smooth. Add remaining nut mixture and bake in a 350 degree oven for 45 minutes (tube pan) or 35-40 minutes (9x9-inch pan). Serves 10.

Spinach and Sorrel Roulade

Stuffing
¼ c. butter or margarine
1 lb. fresh spinach, rinsed, drained and chopped or
1 (10 oz. package) frozen spinach, thawed and drained
2 cups fresh sorrel leaves, rinsed and chopped
1 medium carrot, peeled and diced
1 medium onion, chopped
2 t. each dried thyme and marjoram
1 (6 oz. package) corn bread stuffing mix or 6 oz. any stuffing mix.
2-2½ lb. flank steak, trimmed of excess fat
salt and pepper to taste
¼ c. oil
2¼ cups beef stock
bay leaf

Start by preparing stuffing. Melt butter or margarine in skillet and add vegetables, sautéing until vegetables are just tender, about 4 minutes. Add the stuffing mix, herbs and whatever water stuffing mix calls for. Cover skillet and simmer for about 8 minutes. Set aside. Place the steak on a cutting board and using a very sharp knife butterfly the meat. To butterfly the steak, hold knife parallel to the meat and cut all the way through except for a 1-inch strip along 1 side. Open the steak and pound it flat, using a kitchen mallet and placing the meat between 2 pieces of wax paper. Salt and pepper the meat and cover it with the stuffing, leaving ½-inch around the border. Roll up the meat, with the grain, jelly roll style. When rolled, secure with string about every 2-3-inches. Heat oil in Dutch oven. Add the meat and brown on all sides. Add broth and Bay leaf and simmer, covered until meat is tender, about 1½ hours. To serve, remove from broth, cut off and discard strings and slice into 1-inch slices. Makes 6-8 servings.

Creamed Herring

1 large jar herring in wine sauce
1/3 c. vinegar
2 t. sugar
1 c. sliced sweet onion
1 pint sour cream
1 t. sugar
pumpernickel bread or crackers

Drain herring and reserve liquid. Squeeze gently to remove as much liquid as possible without mashing fish. Cut up any large pieces and add any onion pieces in jar to the mixing bowl. Set aside. Place drained liquid in a saucepan and add vinegar and sugar. Bring to a boil, add sweet onion slices and cook about 15–20 minutes. Drain, cool and add to reserved herring. Combine sour cream and sugar and add to herring mixture. Chill and serve with bread or crackers.

Creamed Spinach

2 (10 oz. package) each, frozen spinach or 2 lbs. fresh spinach, washed and stemmed
1 T. butter or margarine
1 c. milk
2-3 T. flour
salt and pepper to taste
½ t. dill weed

Cook spinach in a small amount of water and drain when heated through or wilted. Return spinach to pot and add butter or margarine. Place milk and flour in jar with tight fitting lid and shake until well mixed. Add to spinach and cook, stirring constantly until thickened and bubbly. Season to taste and serve.

Aunt Tillie's Crock Pickles

1 gallon water (use spring or distilled if your water is hard)
1 c. vinegar
¼-½ c. canning salt
1 T. pickling spice
garlic and fresh dill
fresh pickling cucumbers, washed and ends trimmed

Boil together the water, vinegar, salt and pickling spice. Cool completely. In large, straight-sided crock, stainless steel or food-safe plastic container alternate layers of cukes with dill and garlic according to your taste. You can also eliminate garlic if you choose. Pour over brine to completely cover cucumbers and dill. Place plate or lid on container and weigh down to keep "pickles" submerged. Allow fermentation to take place in a reasonably cool place like a basement, but do not refrigerate. Every couple of days you should skim any scum or foam that forms on the surface. When no scum forms any more, fermentation is complete. The process can take weeks. You can also add more cucumbers as you harvest them, but try to stick the newer ones on the bottom. Pickles can then be placed in sterile jars, covered with fresh brine, sealed and refrigerated. They will keep several months this way. My Mom likes the way they taste after only a few days in the brine and will sometimes enjoy an early taste.

Duck Soup / Czarnina

7 qts. duck stock
1 duck
celery, onion and parsley

Cook together, covered, until duck is very tender. Remove duck, cut into serving pieces, skin if desired, and set aside. Combine the following in a medium bowl, stirring until smooth.

1½ c. flour
1 c. duck blood *
1 c. water
2/3 c. each balsamic vinegar and sugar
¼ c. salt

Add mixture to stock and simmer until thickened and flavors have blended, about 30-45 minutes, stirring often. Strain and return duck pieces to soup.

Also add:
¾ lb. prunes
2 large cans pears, undrained

Heat through and serve with cooked shells or other pasta or kluski. Freezes well. Serves 20.

* Note: If you don't want to use the duck blood you can use ¾ c. unsweetened cocoa and increase the flour to 2 cups. The taste is really close and may be more acceptable to some.

Note: While this soup freezes well you can cut the recipe in half, still using a whole duck.

Sorrel Soup

2 medium onions, chopped
2 T. oil
2 lbs. potatoes, peeled and cubed
1 rib celery, sliced
1 qt. chicken or vegetable stock
1 qt. milk
1/3-½ c. flour
1 lb. sorrel leaves, washed and spun dry, chopped
salt and pepper to taste

In soup pot sauté onions in oil until tender. Add vegetables, stock and 3 cups of the milk. Simmer, covered, until vegetables are tender, about 20 minutes. In a container with a tight fitting lid place the flour with the remaining milk and shake until mixture is smooth. Pour into hot soup and simmer 3-4 minutes. Use more or less flour depending on how thick you like your soup. Toss in sorrel, adjust seasonings and serve. Garnish with snipped chives, if desired. Serves 6-8.

Polish Mushroom Soup

4 qt. water
5 T. paste style, soup base, chicken or vegetable
5 c. dried mushrooms, about 4 oz., **I use Shitake.**
water for soaking
½ c. flour
1 pint sour cream
¼ c. balsamic vinegar
2 T. sugar
1 lb. kluski-style noodles, cooked and drained

Soak mushroom s in water for 1-2 hours. Lift mushrooms carefully out to leave any sand in the bowl of water. Rinse and drain. Set aside. Combine 4 quarts of water with soup base and bring to a boil. Add mushrooms and simmer, covered for about 1½ hours, or until mushrooms reach desired tenderness. Mushrooms will retain some "chewiness". In medium bowl whisk sour cream into flour gradually until smooth. Stir in vinegar and sugar soup until smooth. Add a small amount of the hot soup to the sour cream mixture, whisking until smooth. Continue adding hot soup to the sour cream mixture until sour cream mixture is warm. Add the warm mixture to the pot of soup and stir to combine. Return to simmer and simmer 1 minute, stirring continuously. Place desired amount of kluski into bowls and ladle over the hot soup. Serves 12.

You can use other cooked pasta. Mom said you might want to try spaetzels or even gnocchi. You might also need more than one pound of kluski, depending on how much pasta your family likes in their soup.

Oxtail Soup

5-7 lbs. oxtails
6 qts. water
5 T. beef flavored soup base
1 T. onion flakes or 1 small onion, peeled and halved
¼ c. chopped parsley, or to taste
handful of celery tops
1 large tomato, or three small, fresh or canned, cut-up
4 large cabbage leaves
1 lb. carrots, peeled and trimmed

Simmer all ingredients together, except the carrots for about 1 hour. Add carrots and cook until meat is tender, about 1-2 hours longer. Remove meat and carrots from soup and strain stock. Return to kettle and skim off as much fat as you can. Serve soup with cooked noodles and pieces of the carrots. You can eat the meat right off the bones, or remove some and dice it up to place in the soup. Makes 5-6 qts. Stock can be frozen and recipe can be halved.

Split Pea Soup

1 package split pea soup mix
paste-type soup base to taste
2 c. sweet and sour cabbage (**see next recipe**)
2 medium potatoes, peeled and diced

Prepare soup as directed on package. Season with the soup base rather than salt for richer flavor. When soup is cooked puree in batches until smooth and return to pot. Add cabbage and potatoes and cook over low heat until potatoes are tender, stirring often. To speed things up you can use precooked potatoes. Parboiling the potatoes in a little water or baking them in the microwave are both good ways to cook the potatoes. Serves 4.

Sweet and Sour Cabbage

3 lbs. Sliced cabbage, about a 3½ lb. head or 3 lbs. cole slaw mix
1 onion, sliced
1 T. oil, butter, margarine or even bacon fat
3 c. water
1 T. paste type soup base or to taste
½ t. thyme
1 t. dill weed
1 t. marjoram
1 T. soy sauce
1 T. Worcestershire sauce
¼ c. balsamic vinegar
2 T. sugar
½ c. catsup
1 c. water
¼ c. flour

Sauté onion in oil until wilted. Bring water to boil in large pot. Add soup base and add cabbage. Stir in onions and remaining ingredients, except for the 1 cup of water and flour and cook, uncovered until cabbage is tender. This can take from 15-25 minutes, depending on the age of the cabbage and the size of the pieces. In jar with a tight- fitting lid combine remaining water and flour and shake until smooth. Add to cabbage mixture and cook, stirring until thickened, about 2 minutes. Adjust seasonings. This dish is great served alone, or with pork or chicken dishes or with potatoes.

We always serve Sweet and Sour Cabbage with Pierogis.

Jellied Pigs' Feet

Dad used to love this dish. He would drizzle a little vinegar over it and dig in.

4-5 lbs. pigs' feet, washed well
water
salt
¼ c. pickling spice
1 t. minced garlic
pepper
vinegar

Cover pigs' feet with cold water in soup pot. Add 1-2 t. salt and bring to a boil. Drain and repeat process. Return feet to pot and cover with cold water. Simmer, skimming any foam off the top until meat is getting tender, about 2 hours. Fill tea ball with seasonings and place in pot. Cook until meat is falling off the bone. Remove all meat and bones from pot. Set aside. Remove tea ball and set aside. Strain broth through fine strainer or cheesecloth. Add salt to taste. Remove meat from bones and place meat in a loaf pan. Pour over the stock and chill. Remove fat from top of dish after chilling. Serve with vinegar, if desired.

Red Cabbage Salad

8 oz. shredded red cabbage
salt and pepper
1 small onion, sliced thin
4 tart apples, peeled cored and diced
1 T. each sugar and cider vinegar
2 T. oil
2 t. Dijon mustard

Place shredded cabbage in a colander sprinkling with salt after each layer is added. Allow to stand for a couple of hours, then drain cabbage and squeeze out any liquid. Place cabbage in bowl and toss the cabbage with the onion and apples and pepper to taste. Mix remaining ingredients and toss over cabbage. Serves 4.

Pierogi

Dough
2 c. flour
1 t. salt
½ c. water (you can also use half milk and half water)
1 egg

Potato Filling
2 lbs. potatoes, peeled and boiled
½ onion, minced
2-3 T. cottage cheese or farmer's cheese, optional
salt and pepper to taste

Mix all ingredients together and knead on floured surface until smooth. Cover and let rest at least 15 minutes. Roll out thin and cut into circles. Re-roll scraps. You should get between 20-30. Spoon filling of your choice on center of dough circle. Fold dough in half over filling and press edge with fork to seal. Wetting the edge of the dough will help the dough to stick. Don't overfill or pierogis will split. Test a couple first to get the hang of it. Place a few at a time into salted boiling water and cook until they float. You can eat them as is or brown cooked pierogi in butter in a skillet. Serve with grilled onions and/or sour cream. We would often make a larger batch and then freeze them, uncooked on wax paper-lined baking sheets. When frozen they would be transferred to a freezer bag or container. Place right from the freezer into boiling water when ready to use.

Potato Filling
Mash potatoes with other ingredients and season to taste.

Note: You can also add cheddar cheese if you like.

Sweet and Sour Cabbage Filling
Use the *Sweet and Sour cabbage* recipe, but cool the cabbage before stuffing pierogi.

Lazy Day Pierogi

Layer an 8x12-inch casserole with cooked wide egg noodles. Cover with a layer of sweet and sour cabbage, then add another layer of noodles. Cover with potato filling mixture and add another layer of noodles. Top with buttered breadcrumbs and bake in a 350 degree oven until browned around the edges and heated through, about 40-50 minutes. Serves 8.

Polish Sausage/Kielbasa

A lot of work but the end result is divine.
Make and freeze or share with friends and family.

10 lbs. pork butts
5 T. salt
1 T. pepper
1 T. marjoram
1 t. thyme
2 cloves garlic or more to taste, minced
1½ c. water

Grind pork then combine with seasonings and water. The water helps the ingredients to blend. If you have a sausage maker you can stuff the sausage into casings. Sausage can also be formed into patties or links. To cook sausages in casings, boil until cooked through. You can then serve them as is on buns with bread or on a plate with ketchup and horseradish. You can also take boiled sausages and brown them in a skillet or under the broiler.

Patties and links made without casings can be pan fried until cooked through. You can add a little water and cover the pan allowing them to cook through without getting too brown. Without casings they will fall apart in a big pot of boiling water. Sausages can be frozen cooked or uncooked, but uncooked is preferred.

Angel Wings

8 egg yolks
2½-3 c. flour, plus extra for rolling
½ c. white wine (any table wine or even add a 1-2 T. vinegar)
1 t. salt
oil or shortening for deep frying, shortening is preferred
powdered sugar for sprinkling

Combine egg yolks, wine and salt mixing until smooth. Stir in 2 cups of the flour and continue adding flour until dough is very firm, but still pliable. It is better to add more flour later than to add too much too soon. Knead or mix the dough in a mixer for 5-8 minutes. Kneading dough, or mixing in a stand mixer strengthens the dough. Divide dough into thirds, cover and allow to rest 1 hour. On lightly floured surface roll dough out into thin strips. Cut strips diagonally into 1½-inch wide pieces. Cut a small slit in middle of dough and pull one end through, pulling until dough is long and somewhat twisted. Work with small amount of dough at a time to avoid drying out. Dry dough will tear and be hard to work with. You can use a pizza cutter or a pastry wheel with a zigzag edge. Cook dough, a few pieces at a time in a skillet with either oil or shortening 2-inches deep and heated to a temperature of 375 degrees. Pastry will cook in 30 seconds or so. Remove when lightly brown and drain on paper toweling. Cool and dust with powdered sugar. Makes about 200, depending on how thin you can roll them.

Note: If you have access to a pasta machine, the rolling time will be greatly reduced. Use the machine to roll the dough uniformly and quickly. There is no substitute for experience. After making a batch you will learn just how the dough should feel and how thick to roll the dough. Also, get a friend or two to help you. There are a lot of jobs to do and the time will fly with some assistance.

Potato Pancakes

1½ lbs. potatoes, peeled and grated
¼ c. flour
salt and pepper to taste
1 egg, beaten
oil for frying

When grating potatoes place them in a bowl of ice water to hold their color. Drain and squeeze out all the water you can. Place in a bowl and mix in remaining ingredients. Heat oil in skillet and drop spoonfuls of batter into hot oil. Turn after pancake is starting to brown and is setting up. Cook until both sides are golden brown. Drain on paper towels and serve. Makes about 8 pancakes.

Goldenrod

4-6 hard cooked eggs
2 T. flour
2 T. butter or margarine
1-1½ c. milk
salt and pepper to taste
2-4 slices bread, toasted

Peel eggs and separate whites from yolks. Chop egg whites and set aside. In saucepan cook flour and butter together until smooth. Stir in milk and cook until thickened and bubbly. Be careful not to burn the sauce. Season to taste and add reserved egg whites, heating through. Arrange toast on serving dishes and cover with the sauce. Place reserves egg yolks in a fine sieve and press through over sauce, dusting as evenly as possible. Serves 2-4.

Stuffed Cabbage

1 large head cabbage
1½ lbs. ground beef
1 medium onion, chopped
3 c. cooked rice
2 t. chopped fresh parsley
2 t. dried thyme
2 t. dried marjoram
½ t. salt

Sauce
2 c. tomato sauce
1 t. garlic powder
1 t. dried thyme
½ t. fresh ground pepper

First remove about 12 large leaves from the cabbage. To do it easily you can freeze the cored head overnight then thaw it out and carefully peel the leaves. Another way is to put the whole head, cored, in a large pot of boiling water for 15 minutes. Remove from the pot and plunge in a bowl of ice water. When cabbage is cool enough to handle, peel off leaves. If after a few leaves if it gets difficult, return the cabbage to the boiling water and repeat the earlier process. Cut out the thick base of the leaves to make rolling easier. Set the leaves aside and use the rest of the cabbage in another dish. In a skillet heat the oil and cook the meat until no longer pink. Stir in the onions and cook 5 minutes more. Stir in the rest of the filling ingredients and mix well. Spoon the mixture into the cabbage leaves. You should use about 1/3 c. filling per leaf. Place the filling at the bottom of a leaf. Fold the sides in and then start rolling the leaf up. Secure with a toothpick and place in a casserole dish. Repeat with the remaining filling. In medium bowl combine sauce ingredients and pour over cabbage rolls. Cover the casserole with a tight fitting lid or foil and bake in a 350 degree oven for 40-50 minutes. Serves 6.

Stuffed Peppers

I would be remiss if I did a recipe for stuffed cabbage and neglected stuffed peppers. I also love peppers and grow a lot of them in my garden. About August, I'm looking for any interesting way to use them. Prepare the same filling as for the cabbage. You will need 6-8 large sweet bell peppers, green, red or yellow. Cut off the tops of the peppers and remove seeds. Parboil a few minutes to make them easier to stuff. Place stuffed peppers upright in casserole dish and pour over the sauce used in cabbage recipe. Cover and cook until peppers are heated through and tender, about 45 minutes. Serves 6-8.

Note: My Mom also used to use tomato soup, diluted instead of the tomato sauce. I think it was in a pinch but when we were kids we used to like it that way.

Noodles and Eggs

1 T. butter or margarine
8 oz. cooked noodles
8 eggs
salt and pepper to taste

Heat butter in large skillet and add noodles, cooking until golden and slightly crisped. Beat eggs in bowl and add to hot noodle mixture, stirring until eggs are cooked and dish no longer looks wet. Season to taste and serve. Some like this dish served with catsup. Serves 6-8.

Hint: If you push the noodles to the sides of the pan before adding eggs and pour eggs into center of pan they will cook more quickly. Stir in noodles as eggs set up.

Variations: Add diced cooked ham, bacon or Canadian bacon with the noodles. You can also add 1 c. chopped tomato. Add 1-2 c. shredded cheese just after you add the eggs.

Pork Chops Florentine

5 rib pork chops, or even pork steaks or whole pieces chicken on the bone
1 T oil or other fat
salt and pepper
3 T. butter or margarine
3 T. flour
1 c. milk
1 t. salt
1/8 t. pepper
½ c. grated Cheddar or other favorite cheese
2 (10 oz. package) each, frozen spinach, cooked and drained

Brown pork in fat in skillet. Season to taste with salt and pepper when you turn them over. Remove from pan and set aside. Melt butter or margarine in skillet and stir in flour until smooth. Stir in milk and cook, stirring until sauce has thickened. Stir in seasonings and cheese and cook, stirring until cheese has melted. Stir in spinach and place mixture in a greased 1½ quart casserole. Place chops on spinach mixture and cover. Bake in a preheated 350 degree oven for 30 minutes. Remove cover and bake 15 minutes more.

Kolachky

Dough
3 sticks butter or margarine
8 oz. cream cheese, softened
3 cups flour

Mix all together and chill well before using.

Filling
assorted fruit pie fillings
powdered sugar

Roll out chilled dough into squares or circles. Spoon a little fruit filling into the center and pinch 2 ends or corners together. Bake in 350 degree oven for about 12 minutes, or until golden on edges. Cool and dust with sugar.

Beet Soup

1 large onion, sliced thin
oil
5-6 medium beets or 2 cans of diced beets
5-6 cups beef, chicken or vegetable stock
1 c. dairy sour cream
1 t. dill weed
cooked kluski noodles

Sauté onion in oil until starting to brown. Meanwhile peel and dice the beets. Add beets and stock to pot and bring to boil. Cover and turn down to a simmer. Cook until beets are tender, about 20-25 minutes. If you are using canned beets, just cook until heated through, about 10 minutes. Place sour cream in small bowl and ladle in a little of the hot soup, whisking until smooth. Add another ladle of soup and whisk again. Pour this mixture into pot of soup along with the dill weed. Serve with the kluski. Serves 4-5.

Note: You can also pre-cook the beets. Trim off leaves of beets, leaving 2-inches of stem. Also leave roots intact. Boil beets in water until tender, which can take as little as 20 minutes for tiny beets or 45 minutes for the large ones. Cool in bowl of ice water and then slip off the skins. Dice and add to soup as if the beets were canned. You can also serve the soup with diced boiled potatoes rather than the kluski or with any other cooked pasta. You can also serve the sour cream on the side, rather than incorporating it into the soup, then allow people to add a dollop of sour cream to individual bowls. Polish beet soup usually adds the sour cream and Russian style is to dollop on the top. Both versions taste good.

Iced Mazurek

2 c. flour
2 t. baking powder
½ c. butter
2/3 c. powdered sugar
2 egg yolks

Boiled Frosting
1 c. sugar
2/3 c. water
2 T boiling water
flavoring of your choice

Dried or candies fruit for decoration and sliced almonds

Stir together the flour and baking powder. Cut in butter until mixture resembles coarse crumbs. Stir in sugar and blend in egg yolks to make a soft dough. Press dough into an 8x8-inch greased baking pan and bake in a preheated 350 degree oven for about 35-40 minutes. Cool on wire rack before frosting and decorating.

To make the boiled frosting combine sugar and 2/3 cup water in saucepan. Heat to boiling and cook, stirring until mixture reaches soft ball stage on a candy thermometer (240 degrees.) Place pan in cold water and add boiling water to sugar mixture. Stir in and beat mixture until it turns white. Beat in vanilla, or other flavoring to taste. Frost mazurek and decorate to your own liking. Cut into squares.

Note: If you don't use the frosting right away it gets hard. To soften, just melt in a bowl over warm water for a couple of minutes.

Zakooskas

½ medium onion, diced
2 t. butter or margarine
1 T. flour
1 c. chicken or vegetable stock
½ c. sour cream
1 t. Worcestershire sauce
2 drops Tabasco
2 cooked potatoes
2 t. butter
2 c. ham cut into strips 2x½-inch
2 small dill pickles
1 c. grated cheese

Sauté onion in butter or margarine until tender, but not browned. Stir in flour and cook 5 minutes. Add stock, sour cream, Worcestershire sauce and Tabasco and simmer 10 minutes over low heat. Slice potatoes very thin and sauté in remaining butter 5 minutes. Slice pickles very thin. Combine all ingredients together in casserole and cover with cheese. Cook in a preheated 350 degree oven until cheese has melted and dish is bubbly. Serve with crackers or bread.

Spaetzels

3 eggs
½ c. evaporated milk
½ t. salt
1½ c. flour

Combine all ingredients and let rest 30 minutes. Drop by small spoonfuls into boiling water. Cook until they float and puff up, about 5 minutes. Serve with soups, stews and sauces. They are also good just tossed with a little melted butter.

Polish Butter Cookies

Dough
1 c. butter
¾ c. sugar
5 hard-cooked egg yolks, pressed through a fine sieve
1 t. vanilla
2¼ c. flour
1 t. salt

Glaze
1 egg white
1 t. water
1/3 c. sugar
½-1 t. cinnamon

Beat together butter and sugar until light and fluffy. Beat in egg yolks and vanilla. Stir in flour and salt. Wrap dough and chill for at least an hour. Roll out ¼ of the dough at a time into scant ¼-inch thickness. This dough is soft, so I use a pastry cloth to prevent sticking. Use extra flour sparingly and use a marble rolling pin or one with a cloth sleeve. I also keep extra dough chilled until ready to roll. Cut out with cookie cutters and place on greased baking sheet. Mix egg white with water and brush on cookies. Combine sugar and cinnamon and sprinkle on cookies. Bake in a preheated 350 degree oven for about 10-12 minutes. Cookies will be golden. Makes around 5 dozen, depending on the size of the cutters.

Chapter 5:
Cooking With Tortillas

Wraps

Probably the hottest new food trend recently wraps are simply sandwich fillings wrapped in tortillas or other soft flat breads. They can be eaten hot or cold and the contents are only limited by your imagination.

Most tortillas will roll up just fine, but if yours are a little dry just brush them with a little water and microwave for 10-15 seconds on high. Now they will be pliable.

For easier eating you might want to wrap your wrap. Use foil or plastic wrap (cold wraps only) over your roll to keep it from dripping out. This is extra helpful if you tend to really pack in the fillings.

Filling Ideas

Assorted meats, hot or cold
Cheeses
Chicken, crab, tuna or ham salad
Marinated vegetables
Stir-fried vegetables
Sausages
Grains like rice or quinoa
Cooked beans, peas or lentils

Cinnamon Crisps

tortillas
melted butter or margarine
cinnamon sugar

Brush tortillas with butter or margarine and sprinkle with cinnamon sugar. Cut into wedges and bake in a preheated 400 degree oven until edges turn golden, about 6-8 minutes. Cool and enjoy. Great added to a dish of ice cream.

Turkey and Swiss Wrap

1 small cucumber or ½ an English cucumber
8 (8-inch) flour tortillas
mayonnaise or ranch dressing
8 slices Swiss cheese
8-12 oz. thin sliced turkey
1 c. shredded lettuce or spinach
1 medium tomato, sliced thin or diced

Peel cuke and cut in half lengthwise. Scoop out seeds if not using English cucumber. slice cuke thin. Place 2 tortillas on work surface, overlapping them to form a 12x8-inch shape. Brush with mayo or dressing and top with 2 slices of the cheese, leaving at least 1-inch border all around. Place ¼ of each of the remaining ingredients on the tortillas and roll up tightly, starting at short end. Wrap in plastic or foil and chill for at least 1 hour. Repeat 3 more time with remaining ingredients. Cut in half to serve. Makes 8.

Pizza Rolls

8 oz. pizza sauce
4 (8-inch) flour tortillas
2 c. shredded mozzarella cheese
assorted toppings such as pepperoni, sliced sausage, diced peppers, sliced mushrooms, olives, onions, artichokes, etc.

Place 1 tortilla on work surface and spread with 2 oz. of the sauce, sprinkle with ½ c. of the cheese and add desired toppings. Roll and wrap in foil. Repeat with remaining ingredients. Bake at 350 degrees for 10-15 minutes.

Note: These can also be grilled or wrapped in plastic wrap and cooked in a microwave.

Grilled Vegetable Wraps

2 T. balsamic vinegar
1 T. olive oil
2 t. dried parsley
1 t. dried basil
1 t. honey
1 t. dried thyme
salt and pepper to taste
2 small zucchini
1 medium red sweet pepper, cut in 1-inch cubes
1 medium yellow sweet pepper, cut in 1-inch cubes
1 large sweet onion, cut in ½-inch slices
4 (8-inch) flour tortillas
non-stick spray or oil
½ c. crumbled feta cheese
3 T. cream cheese, softened
1 T. mayonnaise
4 small lettuce leaves
2 T. freshly grated Parmesan cheese

Combine seasonings in plastic bag or medium bowl. Cut zucchini into ¼-inch slices lengthwise. Cut slices in half. Place vegetables in bag or bowl with marinade and refrigerate at least 2 hours. Turn bag occasionally. Drain veggies and reserve marinade.

Brush 1 T, of the marinade on one side of each of the tortillas. Set aside. Place veggies in a grill basket (coated with cooking spray or lightly brushed with oil) and grill over medium high coals for about 7 minutes. Turn basket once during grilling and sprinkle with a little reserved marinade, if desired.

Place tortillas on grill rack, marinade side down, for 3 minutes. They should be lightly toasted and veggies should be tender.

Combine cheeses with mayo and spread over un-grilled side of the tortillas. Top with lettuce and veggies, Sprinkle with the Parmesan cheese and roll up. Makes 4.

Tortilla Spring Rolls

3-4 c. cooked meat such as chicken, turkey, and pork. steak or even shrimp, or a combination
1 large carrot, peeled and julienne
2 ribs Bok choy, sliced thin
2 c. thin sliced Napa cabbage
1 c. fine shredded cabbage, red or green
2 sweet peppers, any color, seeded and julienne
6 T. hoisin sauce
8 (9-10-inch) flour tortillas
olive oil for brushing rolls

Sesame dipping sauce
¼ c. mayonnaise
2 T. sesame oil
3 T. soy sauce
1/3 c. honey

Shred meat and add salt and pepper if needed. Toss with vegetables and hoisen sauce. Place about ¾-1 c. of the mixture in the middle of a tortilla and roll up tightly, folding in the sides. Place seam side down on a baking sheet and repeat with the rest of the ingredients. Brush rolls with oil and bake in the top third of a 400 degree oven for 10-15 minutes, or until golden. Serve with dipping sauce, or sweet and sour sauce. Makes 8.

To make dipping sauce whisk ingredients together in small bowl until smooth.

Layered Enchilada Casserole

2-lbs. lean ground beef
1 large onion, chopped
¼ c. chili powder
salt and pepper to taste
dash hot pepper flakes
12 (5-6-inch) corn tortillas
1 (15 oz.) can kidney or chili beans
1½ c. grated cheddar cheese
3 c. salsa

Cook meat and onion in skillet until meat is cooked and no pink is visible. Drain. Add seasonings and set aside. Oil a 13x9-inch baking dish and line with 6 of the tortillas, covering the bottom completely. Spoon meat mixture over tortillas and top with the remaining tortillas. Sprinkle on the cheese and cover with the salsa. Bake in a preheated 350 degree oven for 1 hour or until the edges are bubbly. Serves 8.

Mini Texas Style Burritos

1 lb. top round steak, cut in 2 x ¼-inch strips
1 T. oil
1/3 c. mild picante sauce or salsa
3 T. barbecue sauce
10 (6-inch) flour tortillas
1 medium onion, chopped
sour cream, optional
additional picante sauce or salsa. Optional

Sauté meat in oil until browned. Drain off fat, add sauces and cook, covered of low heat for 3 minutes. Cut tortillas in half. Spoon 1 heaping tablespoonful onto each tortilla half and top with onion. Roll up jellyroll fashion and keep warm until ready to serve. Tope with additional salsa and sour cream if desired. A nice appetizer. Makes 20.

Asian Burritos

1 lb. ground turkey
½ c. chopped onion
4 cloves garlic, minced
oil
1 (16 oz. package) broccoli slaw
¼ c. hoisin sauce
1 T. each soy sauce, sesame oil and oyster sauce
1-2 t. fresh grated ginger
salt and pepper to taste
2 c. cooked Asian noodles or angel hair pasta
10 (10-inch) flour tortillas

Cook turkey and onion in skillet until meat is cooked. Drain of excess fat and add garlic, cooking 2 minutes more. Place in large bowl. In same skillet stir-fry the broccoli 2 minutes. Add broccoli with seasonings and pasta to meat mixture and mix well. Meanwhile wrap tortillas in foil and bake in a 350 degree oven for 10 minutes to soften.

Place about ¾ c. meat mixture on a tortilla, just below the center and fold bottom of tortilla up to cover. Fold in sides then continue to roll up from the bottom. Secure with wooden toothpicks. Repeat with remaining ingredients. Heat small amount of oil in skillet and brown the rolls, turning as needed until golden. Drain on paper towels and keep warm in 300 degree oven while frying the rest, using additional oil if needed. Serve with additional hoisin sauce or sweet and sour sauce. Makes 10.

Vegetable Tortilla Lasagna

2 T. oil
1 large zucchini, cut into ¼-inch slices
¾ c. frozen corn, thawed
¼ c. ricotta cheese
1¼ c. shredded Monterey Jack cheese
½ t. cumin
1 c. salsa
6 (6-inch) corn or flour tortillas
1 red sweet pepper, seeded and julienned
3 T. fresh cilantro

Preheat oven to 450 degrees and brush 2 shallow baking pans with oil. Arrange zucchini slices in one pan and half of the other and corn in remaining half. Sprinkle with salt and pepper to taste. Place both sheets in the oven and bake 5-7 minutes. Stir corn and switch pan positions in oven and bake 5-7 minutes more, or until lightly browned. Meanwhile combine 1 c. of the Monterey Jack cheese with ricotta and cumin and set aside and drain salsa for 3 seconds.

Trim tortillas to fit 8x4 in loaf pan (3¾x5-inches). Place 2 tortillas in oiled loaf pan, overlapping to cover the bottom. Pour over ¼ c. salsa, half cheese mixture and half of each of the vegetables. Sprinkle with 1 T. of the cilantro. Repeat. Top second layer with last 2 tortillas, reserved Monterey Jack remaining salsa and remaining cilantro. Cover with foil and return to 450 degree oven for about 15 minutes, or until cheese has melted. Let stand 5 minutes before cutting. Serves 2.

Mexican Pizza

flour or corn tortillas
refried beans, or cooked beans, mashed
taco sauce
salsa
cheese, shredded or sliced thin
assorted toppings including diced tomatoes, chopped peppers, sliced olives, chilies

Place tortilla on baking sheet and spread with a layer of the beans leaving about ½-inch around the edge. Add a little taco sauce or salsa, some cheese and whatever toppings you like. Bake in a 350 degree oven until top browns slightly and cheese has melted, about 15 minutes. Cut in wedges or serve whole. These can be made by each person to suit their taste. they also make great appetizers. Serve with shredded lettuce and sour cream on the side, if desired.

Nutty Olive Quesadillas

6 (6-inch) corn or flour tortillas
1 c. shredded mozzarella cheese
2/3 c. crumbled feta
¼ c. chopped walnuts
¼ c. chopped pitted ripe olives
½ t. dried oregano
1 T. olive oil
salsa

Soften tortillas by wrapping in foil and heating in a 350 degree oven for 10 minutes. Combine cheeses with nuts, olives and oregano. Spoon mixture onto half of the tortillas and fold in half, securing with toothpicks. Heat oil in skillet and cook quesadillas, about 4 minutes per side. Cut in half to serve.

Tortilla Blintzes

15 oz. ricotta cheese
3 oz. cream cheese
½ c. confectioner's sugar
½ t. grated orange peel
pinch of salt
4 large tortillas
¼ c. milk
2 T. butter
assorted preserves and sour cream

Combine cheeses with sugar and peel and set aside. Soften tortillas in milk for 1 minute. Place tortillas on wax paper and place ½ c. ricotta mixture on bottom third of the tortilla. Fold in sides and roll up. Repeat with remaining ingredients. Heat 1 T. of the butter in a non-stick skillet and cook 2 rolls at a time. Cook 2 minutes per side and until heated through. Set aside and keep warm. Place remaining butter in skillet and repeat with the remaining rolls. Serve with the preserves and sour cream on the side. Makes 4.

Tortillas with Eggs

1 T. oil
3 (5-6-inch) corn tortillas, halved and cut into strips
4 eggs, lightly beaten
¼ c. canned diced green chilies
2 T. cilantro
salt and hot pepper sauce

Heat oil in skillet and add tortillas. Stir until softened, about in minute. Add eggs, chilies and cilantro, and cook, stirring until eggs are set. Season with salt and hot sauce as desired. Serves 2.

Vegetable Quesadillas

4 large tortillas (burrito size)
1 c. chopped tomatoes
½ c. sliced onions
2 t. fresh lime juice
1 t. olive oil
½ t. salt
¼ t. cumin
1/8 t. ground pepper
1½ c. shredded zucchini
1 c. shredded cheddar cheese
additional olive oil

Heat oven to 425 degrees. Combine tomatoes, onion juice, oil and seasonings in a bowl. Press excess water out of zucchini and add to tomato mixture along with the cheese. Lightly grease a large baking sheet. Place 2 tortillas side by side on sheet. Spread half of the tomato mixture on each tortilla and top with the remaining tortillas. Brush with a little more olive oil and bake 10-12 minutes, until lightly browned and crisp. Cut in wedges to serve.

Corn and Bean Wraps

1 lb. cole slaw mix
oil
1 c. corn
1 c. sliced green onions
1 T. Creole seasoning
1 (16 oz. can) beans, drained
1/3 c. mayonnaise
6 (8-inch) flour tortillas

Sauté coleslaw mix covered, in oil until wilted. Add remaining ingredients (except mayo) and cook until heated through. Remove from heat and stir in mayo. Spoon mixture down center of tortillas and roll up. Serves 6.

Bean and Cheese Quesadillas

1½ cans (15 oz.) kidney or other beans, drained and rinsed
¾ c. chopped onion
½ c. chopped parsley
2 t. chili powder
1 t. cumin
8 (8-inch) flour tortillas
4 oz. cheddar cheese, shredded
oil

Combine first 5 ingredients in food processor and pulse off and on until chunky puree forms. Season with salt and pepper to taste. Place 1 tortilla on work surface and top with ¼ of the bean mixture. Top with 2 T. of the cheese and then with another tortilla. Repeat with remaining ingredients. Heat skillet and brush each quesadilla with oil. Cook, one at a time in skillet until lightly browned and heated through, about 4 minutes per side. Cut in wedges to serve.

Flour Tortillas

2 c. flour
¼ c. shortening
1 t. salt
2/3 c. warm water

Combine flour and shortening by cutting in to resemble coarse crumbs. Dissolve salt in water and stir into flour mixture. Form into a ball and knead on a lightly floured surface 2-3 minutes or until it is smooth. Divide dough into 12 equal pieces and wrap each in plastic wrap. Allow dough to rest 30-60 minutes. On lightly floured surface roll out a piece of dough into a 7-inch circle. Cook dough on griddle or in a skillet over medium high heat until puffy and golden on both sides, 1-2 minutes. Wrap in a kitchen towel and repeat process with remaining dough, stacking and wrapping as you go. Makes 12.

Chimichangas

1 lb. lean ground meat
1 garlic cloves, minced
1 t. cumin
1 t. oregano
¼ c. canned green chilies
¼ c. bottled taco sauce
¼ c. sour cream
2 T. red wine vinegar
½ t. salt
½ c. butter or margarine, melted
6 (7-inch) flour tortillas
4 oz. shredded cheddar cheese
½ c. sour cream
½ c. taco sauce
1½ c. shredded lettuce

Brown meat in skillet, drain. Add garlic and next 7 ingredients and cook 5 minutes longer. Set aside and cool. Place butter or margarine in skillet and dip each tortilla in to coat both sides, allowing excess to drip off. Place tortilla on work surface and top with rounded 1/3 c. of the filling. Fold envelope style and place in a baking dish. Repeat with remaining tortillas. Can be made up to 24 hours ahead and kept chilled and covered until ready to bake. Preheat oven to 500 degrees. Bake uncovered until crispy, about 15 minutes. Sprinkle with cheese and return to oven for a few seconds to melt cheese. Serve with remaining ingredients on the side.

Chicken and Cheese Enchiladas

3 half chicken breasts
2 large onions, sliced
2 T. butter or margarine
1/3 c. chopped green chilies
6 oz. cream cheese, diced
12 flour tortillas
2/3 c. evaporated milk
8 oz. shredded cheese
shredded lettuce and sliced tomatoes
sour cream, sliced olives and green onions, chopped

Poach chicken until cooked. Cool so you can handle. Shred meat, removing bones if needed. Cook onions in butter until wilted. Add to chicken and add chilies and cream cheese. Fry tortillas in oil until just tender, about 5 seconds. Spread about 1/3 c. of filling down center of each tortilla and roll up. Place seam side down in 13x9-inch baking dish. Once all the tortillas are filled and rolled moisten top with the milk and sprinkle with the cheese. Bake uncovered, in a 375 degree oven for 20 minutes, or if made ahead and chilled bake covered 15 minutes and uncovered 15 minutes.

Place 2 enchiladas on each plate and place lettuce and tomatoes on the side. Top enchiladas with sour cream, olives and onions.

Bean Enchiladas

½ lb. hot pork sausage
¼ c. fine chopped onion
1 clove garlic, minced
1 T. oil
1 2/3 c. drained cooked beans
½ t. oregano
¼ t. each salt and pepper
1 (10-11 oz. can) enchilada sauce
8 oz. tomato sauce
6 corn or flour tortillas, heated
½ c. shredded cheddar cheese
sour cream

Sauté sausage with onions and garlic in oil until cooked and crumbly. Drain. Add beans, seasonings and ½ c. enchilada sauce. Heat well, mashing beans slightly with a fork. Combine remaining enchilada sauce with tomato sauce. Dip each tortilla in sauce and place ¼ c. of filling mixture in each. Roll and place in baking dish. Repeat with remaining ingredients and pour extra sauce over enchiladas. Sprinkle with cheese and bake, uncovered in a 350 degree oven for 20-25 minutes, or until hot and bubbly. Serve with sour cream. Serves 3-4.

Tuna Roll Ups

1 (6 oz. can) solid tuna, drained and flaked
1/3 c. diced celery
2 T. mayonnaise type salad dressing
1 t. lemon juice
¼ t. dill weed
4 small tortillas

Combine all ingredients, except tortillas and mix well. Chill until ready to use. Place ¼ of the mixture on each tortilla and roll up. Wrap in foil or plastic wrap. Makes 4.

Brunch Enchiladas

12 oz. cooked ham, or turkey ham ground
½ c. sliced green onions
½ c. chopped sweet pepper
2½ c. shredded Cheddar cheese
8 (7-inch) tortillas
4 beaten eggs
2 c. light cream or evaporated milk
1 T. flour
salt, pepper and garlic powder to taste

In bowl combine ham with vegetables. Place 1/3 c. of the ham mixture and 3 T. of the cheese in each tortilla. Roll up. Place tortillas, seam side down in greased 12x7-inch baking pan. Combine remaining ingredients and mix well. Pour over enchiladas and refrigerate, covered several hours or overnight. Uncover and bake in a 350 degree oven for 45-50 minutes, or until set. Sprinkle with remaining cheese and return to oven for a few minutes to melt. Serves 8.

Chapter 6:
Chicken -
Fun and Easy Recipes

Chicken Facts and Figures

Chickens at the Market

Broiler-Fryer: Range in weight from 2-3½ lbs. Very young birds (10-12 weeks), they are tender and good for broiling, roasting, frying and grilling.

Roasters: Slightly older and larger than broiler/fryers they are still tender. Great roasted as the name implies, but can also be fried, broiled and grilled. Range in size from 3½ -6 lbs.

Capons: Larger still they range in weight from 4-7 lbs. Generous amount of white meat makes them a good choice when a turkey is just too much. Good roasted, grilled, fried and broiled.

Soup Chickens: Sometimes called stewing chickens or heavy hens. Older still than the other birds, soup chickens are too tough for dry cooking methods. As the name implies they need to be cooked in moist conditions like stewing and in soups or casseroles. Great choice to make homemade chicken stock. Meat will not be as tender as other choices, but adds great flavor to soups.

Rock Cornish Hens: These are young specially bred chickens that are quite small. Range in size from about 1-2 lbs. Allow a small bird per person or cut larger birds in half to serve 2. Tender and cook by baking, grilling, broiling and frying

Free Range: This term is used to describe chickens that are raised in larger, more open areas. These birds are allowed to walk around, often outdoors enjoying a more natural life. This method is more humane than the cage-bound birds.

Natural: Can mean that there are no additional liquids injected into the birds for flavor. Does not insure that the birds were raised without hormones or antibiotics. Only birds clearly labeled as antibiotic and hormone free are definitely so.

Many companies inject additional liquids into chicken to make them more tender. Read the label. You are sometimes buying chicken where 15% of the weight is made up of these "juices". They can also add sodium to the chicken. There will be more shrinkage from these injected chickens during cooking. If you like the taste and texture there is no problem but be aware of what you are paying for.

Unless marked as "never frozen" there is also a good chance that the chicken you are buying has been frozen and thawed out. Since texture changes with re-freezing you should not purchase previously frozen chicken and put it in the freezer. You can also get a good buy on already frozen chicken and that is fine, but make sure pieces are separate. Frozen chicken pieces that are stuck together suggest that chicken began to thaw out at some point and was re-frozen.

Color of the bird's skin can range from white to yellow. The diet determines what color the skin will be. Color preference is often regional and may vary from one part of the country to another. Color does not affect flavor but consumers may have a preference.

Serving Sizes

When deciding how much chicken to cook keep in mind general serving sizes.

Of course, you know your own audience best but here are some guidelines.

One serving could be any of the following:
- ½ a breast (whole breast cut in half, 2 per chicken)
- 1 whole leg
- 2 drumsticks
- 2 thighs
- 3 wings

Allow about ¾-1 lb. of uncooked chicken per person, allowing for skin, bone and shrinkage. Allow about 6-8 oz. uncooked boneless chicken per person. Larger birds yield more meat per pound and generally cost less than pieces, but watch for sales in your area. Whole birds are no bargain if everyone wants white meat. Buy what you like.

The most expensive chicken cuts will be boneless, skinless breasts. Easy to use and no waste. Often bone-in chicken breasts are a good buy. You can remove skin and bones easily yourself saving them for soup stock.

A broiled 3 oz. chicken breast (weight after cooking) has only 115 calories and even skin-on is a reasonable 185 calories. Chicken has one of the lowest fat contents of all meats and offers an excellent source of protein at a good price. It is also easy to digest and can be eaten even by those on bland diets.

Q's and A's about Chicken

How long can chicken be kept in the fridge?
Raw chicken can be kept in the refrigerator for 2 days. After that it should be cooked or frozen. Whole cooked chicken can be kept for about 3 days and cut up pieces should be used within 2 days of cooking. Remember to always promptly refrigerate leftovers for best safety.

How long can chicken be frozen?
Whole frozen raw chicken can be frozen for up to a year. Cut up pieces should be frozen no longer than 4-6 months for best flavor

How should chicken be frozen?
Chicken can be frozen whole or in pieces. Pack in freezer wrap, foil or plastic freezer bags and get as much air out as you can. Seal, label and freeze. Unless purchased already frozen, chicken should not be frozen in the store packaging.

How should chicken be thawed?
The best method is to loosen the wrapping and defrost in the fridge. Small pieces will take 6-9 hours and small chickens from 12-19 hours. Larger birds can take 1½ days or longer. You can also defrost by submerging in cold water on the counter or in the sink. This is a faster method although not preferred. You can also defrost in the microwave, but this can cause uneven results. Always be sure to provide a dish or tray to contain raw chicken juices. Raw juices dripping in the fridge can cause a lot of cross contamination.

Can thawed chicken be re-frozen?
Generally, chicken should not be re-frozen. While not a safety factor the texture will suffer. If you have to re-freeze chicken cook it first. Use cooked chicken within a couple of months of freezing.

Can I stuff my chicken ahead of time and refrigerate it or freeze it for later?

No. Because you can get additional bacterial growth in the stuffing you should loosely stuff a bird just before placing it in the oven.

How can I be sure my chicken is cooked enough?

Chicken must reach an internal temperature of 185 degrees to be safe. Use an instant read thermometer inserted in the thickest meat (thigh near the breast in whole birds) or use a meat thermometer. In small pieces you can pierce the thickest part with a fork and check the juices. Fully cooked chicken with have juices with no trace of pink. Pink or red bones are not a sign of under doneness. Chicken that has been frozen will have red or pink bones. Always err on the side of caution. Cook a little longer if you are unsure.

Does freezing kill salmonella?

No. Unfortunately only thorough cooking kills salmonella. Since there are no visible signs you must assume that every chicken you purchase could be contaminated and treat it as such. Wrap separately at the store. Handle carefully and wash all surfaces well after contact. Bleach is an excellent cleaner as well as hot soapy water or even vinegar. Don't use sponges to clean surfaces touched by raw chicken as they will spread the germs. Use paper towels instead and then discard. Wash knives well and designate a cutting board that is only used for raw meat to reduce the risk of cross contamination.

Chicken Breasts in Hot Tomato Vinaigrette

1 (14 oz. can) tomatoes, stewed, diced or whole, large pieces broken up, if needed
1 clove garlic, minced
1 T. balsamic or red wine vinegar
1 T. lemon juice
1 t. sugar
½ t. lemon zest
1/8 t. crushed red pepper flakes
salt to taste
1 T. chopped fresh basil or 1 t. dried
1 T. chopped parsley or 1 t. dried
2 whole boneless, skinless chicken breasts, halved
1 T. oil
1 T. butter
additional parsley for garnish

Combine first 7 ingredients and simmer together until thickened, about 20 minutes. Add salt to taste and herbs. Simmer 5 minutes longer. Meanwhile pound chicken breasts between sheets of plastic wrap ¼-½-inch thick. Heat oil and butter in skillet and sauté chicken about 3 minutes per side. Add sauce and simmer about 2 minutes longer. Remove chicken pieces to platter and pour over sauce. Serves 4.

Cooking Tip
Some good herbs and spices to use with chicken are: Allspice, basil, bay, celery leaves, cinnamon, chives, curry, dill, garlic, ginger, lavender, lemongrass, lemon peel, lovage, marjoram, mint, orange peel, paprika, parsley, pepper, pineapple sage, rosemary, saffron, sage, tarragon.

Southwest Chicken

2 whole boneless, skinless breast, halved
1 T. butter or margarine
1/3 c. sour cream (reduced fat is OK) or strained yogurt
1 small can green chilies, diced and drained
½ c. shredded Monterey Jack cheese
avocado slices for garnish, optional

Place chicken breasts between layers of wax paper or plastic wrap. Pound chicken breasts to ¼-½-inch thickness. Sauté breasts in butter or margarine about 3 minutes per side. Remove chicken from pan and place on foil-lined broiler pan. Combine sour cream, chilies and cheese and divide among breasts spreading slightly. Place 6-inches from boiler and cook 5 minutes. Garnish with avocado slices, if desired. Serves 4.

Baked Chicken Salad

2 c. cooked cubed chicken
2 c. diced celery
½ c. toasted slivered almonds
½ c. mayonnaise or salad dressing, low-fat works well
½ c. yogurt or sour cream
1 T. lemon or lime juice
2 T. chopped green onion
2 c. toasted bread cubes
8 oz. shredded cheddar cheese, reduced fat works fine

Combine all ingredients, except bread cubes and cheese and place in a casserole dish. Cover with bread and cheese and bake in a 350 degree oven for 25 minutes. Serves 4

Chicken Sate

½ c. cream of coconut
3 T. lime juice
1 T. oil
2 t. soy sauce
2 cloves minced garlic
1/8 t. crushed red pepper flakes
2 whole boneless chicken breasts, skinned and cut into thin strips
1/3 c. peanut butter
1/3 c. water
2 T. soy sauce
1 T. sugar
1 T. red wine vinegar
1/8 t. red pepper
2 cloves minced garlic
thin bamboo skewers, soaked in water 30 minutes before use.

Combine first 6 ingredients in a shallow dish and add chicken strips stirring to coat. Cover and refrigerate at least 4 hours and up to 24. Combine remaining ingredients for dipping sauce and chill until needed. Skewer chicken onto bamboo and place in broiler about 4-inches from unit. Cook about 2-3 minutes per side. Discard unused marinade. Serve with dipping sauce. Serves 4.

Szechwan Chicken

oil
½ c. slivered almonds
2 whole boneless skinless chicken breasts cut into ¾-inch cubes
2 T. cornstarch
 2 cloves minced garlic
2-3 t. fresh grated ginger root
1 sweet pepper, seeded and cut into chunks
½ c. sliced green onions
¼ t. crushed red pepper flakes
3 T. soy sauce
1 t. sugar
1 t. vinegar

In skillet heat 1 t. oil and toast almonds until lightly browned. Set aside. In medium bowl toss chicken with cornstarch until well coated. Heat a couple of tablespoonfuls of oil in a skillet and add the chicken and half the ginger and garlic. Cook chicken until done. Remove chicken and set aside. Add 2 t. more oil to skillet and cook remaining garlic, ginger, pepper and onions 3 minutes. Add remaining ingredients and chicken and heat until sauce is thickened and bubbly. Toss in almonds right before serving. Serve over rice or pasta. Serves 4.

Chicken Florentine

6 boneless chicken breast halves, skinned if desired
¼ c. butter
¾ c. chicken stock
½ c. chopped onion
¼ c. flour
salt and pepper to taste
dash of nutmeg
2 c. milk
1 whole egg
1½ c. grated Parmesan cheese
2 (10 oz. packages) each, frozen spinach cooked and drained or 2 lbs. fresh spinach, blanched and chopped

Place chicken between wax paper or plastic wrap. Pound breasts slightly to even up thickness. Sauté chicken in half of the butter, browning a little on each side. Add stock to pan and simmer 10 minutes. Meanwhile in another skillet sauté onion in remaining butter until browned. Add flour and toss to coat. Season with salt and pepper and add nutmeg. Combine milk with egg and add to onion mixture stirring constantly until sauce thickens. Stir in ½ c. of the cheese. In oven proof dish place spinach and top with ½ c. of the cheese. Add chicken then cover with the sauce and remaining cheese. Bake in a 350 degree oven for 30-45 minutes until hot and bubbly. Serves 6.

Chicken Cordon Bleu Stir Fry

1 lb. boneless, skinless chicken breast
1 T. each cornstarch and sherry
3 T. oil
6 oz. cooked ham, turkey ham or even turkey pastrami, julienned
¼ t. white pepper
2 T. dry bread crumbs
1 c. shredded Swiss cheese

Cut chicken into julienne strips and mix with cornstarch and sherry. Heat oil in wok or skillet: toss in chicken and stir-fry for 3-5 minutes. Add ham and stir-fry for about 30 seconds. Stir in white pepper and bread crumbs. Sprinkle with shredded cheese, cover, and let stand until cheese has melted. Serves 4.

Chicken Diane

4 chicken breast halves
½ t. each salt and pepper
1 T. oil
2 T. butter or margarine
3 T. fresh chives or green onions, chopped
juice of ½ a lime or lemon
2 T. brandy or cognac, optional
3 T. fresh parsley, chopped
2 t. Dijon style mustard
½ c. chicken broth

Place chicken between plastic wrap and pound to flatten and even thickness. Sprinkle with salt and pepper and sauté in oil and butter for about 4 minutes per side. Remove from pan and keep warm in oven while finishing sauce. To make sauce add remaining ingredients to pan and cook 5 minutes. Pour over chicken and serve. Serves 4.

Lemon Chicken

4 chicken breasts, cut into 2 oz. pieces
flour
2 T. oil or butter
1 lemon, sliced thin

Batter
3 eggs
¼ c. grated Parmesan cheese
1 T. lemon juice
salt and pepper

Combine batter ingredients and chill several hours. Pound chicken pieces to ½-inch thickness and dredge in flour. Dip in batter and sauté in oil or butter until golden on both sides and cooked through. Place lemon slices on top and bake in 375 degree oven for 5 minutes. Serves 4.

Creamy Oven Baked Chicken

8-10 assorted chicken pieces
1 can condensed cream of mushroom soup
3 T. dry onion soup mix
½ c. white wine, sherry or chicken broth
paprika or slivered almonds
1 c. reduced fat sour cream or yogurt

Place chicken skin side up in a baking dish. Combine next 3 ingredients and pour over chicken. Bake in a 350 degree oven for about 1 hour. Place chicken on serving platter and sprinkle with paprika or nuts. Add sour cream or yogurt to pan juices and stir until smooth. Serve as gravy on the side. Serves 4.

Note: You can use boneless breasts instead but reduce cooking time 10-15 minutes.

Pacific Rim Stir Fry

1 T. oil
2 medium carrots, cut into julienne strips
2 c. broccoli flowerets
1 sweet pepper seeded and cut into 1-inch strips
12 oz. boneless, skinless chicken, cut in thin strips
¼ c. cashews or peanuts
hot cooked vermicelli

Sauce
½ c. chicken broth
2 T. soy sauce
2 T. fresh basil, chopped or 2 t. dried
2 t. cornstarch
½ t. crushed red pepper
½ t. ground turmeric

Combine sauce ingredients and set aside.

Heat oil in skillet and stir-fry carrots one minute. Add broccoli and stir-fry two minutes more. Add pepper and cook three more minutes. Remove vegetables and stir-fry chicken until no pink is visible, about 2-3 minutes. Push chicken to side of wok and add sauce, stirring until thickened. Return vegetables to pan and heat together 3-4 minutes. Add nuts and serve over pasta. Serves 4.

Cooking Tip
When cutting chicken into thin strips it is easier to cut if the meat is partially frozen. The firmness will make cutting a breeze. Place chicken in freezer for about 30 minutes before cutting. Remember, too to always keep knives sharp.

Minnesota Wild Rice Stuffed Chicken

1 (6 oz. package) long grain and wild rice mix
2 medium apples, peeled and chopped
3 c. fresh sliced mushrooms, about 12 oz.
1 c. shredded carrot
½ c. chopped green onion
½ t. pepper
1 (4 lb.) whole chicken
2-3 T. apple jelly

Prepare rice according to package directions, except mix with apples, vegetables and pepper. Place stuffing loosely in bird using a skewer to secure skin at neck opening. Place prepared chicken in roasting pan on a rack and insert thermometer in thick part of muscle, unless using instant thermometer. Roast uncovered in 375 degree oven for 1¾-2¼ hours. Juices should run clear and drumstick should move easily in socket. During last 10 minutes of roasting, brush bird with jelly. Serves 6.

Easy Chicken Marinade

16 oz. Italian dressing
2 t. Italian seasoning
2 cloves minced garlic
2 T. fresh basil, chopped or 2 t. dried
4-8 chicken breasts

Combine all ingredients (except chicken) in shallow pan. Add chicken, cover and refrigerate 6-24 hours. Prepare chicken any way you like. Grilling and broiling work great.

Northwestern Chicken Salad

2 boneless skinless chicken breast halves
8-10 asparagus spears
lettuce leaves
4 c. mixed salad greens, washed and torn
2 T. chopped sweet onion
6-8 whole strawberries, stemmed and sliced
1 pear, cored and sliced
8-10 whole pecan halves, toasted

Raspberry vinaigrette
¼ c. pear or apricot nectar
2 T. oil
2 T. raspberry vinegar
1 t. dried basil
1 t. Dijon-style mustard
1 t. sesame oil
¼ t. pepper

Combine vinaigrette ingredients and set aside.

Marinade chicken in half the vinaigrette for 30 minutes, reserving the rest for dressing. Meanwhile, cook the asparagus until crisp-tender and plunge in ice water to stop cooking. Drain. Grill or broil chicken until no longer pink, basting with marinade. Discard any leftover marinade. To serve place lettuce leaves on 2 lunch or dinner plates and top each with half of the salad greens. Slice the breasts into 6-8 strips and place one breast on each plate. Place half of remaining ingredients on each plate, arranging decoratively. Drizzle with remaining vinaigrette. Serves 2.

Country Captain

1 (3 lb.) broiler, cut up
1 (14 oz. can) diced tomatoes or stewed tomatoes
¼ c. currants or raisins
2 t. curry powder
½ t. paste-type chicken soup base
½ t. ground nutmeg
½ t. sugar
¼ c. snipped parsley
1 T. cornstarch
1 T. cold water
hot cooked rice, made from 1½ c. raw rice

Place chicken in large skillet. Combine tomatoes with currants, seasonings and sugar and pour over the chicken. Heat to a boil and reduce to simmer. Cook, covered 35-45 minutes. Add parsley during last 5 minutes of cooking. Remove chicken and skim fat off sauce. Combine cornstarch and water and add to sauce in pan heating to boil and cooking until thickened, about 2 minutes. Pour sauce over rice and serve with chicken. Serves 4-6.

Note: You can skin the chicken, if you like and you can substitute boneless breasts (2 lbs.) for the whole chicken. Reduce cooking time for breasts to 20-30 minutes.

Chicken Cacciatore

6 chicken breast halves, boned and skinned, cut in 2 oz. pieces
salt and pepper to taste
flour
oil
1 large onion, chopped
3 garlic cloves, minced
12 oz. sliced mushrooms
1 sweet pepper, seeded and chopped
3-4 c. spaghetti sauce, bottled or homemade
hot cooked pasta
Parmesan cheese
fresh chopped parsley, basil and marjoram, if desired

Season chicken pieces with salt and pepper and dredge in the flour. Heat oil in skillet and brown chicken pieces about 3-4 minutes per side. Remove chicken and brown onion in skillet. Add garlic, mushrooms and pepper and cook 3 minutes longer. Return chicken to pan along with sauce and cook, covered on a simmer for 10-15 minutes. Add fresh herbs, if desired and spoon over pasta. Serve Parmesan cheese on the side. Serves 6.

Sweet and Sour Chicken

1-2 lbs. boneless chicken
1 egg
1 t. cornstarch
¼ t. salt
1 t. soy sauce
additional cornstarch for dredging
2 T. oil
1 medium onion, chopped
1 medium carrot, peeled and sliced thin
1 sweet green pepper, seeded and chopped
1 sweet red or yellow pepper, seeded and chopped
1 (20 oz.) can pineapple chunks, drained, reserving juice for sauce (see recipe for sauce in Saucy Sauces)

Cut chicken into cubes and place in bowl. Combine egg, 1 t. cornstarch, salt and soy sauce and pour over the meat, stirring to coat. Allow to marinade at least 1 hour in fridge. When ready to cook, heat 1 T. oil in large skillet or wok. Sauté onions on high until tender. Add carrots and stir fry 3 minutes. Add peppers and sauté 3 minutes more. Remove to bowl and stir in pineapple. Dredge chicken in additional cornstarch and sauté in remaining oil until browned and when juices run clear when pierced with a fork. Meanwhile, combine sauce ingredients in a saucepan and heat to boiling. Return vegetables to pan with chicken and pour over sauce to desired amount. Serve over rice, makes 4-6 servings.

Note: If you make the sweet and sour sauce ahead of time it will get runny when reheated if made with regular cornstarch. Either use modified cornstarch (Clear Gel A) or make sauce just before using. You may also want to use only some of the sauce and save the rest for another use.

Chicken Marsala

6 chicken breast halves, boned and skinless, pounded thin
oil
1 onion, chopped
8 oz. sliced mushrooms
salt and pepper to taste
flour
½ c. Marsala wine, or more to taste
fresh chopped parsley

Heat oil in skillet and cook onions until browned. Add mushrooms and cook 3 minutes longer. Meanwhile, season chicken with salt and pepper and dredge pieces in flour. Remove onion mixture from skillet and add more oil if needed. Cook chicken until browned on both sides and cooked through. Add wine and vegetables and cook until sauce thickens, about 5 minutes. Sprinkle with parsley. Serve over rice or pasta. Serves 4-6.

Sesame Chicken Salad

3 whole chicken breasts
4 c. water or chicken stock
1 T. soy sauce
salt to taste
1 t. fresh grated ginger
3 ribs celery, cut in to thin diagonal slices
1 T. sesame oil
1 T. oil
1 T. soy sauce
1 T. rice vinegar
pepper to taste
1 T. toasted sesame seeds
chopped green onions, optional

Poach chicken in water or stock with soy sauce, salt, if needed and ginger until cooked. This will take 15-20 minutes. Allow chicken to cool and remove bones, if needed. Cut into small pieces and place in bowl. Meanwhile cook celery in chicken broth for 1-2 minutes. Drain. Add to chicken. Combine oils with soy sauce and vinegar. Season to taste with pepper and toss with chicken. Chill until ready to serve. Spoon onto serving platter lined with lettuce leaves, if desired and sprinkle with sesame seeds and onions. Serves 4.

Cooking Tip
To toast sesame seeds place in a skillet and cook over medium heat until seeds brown a little, tossing pan often. Takes about 4 minutes.

Crispy Chicken Bites

1 lb. boneless skinless chicken white meat or dark
¼ c. flour
1 t. dried parsley flakes
½ t. poultry seasoning
1/8 t. salt
dash pepper
1 beaten egg
2 T. milk
about 30 crackers, regular or whole wheat, crushed, not saltines
assorted sauces for dipping

Cut chicken into 1-inch cubes and set aside. Combine flour with seasonings in a plastic bag. In shallow bowl beat together egg and milk. Place cracker crumbs in a plastic bag. Place chicken pieces in flour bag and shake to coat. Dip floured chicken pieces in egg wash a few at a time. Place egg dipped pieces in bag with cracker crumbs a few at a time and toss to coat. Place chicken pieces on an ungreased baking sheet in a single layer and bake in preheated 400 degree oven for about 12 minutes or until chicken is cooked through. Makes 8 appetizer servings. Serve with dipping sauces like BBQ sauce, honey mustard or ranch dressing.

Buffalo Wings

12 chicken wings
2 T. butter or margarine, melted
2-3 T. bottled hot pepper sauce
1 t. paprika
salt and pepper to taste
celery sticks, optional
blue cheese dressing, optional

Cut wings into three segments, saving wing tips for another use. Place remaining 24 pieces into a shallow pan. Combine butter or margarine with hot sauce and seasonings and pour over wings, allowing to marinade at least 30 minutes. Drain.

You can cook the wings one of two ways. You can place them on a baking sheet and bake in a 400 degree oven for about 25-35 minutes. Brush with the extra marinade a few times as they cook. You can also broil the wings placing them on a broiler pan and cooking 4-5-inches from heat source for 10-15 minutes per side, brushing with extra marinade a few times. Discard unused sauce as it contains raw chicken juices. Serve with celery and bleu cheese dressing. Makes 8 appetizer servings. Can also be served with extra bottled hot sauce for the fire-eaters.

Chicken Salad California

4-5 c. cubed, cooked chicken
1 c. shredded Monterey Jack cheese
1 c. diced celery
1 c. seedless red grapes
½ c. peeled, seeded, diced cucumber
¼ c. chopped green onion
½ c. reduced fat sour cream or strained yogurt
¼ c. reduced fat mayo
½ t. grated lemon peel
salt and pepper to taste
toasted slivered or sliced almonds

Combine chicken with cheese and next four ingredients in medium bowl. Combine sour cream with mayo, peel and seasonings. Toss with chicken mixture and chill until ready to serve. Can be served on lettuce bed or in pitas. Sprinkle with almonds just before serving. Serves 4-5.

Chicken Marengo

4-6 chicken breast halves, boned and skinned
salt and pepper to taste
flour
oil
1 onion, chopped
2 cloves minced garlic
½ c. white wine
1 (14 oz. can) diced tomatoes or 2 c. chopped fresh tomatoes
1 c. sliced mushrooms

Season chicken with salt and pepper and dredge in the flour. Brown in hot oil in skillet. Set chicken aside and brown onion in pan juices. Return chicken to pan along with remaining ingredients and bring to a simmer. Cover and cook until chicken is done, about 20-25 minutes. Serve over pasta or rice. Serves 4-6.

Chicken Curry

½ c. plain yogurt
1 medium onion, cut in chunks
2 garlic cloves, minced
1 T. fresh cilantro
1 t. curry powder, or to taste
½ t. cumin
½ t. salt
1/8 t. cayenne pepper
4 boneless skinless chicken breast halves
2 T. oil
½ c. plain yogurt
½ c. peeled, seeded and chopped cucumber
1 t. fresh cilantro, chopped
¼ t. salt

Combine first 8 ingredients in blender or food processor and blend until smooth. Place half the mixture in a shallow baking pan. Pound chicken breasts until ½-¼-inch thick and place on yogurt mixture. Spread with remaining mixture, cover and refrigerate overnight. Baste with oil and grill or broil until done. Broil about 4-inches from heat source. Combine remaining ingredients (raita) and serve as a dipping sauce with the chicken. Serves 4.

Cooking Tip
To toast nuts (almonds, pecans, walnuts etc.) place on a baking sheet and bake in a 300 degree oven until you can smell them. About 10 minutes for sliced or slivered almonds and 15 minutes for whole pecans and walnuts. Toasting intensifies the flavor.

Chicken with Mangoes

1 c. flour
1¾ c. water
½ t. salt
¼ t. baking powder
3 whole chicken breasts, boned, skinned and cut into thin strips
oil
8 green onions, chopped
2 T. fresh grated ginger
2 large mangoes, peeled, pit removed and flesh chunked
3 T. rice vinegar
3 T. dry sherry
1½ T. soy sauce
1 T. sugar
2 t. cornstarch
2 t. paste-type chicken soup base
1 t. sesame oil

Combine flour with 1 c. of the water, salt and baking powder and let sit 15-30 minutes. Dip chicken strips in flour mixture and cook in skillet in hot oil until browned and cooked through. Set aside. In 1 T. of oil cook onions and ginger in skillet 2 minutes. Meanwhile, combine remaining water with the remaining ingredients and add to skillet. Heat until sauce is thickened and bubbly. Add chicken and heat 3-5 minutes more. Serve over rice. Serves 4-6.

Luxury Baked Chicken

8 chicken breast halves, boneless and skinless
1 c. strained yogurt or reduced fat sour cream
¼ c. lemon juice
1 T. Worcestershire sauce
2 t. each salt, celery seeds and paprika
2 cloves minced garlic
½ t. pepper
1¾ c. bread crumbs
2 T. melted butter, optional

In bowl combine yogurt with juice, sauce and seasonings. Dip chicken breasts in this mixture and roll them up, securing with toothpicks. Cover and refrigerate overnight. Roll chicken in bread crumbs and bake in a 400 degree oven for 45 minutes. Spoon over melted butter, if desired and bake 10 minutes more. Serves 8.

To strain yogurt place coffee filter in strainer and spoon in yogurt. Place over a bowl in fridge overnight. Mixture will be thick and creamy and reduced in volume by half. Tastes more like sour cream.

Orange Rosemary Chicken

1 frying chicken, cut up
salt and pepper
3 T. oil
2 T. fresh rosemary or 2 t. dried
½ t. garlic powder
½ t. paprika
1½ c. orange juice
¼ c. lemon juice
½ c. brown sugar
1 orange, sliced thin

Season chicken pieces with salt and pepper and brown in skillet in hot oil. Place in casserole dish and sprinkle with the seasonings, including more salt and pepper to taste. Combine the juices and sugar and pour over the chicken. Place orange slices on top and bake in a 350 degree oven for 35 minutes. Turn up heat to 425 and bake 15 minutes longer. Chicken should be nicely glazed. Serves 6-8.

Chapter 7:
Seafood Made Easy

Preparing Fish

Poaching Fish

To poach fish choose the poaching liquid. You can use water, wine, tomato juice, broth (chicken, vegetable, or fish) or even milk. Flavor with salt, pepper lemon, lime or herbs such as basil, parsley, chives, dill weed, dill seed, celery leaves, celery seeds, thyme, paprika, savory, cumin etc.

Warm the liquid first then place some seasonings in, if desired then add the fish. Most any fish works, thicker pieces will take a little longer. Cook at barely a simmer, cooking at a boil will make the fish tough. Most fish is poached in 10-15 minutes. Check to see when fish flakes. Don't overcook.

Broiling Fish

Place fillets or steaks on a heat proof dish that has been lightly oiled. You can preheat the dish to make sticking less likely. Leave room between fish and season as you like. Brush with a little oil or butter, if you like. Broil fish only on one side. It cooks so quickly that there is no need to turn it over. Allow 5-8 minutes for most fillets, a little longer if the steak is more than an inch thick.

Baking Fish

Fish cooks quickly, so keep an eye on it. Some people like to brush a little milk on fish before baking. You can also dab with butter, if desired, season to taste and even sprinkle on some breadcrumbs. At 375 degrees an average fillet will take 10-15 minutes to bake. Fish should flake and be slightly firm in the middle.

Marinating Fish

Unlike meats, fish should never be marinated for longer than 30 minutes. The flesh is so tender that longer marinating can make the fish too mushy. Marinades can include tomato juice, milk, lemon; lime or orange juice and of course wine. Use a light hand with seasonings, as the marinating tends to make the flavors more intense. You can also use the same liquid to poach the fish if you want.

Frying Fish

There are several easy rules to follow for perfect fried fish every time. First, fry fish soon after breading and immediately after dipping in batter for best results. Fry in hot oil. Don't rush the job and throw the fish in if the oil is less than 375 degrees or the fish will soak up oil like a sponge. You don't have to deep fry fish; you can also pan fry with just a touch of oil in the bottom of the pan. Cooks fast 5 minutes or less sometimes. Drain on paper towels and serve hot.

Creole Seafood Seasoning

3 T. paprika
3 T. dried minced onion
2 T. salt
2 T. dried minced garlic
1 T. freshly ground black pepper
1 T. cayenne pepper
1 T. dried thyme

Combine all ingredients and store in a cool, dry place. Use with any seafood.

Parchment Fish

4 (6 oz.) fish steaks or fillets, almost any kind will work
salt and fresh ground pepper
fresh chopped herbs, such as basil, dill, cilantro, thyme, parsley etc.
fresh minced garlic
butter
4 sheets parchment paper, about 12x12-inches
lemon wedges
edible flowers for garnish, optional

Place each piece of fish in the middle of a piece of parchment. Salt, pepper and season with garlic to taste. Add a dab of butter to each fish and sprinkle liberally with fresh herbs. Wrap parchment bundles by folding in sides and then rolling up from one side. End with corner of parchment tucked under. Place bundles on baking sheet and bake in 375 degree oven for 20 minutes. To serve, place bundles on individual serving dishes, tear open down the middle and garnish with lemon and edible flower. You can also remove the parchment before serving, but it's not as much fun. Serves 4.

Smelts

smelts
oil
flour
salt and pepper

Clean smelt by gutting, beheading and washing well. Add salt and pepper to flour in a plastic bag. Heat oil in skillet. Shake fish, several at a time in the flour then fry in oil, turning to brown both sides. Drain on paper towels, serve with tartar sauce.

Creole Jambalaya

1 lb. smoked sausage, sliced into 1-inch pieces
1 c. chopped onions
2 garlic cloves, chopped
¼ c. oil
2 c. cubed uncooked chicken
3 c. water
1½ c. uncooked rice
1 (16 oz. can) tomatoes
2 T. instant chicken base or 6 bouillon cubes
2-3 t. paprika
cayenne pepper to taste
black pepper to taste
¼ t. ground turmeric
1 lb. medium shrimps, peeled and deveined, uncooked
1½ c. frozen peas
½ c. chopped red pepper
1 lb. mussels, optional

In Dutch oven cook sausage, onion and garlic in oil until onion is tender. Add remaining ingredients, except shrimp, peas, sweet red peppers and mussels. Bring to a boil, turn down to simmer and cook 20 minutes. Stir in shrimp, and peppers, cover and cook 10 minutes. Stir in peas and stick in mussels, if desired. Cover and cook 5 more minutes. Discard any mussels which have not opened in 5 minutes. Serves 8.

Fish Chowder

1 medium carrot, sliced
2 ribs celery, diced
2 medium potatoes, peeled and sliced
1 large leek, white part only, cleaned and chopped
5 c. chicken, vegetable or fish stock
2 c. plum tomatoes, drained, chopped
salt and pepper to taste
1½ lb. firm white fish cut into ½-inch cubes
¼ c. flour
½ t. paprika
2 T. oil

In broth cook the carrot, celery and leeks 10 minutes. Add tomatoes and potatoes and simmer, covered, for 15 minutes longer. Season to taste. Meanwhile mix the flour and paprika together and dredge the fish in it. Heat oil in a skillet over medium high heat and cook the fish until lightly browned on both sides. Drain on paper towels. Before serving add fish pieces to the soup and simmer 5 minutes. Serve with crusty bread. Serves 6.

Salmon Bake with Pecan Crunch Coating

2 T. Dijon mustard
2 T. melted butter
4 t. honey
¼ c. fresh bread crumbs
¼ c. finely chopped pecans or walnuts
2 t. chopped parsley
4 salmon fillets
salt and pepper
lemon wedges for garnish

Mix together mustard, butter and honey and set aside. Mix together bread crumbs, nuts and parsley and set aside. Season each fillet with salt and pepper. Place on lightly greased baking or broiling pan. Brush each fillet with mustard mixture. Divide crumb mixture among fillets, patting to hold. Bake in 450 degree oven for 10 minutes per inch thickness of fillets. Serves 4.

Salmon Quiche

1 c. whole wheat flour
2/3 c. shredded sharp cheddar cheese
¼ c. chopped almonds
½ t. salt
½ t. paprika
6 T. oil
1 (15 oz. can) salmon, flaked, drained, liquid reserved, bones and skin removed
3 eggs, beaten
1 c. sour cream
¼ c. mayo or salad dressing
½ c. shredded sharp cheddar cheese
1 T. grated onion
½ t. dill weed
3 drops Tabasco

For crust, combine first 5 ingredients in a bowl. Add oil and mix well. Press into a 9-inch pie plate. Bake in a 400 degree oven for 10 minutes. Remove pie crust from oven and reduce oven temperature to 325 degrees. Meanwhile, begin filling. If needed, add water to reserved salmon juice to measure ½ c. Combine remaining ingredients in a bowl, including reserved liquid. Pour into prepared crust and bake for 45 minutes or until set in the center. Makes 6 servings.

Linguine with Clam Sauce

1 T. oil
2 cloves garlic, minced
2 (10 oz. cans) each, whole clams, drained
1 c. finely chopped parsley
1 c. skim milk
1 T. lemon juice
pepper to taste
1 lb. linguine

Heat oil in Dutch oven and sauté garlic until tender. Add clams and parsley and cook over medium heat 5 minutes. Add milk, lemon juice and pepper and simmer 5 more minutes. Meanwhile prepare linguine al dente. Drain pasta and transfer to a large warm serving bowl. Toss with the sauce and serve. Makes 6 servings.

For linguine with a red clam sauce just substitute 1-2 c. of your favorite spaghetti sauce for the milk and lemon juice. Serve with fresh grated Parmesan cheese.

Surimi Salad

12 oz. surimi (fake crabmeat) well flaked
1 small avocado, seeded, peeled and diced
½ c. celery diced
1 or 2 green onions, chopped
2 T. reduced calorie mayo
2 T. plain yogurt
2 T. creamy horseradish
1 t. lemon juice
4 large romaine lettuce leaves

Combine first four ingredients in medium bowl and toss together. Combine remaining ingredients, except lettuce and pour over surimi mixture, tossing to coat well. Place leaves on 4 serving plates and divide salad between them. Serves 4.

Stuffed Baked Bass
(Or Any Large Fish)

1 (3-4 lb.) fish, split and cleaned

Stuffing
¼ c. chopped onion
¼ c. butter
2 c. bread cubes
1/3 c. dill pickle relish
salt and pepper to taste

Sauce
1 (6 oz. can) tomato paste
2 c. water
1 T. lemon juice
¼ c. shopped parsley
salt and pepper to taste

Sauté onion in butter until tender. Add remaining stuffing ingredients and toss to blend. Pat fish dry inside and stuff with bread mixture. Sew or skewer fish closed and place in greased baking dish. Mix sauce ingredients, except parsley and bring to a boil. Pour over fish and sprinkle with parsley. Bake in a 350 degree oven for 50 minutes, or until fish flakes. Garnish with lemon when serving. Serves 6.

Paella Salad

12 oz. fresh or frozen shrimp in shells
½ t. salt
1 6 oz. package long grain and wild rice mix
1 c. frozen peas, thawed and drained
4 oz. fully cooked smoked sausage, cut into 1-inch slices
1 oz. jar sliced pimento, drained
1 garlic and herb dry salad dressing mix
1 (6 oz. can) crabmeat, drained
lettuce leaves and tomato wedges, optional

Peel and de-vein shrimp. Cook in 2 c. boiling salted water for 1-3 minutes. Rinse shrimp under cold water to cool. Set aside. Prepare rice mix according to directions on box. Set aside and allow to cool. Prepare salad dressing according to package directions. Combine ingredients, except crabmeat, dressing, lettuce and tomatoes. Toss to blend. Add ½ of dressing and toss to coat. Gently fold in crabmeat. Chill several hours before serving. Serve over lettuce and garnish with tomato wedges, if desired. Makes 6 main dish servings.

Fish Parmesan

1 (14 oz. can) chunky Italian style tomatoes
1 egg
1 T. water
½ c. Italian flavored bread crumbs
¼ c. fresh grated Parmesan cheese
1 lb. flounder, sole, cod, or other mild white fish fillets
1 T. oil
cooked pasta

Bring sauce to a simmer and keep warm. Combine egg and water and place on plate. Combine crumbs and cheese on a sheet of wax paper. Dip fillets in egg mix then in crumbs. Sauté fish about 3 minutes per side, more for thicker fillets. Serve with sauce over pasta. Makes 4 servings.

Flounder Florentine

1 lb. flounder or other mild fish fillets
1 package frozen spinach
¼ c. chopped onion
½ t. marjoram
1 c. skim milk
2 T. flour
salt and pepper to taste
2 T. fresh grated Parmesan cheese

Pour 1 c. of water into a skillet and bring to a boil. Add fish and simmer 2 minutes. Remove filets and set aside. Add spinach and onion to the water and cook until spinach is thawed. Drain and return to the pan. Place milk and flour along with seasonings in jar with tight fitting lid. Shake until flour is mixed in. Pour over spinach mixture and cook over medium heat until sauce thickens. Adjust seasonings. Spoon out spinach and place in bottom of casserole. Place fish on top and pour over the sauce. Sprinkle with the cheese. Place in a 400 degree oven for 15-20 minutes, sauce should start to brown a little. Four servings.

Maryland Clams Casino

12 cherrystone clams in shell
1-2 drops Worcestershire sauce
1-2 drops hot sauce
3 strips partially cooked bacon, cut in thirds
seasoned bread crumbs for topping

Open clam leaving them on one shell. Discard other shell half. Arrange clams in shallow baking pan. On each clam place Worcestershire, hot sauce, bacon and bread crumbs. Broil 4 inches from heat source until edges of clams begin to curl and bacon is done. Makes 12 appetizers.

Greek Seafood Salad

1 lb. cooked shrimp
1 ripe avocado, peeled, pitted and sliced
1 (11 oz. can) drained Mandarin oranges
1 lb. fresh spinach, washed and torn into bite sized pieces
4 strips bacon, cooked and crumbled
Russian dressing
2 hard cooked eggs, sieved

If shrimp are large cut in half. In medium bowl add all salad ingredients, except dressing and eggs. Mix well and divide among 4 serving bowls. Sprinkle with the eggs and serve with dressing on the side. 4 Servings.

Asian Steamed Tuna with Vegetables

1 lb. boneless tuna steak (1-inch thick)
1 green onion, chopped fine
1 t. fresh grated gingerroot
1 garlic clove, minced
2 t. cornstarch
2 t. each soy sauce and dry sherry
8 oz. pea pods
1 small head Chinese cabbage, about 1 lb., sliced
2 carrots, julienne

Cut tuna into 1-inch cubes. In small bowl combine green onion, ginger and garlic. In separate bowl combine cornstarch, soy and sherry. Add half the green onion mixture to the cornstarch mixture, add the tuna and toss to coat. Set up steamer in large kettle or in steamer. Place vegetables in steamer, sprinkle with remaining green onion mixture and stem until veggies are just tender. Remove vegetables and keep warm. Place tuna on foil placed on steamer rack. Cover and steam until fish is opaque, about 8-10 minutes. Arrange fish and vegetables on serving plate. Serves 4.

Mussels in White Wine

2 lbs. mussels
2 T. butter or margarine
2 cloves garlic, minced
1 c. dry white wine
¼ c. packed fresh basil, chopped
¼ c. packed parsley, chopped

Scrub and rinse mussels. In medium saucepan melt butter or margarine. Add garlic and sauté 30 seconds. Add mussels and remaining ingredients and bring to a boil, covered. Simmer 4-5 minutes, tossing pot a couple of times until shells open. Discard any mussels that do not open. You can serve with the broth, or you can remove the mussels, keeping them warm and boil the broth to reduce it by a third to make it more intense. Serves 4.

Lime Garlic Broiled Shrimp

2 lbs. raw shrimp, peeled and de-veined
3 cloves garlic, minced
½ c. butter or margarine, melted
2 T. lime juice
½ t. salt
fresh ground pepper and chopped parsley

Cook garlic in butter until tender. Remove from heat and stir in lime juice and salt. Place shrimp in single layer in heat proof dish. Pour over sauce and broil shrimp 4 inches from heat source for 8-10 minutes. Shrimp will turn pink, but still be tender. Sprinkle with pepper and parsley and serve. Makes 6 servings.

Note: On this recipe you can marinade the shrimp for 30 minutes in sauce (including pepper and parsley) and then place shrimp on skewers and grill. Allow 4-5 minutes per side, turning once during cooking.

Surimi with Melon

4 cantaloupe halves
1 lb. surimi (fake crabmeat)
½ c. mayo
1 c. diced celery
2 green onions, diced
2 t. mustard
1 t. wine vinegar
8 small wedges watermelon
2 oranges
Romaine lettuce leaves

Trim some skin off the sides of melon halves to allow them to rest on their sides. Combine "crabmeat" with vegetables, mayo, mustard and vinegar. On each of four serving plates place cantaloupe half. Place lettuce leaves around edge of melon. Place ¼ of salad in each of the melon halves. Place 2 watermelon slices on each plate and decorate with sections from the oranges (½ orange per plate). Makes 4 servings.

Basic Seafood Seasoning

3 T. parsley flakes
3 T. dried minced onion
1 T. dill weed
1 T. savory or thyme
2 t. basil
2 t. oregano
2 t. celery seed
1 t. dill seed
1 t. dried minced garlic

Combine all ingredients and store in a cool, dry. Dark place. Use on any seafood or mix into mayo for a nice seafood sauce. I like to dust fillets with this mixture before cooking.

Crab Cakes

1 lb. lump crabmeat, picked over
½ c. fresh bread crumbs
2 T. fresh chopped parsley
2 T. heavy cream
1 T. fresh lemon juice
2 t. fresh chives, snipped or green onion, minced
1 t. Dijon mustard
½ t. grated lemon zest
1/8 t. cayenne pepper
1 egg
1 egg yolk
1/3 c. dry bread crumbs
4 T. butter
Tartar sauce

Set oven on warm. Place all ingredients except dry bread crumbs, butter and tartar sauce in medium bowl and mix well. Form into 8 balls, squeezing out extra moisture. Place bread crumbs in shallow dish and coat crab cake sin the crumbs, turning gently to coat both sides. Heat half the butter in a skillet and cook 4 cakes at a time, turning carefully. Brown both sides and keep finished cakes in warm oven while finishing the remaining 4 cakes. Serve with tartar sauce. Makes 8 cakes.

Shrimp and Asparagus Pizza

1 prepared pizza crust
2 T. oil
1 lb. asparagus, trimmed into 1-inch pieces
¾ lb. medium shrimp, cleaned and deveined
½ t. each salt, garlic and lemon peel
1½ c. shredded Muenster cheese
2 plum tomatoes, diced

Heat oil in skillet. Cook asparagus in oil until tender. Add shrimp and cook until shrimp are just turning pink. Add seasonings and remove from heat. Place ½ of the cheese on crust. Spread the shrimp mixture over the cheese. Top with the remaining cheese and top off with tomatoes. Bake in 450 degree oven for 10 minutes.

Cooking Scallops

There are two types of scallops on the market, bay and sea. Sea scallops are the larger and more expensive, bay scallops are smaller and generally more affordable. Both can be cooked in similar ways, but obviously bay scallops cook for a shorter time. The secret to having good scallops is starting off with fresh scallops. They should have nothing but a fresh aroma or no smell at all. Smelly scallops have been around too long or have been mishandled. The scallops you get at most stores have been previously frozen, then thawed out for sale. Do not refreeze them unless they are cooked first. The next step is to cook them properly. Like mussels, scallops cook very quickly and once overdone are really bad. This is more critical in smaller scallops. Barely cook scallops for best flavor. Good methods include baking, broiling, stir-frying and even grilling. As with shrimp, if you want to add them to soup, stew or casserole adds at the last few minutes of cooking. Scallops will go from translucent to opaque when cooked and with small scallops in a stir-fry they can be cooked in as little as 2 minutes. I always test one to be sure. Still, don't get too cautious. For safety's sake all shellfish should completely cooked before eating.

Scallop Stir-Fry

1 T. oil
1 onion, sliced
1 carrot cut into matchstick pieces
1 rib celery, sliced thin
½ lb. sliced green beans or pea pods
1 sweet pepper, seeded and cut in thin strips
1 c. mushrooms, sliced
1 lb. bay or sea scallops
2 t. soy sauce, or to taste
2 t. sesame oil
1 t. fresh grated ginger
½ c. chicken or vegetable stock
1 T. cornstarch
½ c. sliced green onions
hot cooked rice or vermicelli

Heat oil in large skillet or wok. Add onion and stir-fry over high heat for 3 minutes. Add carrots, celery and beans or pea pods and cook 3 minutes more. Add pepper and mushroom and cook 2 more minutes. Add scallops and cook 1-2 minutes for bay scallops and 4-5 minutes for sea scallops. Add soy sauce, sesame oil and ginger. Dissolve cornstarch in stock and add to vegetables stirring until thickened and bubbly. Sprinkle with the green onions and serve over pasta or rice. Serves 4-6.

Crab Puffs

2 T. butter
1 medium onion, diced fine
1 sweet pepper, any color, seeded and diced fine
1 rib celery, minced
1 t. cumin
1 t. dry mustard
½ t. salt
dash cayenne
1½ T. flour
½ c. evaporated milk
6 oz. crab meat, cooked
1 t. Worcestershire sauce
1 t. paprika
tiny baked cream puff shells, split

Sauté vegetables in butter until onions are translucent. Add seasonings and cook 3-4 minutes. Stir in flour and then add milk and cook, stirring, until mixture is thickened and bubbly. Stir in crabmeat, Worcestershire sauce and paprika. Add more milk if mixture seems too thick. Mixture can be made day ahead, chilled, and then warmed right before using.

To serve: Spoon warm filling in puffs and place in 350 degree oven to heat through. Makes 18-24 puffs.

Chapter 8:
Saucy Sauces

Sweet and Sour Sauce

½ c. vinegar
½ c. sugar
½ pineapple
3 T. catsup
2 T. soy sauce
2 T. cornstarch
1 t. dried minced garlic
1 t. fresh grated ginger
hot pepper flakes to taste

In saucepan combine all ingredients. Cook over medium heat, stirring as mixture gets hot, until sauce begins to bubble. It will also get much clearer. Boil gently 1 minute, stirring constantly before removing from heat. Makes 1½ cups. Keeps in the fridge for a couple of weeks.

Plum Dipping Sauce

½ c. plum jam
3 T. soy sauce
½ t. mustard

Combine ingredients in saucepan and heat until bubbly. Serve with pork, lamb and poultry.

Cranberry Barbecue Sauce

1 (14 oz. can) diced tomatoes
2 T. brown sugar
1 T. minced dried onion
1 T. vinegar
1 T. molasses
1 t. each dried basil, dried oregano and garlic powder
½ t. each cumin, paprika and pepper
dash salt
1 (15 oz. can) whole-berry cranberry sauce

Combine all ingredients, except cranberry sauce in food processor and pulse a few times to chop up a bit. Combine this mixture with cranberry sauce in saucepan and cook over medium heat about 30 minutes or until thickened. Stir to prevent sticking. Makes about 2½ cups.

To use: Brush on chicken, ribs or beef kebobs last 15 minutes of cooking.

Chicken Sauces

If you are eating chicken more you may want some quick sauce ideas to dress up breasts, legs or even boneless chicken. When cooking chicken without bones cooking time will be reduced. You can bake, grill, poach or sauté chicken, depending on your mood, and what sauce you are using. You can also purchase an already cooked chicken, then freeze some for later. These sauce recipes are generally enough for a couple of servings. You can of course make more as needed.

Italian: 8oz. can tomato sauce, Italian seasoning and 1 c. sliced mushrooms for Italian Chicken, serve over pasta.

Sweet and Sour: ¼ c. each sugar, pineapple juice and vinegar. Add a little ketchup, soy sauce and about 1 T. of cornstarch to thicken.

Marsala: Add ¼-1/3 c. Marsala wine per chicken piece to the pan. Add onion, mushrooms and a little tarragon. Thicken with flour.

Cantonese: Sauté chicken with celery, onion and mushrooms. Add ½ c. chicken stock mixed with 1 T. cornstarch and cook until thickened. Add soy sauce to taste. Serve over rice

Lemon: Dredge chicken in flour, sauté until cooked. Add 1-2 T. lemon juice and a little water or broth. Simmer until the flour on the chicken thickens liquids into a sauce. Add a little grated Parmesan cheese, if you like.

Jelly: Many fruit jellies and preserves make a quick and tasty glaze for chicken, try apple, raspberry, pineapple, apricot and even strawberry. Add salt and pepper to taste and a little garlic powder.

Florentine: Add 1 package of frozen spinach for every 2 pieces of chicken in the pan. Season with salt, pepper and a little dill. This dish works well as a baked dish with spinach on bottom of the pan and seasoned, and then chicken added and seasoned. Bake until chicken is cooked.

Orange: Add 1-2 T. orange juice concentrate, 1 T. vinegar and 2 T. brown sugar. Salt and pepper to taste.

Honey-mustard: Add equal parts of honey and mustard to chicken. A pinch of ginger goes well here, too.

Orange Barbecue Sauce

½ c. chopped onion
oil
½ c. water
1 c. catsup
1/3 c. frozen orange juice concentrate
juice of ½ a lime (about 1-2 T.)
2-3 T. brown sugar
1 T. Worcestershire sauce
1 T. mustard

Cook onion in oil until tender. Add remaining ingredients and simmer, covered for about 30 minutes. Remove lid and continue to cook, if needed, to reach desired thickness. Stir often to prevent sticking. Makes about 1¾ cup.

Cherry Dipping Sauce

12 oz. cherry jelly
2 T. lemon juice
dash of cloves

Combine all ingredients in saucepan and warm up. Use as a dipping sauce or as a glaze for beef, poultry, lamb and pork.

Raspberry Sauce

2 (10 oz. package) each, frozen raspberries, thawed
2 T. brown sugar
1 T. lemon juice
2 t. cornstarch

Press one package of the berries through a sieve to remove the seeds. You can do both packages, if desired. Press out as much of the pulp as possible. Place all ingredients in saucepan and heat to a simmer, stirring often to prevent sticking. This will take about 5 minutes. Serve as a glaze on meats and poultry, especially duck or serve warm as a sauce on the side.

Rhubarb Glaze

4 c. sliced fresh or frozen rhubarb
¾ c. cran-apple juice drink concentrate
2 T. cornstarch
2 T. water
1/3 c. honey
2 T. mustard
1 T. cider vinegar

Cook rhubarb in juice until it is very tender, about 15 minutes. Press this mixture through a strainer to extract pulp. Return this pulp to saucepan. Combine cornstarch and water and add to saucepan along with remaining ingredients and cook until thickened and bubbly, stirring often. Use on pork, beef, lamb and poultry.

Cranberry Mayo

Combine equal amounts of whole berry cranberry sauce and mayonnaise and blend until smooth. Use as a salad dressing, for pasta and poultry salads. Tastes good with ham salads, too.

Mango Chutney

Major Grey move over!

1 c. vinegar
3¼ c. sugar
6 c. of peeled, sliced green mangoes
¼ c. peeled freshly grated ginger root
1½ c. raisins
2 chili peppers, seeded and finely chopped
1 clove of garlic, minced
1/3 c. sliced onion
½ t. salt

Boil vinegar and sugar in large pot for five minutes. Add remaining ingredients, and cook for about 30 minutes, or until thick. Pack into clean hot jars, leaving ½-inch head space, and seal. Process in a boiling water bath for 10 minutes. Yields 8 half-pints.

British Mint Sauce

¼ c. white wine vinegar
2 T. water
2 t. sugar
1 c. fresh chopped mint, or 1/3 c. dried
salt to taste

Combine vinegar, water and sugar and stir until sugar is dissolved. Stir in mint and season to taste. Store in fridge and use within a few days. Use with lamb, chicken or pork. Makes ½ cup.

Vidalia Onion Relish

1½ gallons ground Vidalia sweet onions (14 to 16 med. onions)
½ c. salt
¼ gallon cider vinegar
1 t. turmeric
1 t. pickling spice
1 t. pimento, chopped
4½ c. sugar

Grind enough Vidalia onions to yield 1½ gallons. Add ½ c. salt and let stand thirty minutes. Squeeze juice from onion-salt mixture and discard juice. Sterilize canning jars. To onions, add vinegar, sugar, spices, and pimento. Bring to boil and cook for thirty minutes, stirring often. Pack both onions and cooking liquid to cover in hot jars, leaving ½-inch head space. Remove air bubbles. Wipe jar rims. Adjust lids. Process 10 minutes in a boiling water bath. Yields about 8 pints.

Sweet and Sour Peach Salsa

3 lb. ripe tomatoes (about 7 medium)
2 c. celery, sliced
2 c. onions, chopped
2 green peppers, seeded and chopped (1½ c.)
3 fresh peaches, sliced
1 c. sugar
1 c. white vinegar
1½ tsp. salt
1½ tsp. mixed pickling spice, tied in cloth bag (or tea or spice ball)

Pour boiling water over tomatoes; leave for 1 minute. Drain and cover with cold water. Peel, chop and measure to get 1½ quarts pulp. Put into heavy pan (at least 8-quart size) with all other ingredients. Boil slowly, stirring often, until thickened, about 2 hours. Remove spices and discard. Pour into sterilized pint or ½ pint jars, leaving ¼-inch headspace. Process in boiling water bath for 10 minutes; cool and store. Makes 3 to 4 pints.

Notes: Recipe may be doubled, but boiling time will need to be increased to thicken relish. Good on chips and crackers, but excellent as accompaniment to pork roast or fowl and also as baking sauce on oven cooked chicken.

Cilantro Sauce

½ c. sour cream or strained yogurt
2 T. minced cilantro
pinch of cumin

Combine all ingredients and mix well. Use as a topper for tacos, baked potatoes or in fajitas. Makes ½ cup.

Easy Cranberry Glaze

1 can whole berry cranberry sauce
1 T. each orange and cranberry liqueurs
1 c. French dressing

Combine ingredients and spoon over chicken, turkey, pork or lamb before cooking.

Easy Barbecue Sauce

½ c. packed brown sugar
1 T. cornstarch
1 t. chili powder
1 c. tomato sauce
½ c. vinegar, preferably herb-flavored
½ c. catsup
½ c. corn syrup
½ c. water
¼ c. orange or other fruit-flavored liqueur

In saucepan combine sugar, cornstarch and chili powder. Stir in all ingredients, except the liqueur and bring to the boil. Reduce heat and simmer, uncovered, 30 minutes. Stir in liqueur and simmer, covered, five minutes longer. Use with pork, beef, lamb or poultry. Makes 2½ cups.

Sofrito

¼ c. oil
4 green peppers, seeded and chopped
1 medium onion, chopped
1 c. chopped cilantro
4 cloves garlic
2 t. dried oregano

Combine all ingredients and blend until smooth. Store in refrigerator and use within a few days or freeze until needed. Sofrito is almost a Latin pesto. Used in Hispanic households to flavor rice, beans and meat dishes. Keeps for a few days in the fridge and can be frozen. For a grilled flavor you can also sauté the sofrito before using. Makes 1½ cups.

Chili Con Queso

1 T. olive oil
1 medium onion, chopped
1 sweet green pepper, seeded and chopped, or 5-6 green chilies, seeded and chopped
1 sweet red or yellow pepper, seeded and chopped
3 cloves garlic, minced
1 c. peeled, seeded and chopped tomatoes (2-3 medium fresh or canned tomatoes)
1 lb. Colby or Cheddar cheese cut into cubes
½ c. chopped fresh cilantro
2 t. cumin
2 t. chili powder
1 t. red pepper flakes, or to taste

In medium saucepan heat the oil and sauté the onion until it is tender. Stir in peppers and garlic and sauté 3 minutes. Add remaining ingredients, including any juices in the tomatoes and heat, stirring constantly over medium low heat. Stir until the cheese has melted. If the sauce is too thick add a little milk.

This is usually not necessary because the veggies give off liquid when they cook. Serve sauce with tacos and tortillas, over hot vegetables and potatoes. It can also be used as a dip for raw veggies and tortilla chips and as a topper for chili.

Mango Salsa

2 large mangoes, seeded, peeled and cut into small cubes
¼ c. sugar
2 T. lime juice
2 T. fresh minced mint leaves
2 T. fresh chopped pineapple sage leaves (or extra mint leaves)
1 t. red pepper flakes

Combine all ingredients in medium bowl. Cover and chill several hours or overnight. Serve with poultry and seafood. Makes 2 cups.

Herb Dipping Sauce

Originally I used this recipe as a dip for veggies. They can be used on grilled meats, seafood or vegetables. They can also be used in chicken, tuna or vegetable salads. Start with the base recipe and add the options of your choice.

Sauce Base
½ c. each mayo and strained yogurt or sour cream
2 T. minced green onion
2 t. fresh lemon or lime juice
salt and pepper to taste
dash red hot pepper sauce

Variations

Dill: 2 T. fresh chopped dill or 2 t. dill weed, dash of Worcestershire sauce, 1 t. dried minced garlic or 1 garlic clove, minced. This is good with veggies or fish.

Sorrel: ½ c. fresh chopped sorrel leaves, 1 T. chopped parsley, dash of cayenne pepper. This sauce is good with fish and chicken or on baked potatoes.

Tarragon: 1-2 T. fresh chopped tarragon or 1-2 t. dried, 1 clove minced garlic and 1 t. honey. Tarragon enhances the taste of poultry and meats and is good with grilled foods.

Marjoram: 2-3 T. fresh chopped marjoram or 2-3 t. dried and 1 T. fresh chopped parsley. This is good with meats especially sausages and burgers.

Italian: Use 2 T. Italian seasoning and 1 T. fresh chopped basil or 1 t. dried, 2 cloves minced garlic and ¼ c. grated Parmesan cheese. This goes with both meat and veggies and is excellent on sandwiches and baked potatoes.

Mint: 2/3 c. fresh chopped mint leaves, dash of ground coriander. Good with meats, lamb and curry dishes.

Curry: 2 t. curry powder, 1 t. cumin and 3 T. creamy peanut butter. Good with any meat, especially grilled lamb and chicken and with battered vegetables.

Pesto: In blender combine ½ c. chopped fresh basil 2-3 cloves minced garlic, ¼ c. Parmesan cheese and 3 T. of pine nuts, sunflower seeds or pecans. Stir into dip base. Good with meat, chicken and with fresh veggies.

Mexican: 2 T. fresh chopped cilantro,1 t. cumin, 1 t. chili powder, 1 t. dried oregano and 1 clove minced garlic. Good on tacos and enchiladas or on a taco salad.

Herb: 1 T each of fresh chopped parsley, thyme and chives and 1.2 t. fresh rosemary. Excellent on chicken or with rice salads.

Dill Gravy

This recipe is from Anna Welker, an excellent cook, a terrific gardener and a dear friend.

1 T. oil
2 T. flour
½-1 c. fresh chopped dill
2 T. vinegar
1 t. sugar
salt and pepper to taste
about ½ c. water

In small skillet heat oil and brown the flour. Stir in all ingredients until dill wilts. Start adding the water, over medium high heat, stirring constantly. Add the water slowly, allowing the gravy to come to the boil and thicken as you go. You may need a little more or less water according to you taste. You can use stock in place of water if you prefer. Serve with meat and potatoes. Makes ½ cup.

Green Sauce

1 c. lightly packed spinach leaves
½ c. lightly packed parsley leaves
¼ c. lightly packed cilantro leaves
2 green onions, trimmed and chopped
½ t. ground pepper
1 c. mayonnaise, reduced fat works fine

In small saucepan, combine the spinach, herbs, onions and pepper. Cover with a little water and bring to a boil. Boil 30 seconds and remove from the heat. Drain and squeeze out the liquids from the spinach mixture. Discard liquid. Chop spinach mixture fine and combine with the mayo. Cover and chill several hours or overnight. Serve with fresh veggies and bread. Makes 1¼ cup.

Onion Relish

4 large onions, chopped
1 c. tomato juice
¼ c. catsup
¼ c. brown sugar
¼ c. cider vinegar
4 cloves garlic, minced
1 t. salt, or to taste
1 t. red pepper flakes, or to taste
2 T. chopped fresh cilantro
2 T. chopped fresh parsley
1 t. dried oregano
1 t. fresh lemon thyme or regular thyme

In saucepan combine all ingredients except herbs. Heat to simmering and cook, covered, until onions are very tender, about 20 minutes. Remove cover and continue simmering until relish thickens a little, about 5 minutes. Stir in cilantro, parsley, oregano and thyme. Remove from heat and chill well before serving. Makes about 3 cups.

Tomato Chutney

2 large onions, chopped
4 cloves garlic, chopped
4 lbs. plum tomatoes, peeled, seeded and chopped
1½ c. sugar
2 c. white wine vinegar
1 c. raisins
1 T. ground ginger
2 t. salt
1 t. cumin
½ t. ground allspice
½ t. red pepper flakes, or to taste
¼ t. ground cloves
½ c. fresh chopped cilantro,

In large saucepan combine the onions, garlic and tomatoes. Cook over low heat, stirring occasionally until onions start to soften and tomatoes are soft. Add remaining ingredients, except the cilantro and turn up the heat until chutney reaches a low boil. Simmer, uncovered until the chutney begins to thicken, at least an hour, probably longer. Stir more often as chutney thickens to prevent scorching. When it is thick remove from the heat and stir in cilantro. Cool to room temperature and then chill. Keeps in the fridge for a couple of weeks, and chutney can be frozen for a couple of months. Serve with meats, particularly grilled meats, and with cheeses. Makes about 3 cups.

India Sauce

This versatile sauce is great as a sauce for curried dishes or as a dipping sauce for tempura seafood and veggies.

1 c. mayonnaise, reduced fat works well
¼ c. tahini (sesame seed paste, you can find it in larger supermarkets and some ethnic stores)
¼ c. minced mint leaves
1 T. fresh lemon juice
1 T. fresh lime juice
1 t. crushed coriander seeds
½ t. dried minced garlic
¼ t. red pepper flakes

Combine all ingredients in a bowl and chill, covered, several hours. Makes 1 cup.

Dill Marinade

¼ c. white wine
juice of half a lemon or lime
1/3 c. olive oil
2 T. balsamic vinegar
2 T. chopped fresh dill
2 T. Dijon style mustard
salt and pepper to taste

Combine all ingredients in a blender until smooth. Use with chicken, swordfish, tuna or shark steaks.

Salsa Verde

1 lb. fresh tomatillos, husked and rinsed
½ c. chopped fresh cilantro
½ c. chopped sweet onion
½ c. chopped sweet red or yellow pepper
3-4 seeded and chopped green chilies
2 T. cider vinegar
1 T. sugar
1 t. cumin
1 t. dried minced garlic
½ t. red pepper flakes
salt to taste

Simmer tomatillos in water until tender, about 15 minutes. Drain well and puree in blender until smooth. Stir in remaining ingredients and chill, covered, several hours or overnight. Serve with tortilla chips or as a side with Mexican food. Makes 2 cups.

Salsa

4 lbs. tomatoes, peeled, seeded and chopped)
1 T. olive oil
1 large onion, chopped
4-5 cloves garlic, minced
1 c. finely chopped sweet red, yellow or green peppers
1-2 t. cumin, or to taste
1 t. chili powder
salt to taste
chopped hot peppers to taste, or hot pepper flakes or hot sauce
½ c. chopped fresh cilantro

Place oil in heavy saucepan and add onion, cooking until onions are translucent. Add tomatoes and garlic and cook until tomatoes are softened, about 10 minutes. Remove from heat and stir in remaining ingredients, except the cilantro. Cool salsa and stir in cilantro. Chill until ready to use. Great with chips, tacos and as a side dressing for grilled meats, poultry and seafood. Makes 3-4 cups.

Favorite Barbecue Sauce

2 qts. tomato sauce
1 (28 oz. can) whole tomatoes, undrained
½ c. pickling spice
2 sticks cinnamon
2 t. whole allspice
1 t. whole peppercorns
½ t. whole cloves
7 c. cider vinegar
2 c. sugar
2 c. brown sugar
1/3 c. Worcestershire sauce
¼ c. prepared mustard
¼ c. lime juice
¼ c. lemon juice
3 large onions, minced
6 cloves garlic, minced
2 T. red pepper flakes
2 T. chili powder
1 T. paprika

Begin to heat together the tomato sauce and whole tomatoes, crushing the tomatoes with the back of your spoon. Place pickling spice, cinnamon, allspice, peppercorns and cloves together in a piece of food-safe cheesecloth and tie securely. Place in kettle with tomato sauce and all remaining ingredients. Cook over high heat, stirring as sauce thickens until sauce reaches desired thickness. Remember you put in 7 c. of vinegar, this is going to take a while. Of course, it's so thin in the beginning, at least you won't have to stir it very often. My experience has been that the whole process takes 2-3 hours, but it could take less if you keep stirring and keep the burner on high. The sauce will cook down to about 5-6 pints, give or take a little. Freezes well or can be processed in pints in a hot water bath for 10 minutes.

Seafood Marinade

1 c. packed parsley leaves
2 green onions, trimmed and chopped
3 cloves garlic
1 T. lemon thyme or regular thyme
¼ c. olive oil
¼ c. clam juice
¼ c. white wine
1 T. vinegar

Place all ingredients in a blender and mix until smooth. Refrigerate several hours before using. Use for seafood. Marinade 30 minutes then grill or broil.

Meat Marinade

½ c. red wine
¼ c. parsley leaves
4 cloves garlic
2 t. thyme leaves
2 t. savory leaves
1 t. basil leaves
1 t. marjoram leaves
1 T. soy sauce
¼ t. red pepper flakes
½ c. olive oil

Combine all ingredients in a blender until smooth. Use with beef, pork or lamb.

Marinade for Lamb or Pork

½ c. red wine
½ c. olive oil
¼ c. balsamic vinegar
2 T. thyme leaves
3 cloves garlic
1 T. soy sauce
2 t. pineapple sage, or 1 t. mint leaves and 1 t. sage
1 t. ground ginger
1 t. rosemary
pepper to taste

Mix all ingredients in blender until smooth. Use with lamb or pork. Works with poultry, too.

Basic White Sauce (Béchamel)
The start of many a classic dish.

2 T. butter or oil
2 T. flour
1¼ c. warmed milk
salt and pepper to taste

In saucepan melt butter or heat oil and add flour, stirring until smooth. Slowly whisk in milk, stirring constantly until thickened and bubbly. Turn heat down and continue to cook, stirring constantly for a couple minutes longer. Season to taste. If you are going to store the sauce for later use place a layer of wax paper on top, store in a container with a lid or pour a little milk over the top to prevent a skin from forming. Makes about 1 c.

Variations

Thick and Creamy: Use 3 T. of flour and only 1 c. milk.

Curry: Add 1 t. curry powder and ½ t. ground ginger.

Lemon: Add zest of a lemon, 2 T. lemon juice and 2 T. butter just before serving.

Cheese: Add ½-2/3 c. shredded Cheddar cheese near end of cooking process. You can also add a dash of red hot pepper sauce, if desired.

Mornay: Add 2 T. grated Parmesan cheese and 2 T. grated Swiss cheese just before finished cooking. Turn off heat. Place an egg yolk in a small bowl and beat in 2-3 T. of the sauce. Add this to the pan and add 3 T. butter. Return to heat and cook 1 minute longer, stirring often.

Herb: Add ¼ c. chopped fresh parsley and ½ t. dried thyme near and of cooking

Spring Herb: Add ½ c. chopped chives and 1 T. chopped mint near end of cooking.

Mushroom: Add 1 (8 oz. can) sliced mushrooms, well-drained near end of cooking.

Chapter 9:
Pasta Sauces

Broccoli Pesto

1 stalk broccoli, cooked
1-2 cloves garlic
¼-1/3 c. fresh grated Parmesan cheese
¼ c. pine nuts, walnuts or sunflower seeds
salt and pepper to taste
½ t. crushed red pepper, or to taste
¼ c. olive oil

Combine all ingredients, except oil in food processor and mix until evenly chopped. Drizzle in oil with processor running until mixture is smooth. Toss with hot pasta.

Creamy Tomato Sauce with Cheese

3 T. butter or oil
3 T. flour
¾ c. milk
½ c. chicken broth
1 (14½ oz. can) diced tomatoes, drained
½ t. red pepper flakes
½ t. pepper
1 t. oregano
2 c. shredded cheddar cheese
1 c. grated Romano cheese
hot cooked pasta

Combine butter and flour in pan and stir together over medium heat. Add milk and broth and bring to a simmer, stirring frequently. Add tomatoes and seasonings and simmer 5 minutes. Add cheeses; stir until melted and smooth. Serve tossed in hot pasta.

Walnut Cheese Sauce

¼ c. chopped walnuts
1 T. oil
1 c. ricotta cheese
½ c. cream or evaporated milk
¼ c. chopped parsley
1 garlic clove
salt to taste.

Sauté walnuts in oil 2-3 minutes. Combine with remaining ingredients in food processor or blender and puree until smooth. Toss warm over hot pasta. Serves 2-3.

Orange Beef Sauce

1-1½ lbs. lean ground beef (turkey or chicken would also work)
1 T. olive oil
1-2 garlic cloves, minced
½ c. chopped onion
¼ c. grated carrot
½ c. orange juice
1 c. beef, chicken or vegetable stock
½ t. caraway seeds
½ t. orange peel
1 T. brown sugar
1 T. vinegar
salt and pepper to taste
¼ c. water
2 T. cornstarch

Brown meat in oil until no longer pink. Drain and place in Dutch oven with the vegetables Cook until onions are tender. Add remaining ingredients, except water and cornstarch and simmer, covered, 30-60 minutes. Five minutes before serving dissolve cornstarch in water and add to sauce to thicken. Cook until sauce is thickened and bubbly. Serve over pasta.

Spinach Sauce

¼ c. butter or margarine
1 (10 oz. package) frozen spinach, cooked and drained
1 t. salt
1 c. ricotta cheese
¼ c. grated Parmesan cheese
¼ c. milk

Heat spinach in butter for 5 minutes. Add remaining ingredients and heat gently until warmed through. Do not boil sauce. Makes 2½ cups.

Carrot Sauce

1 T. oil
1 onion, chopped
1 garlic clove, minced
1 lb. carrots, peeled and sliced
2 c. chicken or vegetable stock
salt and pepper to taste
½ c. cream, half and half or evaporated milk
1 T. fresh dill or 1 t. dried
hot cooked pasta

Sauté onion in oil until tender. Add garlic, carrots and stack and cook until carrots are very tender. Much of the liquid should have evaporated by then. Place mixture in blender and add cream or milk, mixing until smooth. Add dill and adjust seasonings, tossing over hot pasta to serve.

Variations: Use sweet potatoes, pumpkin, winter squash or even peas for different tastes.

Pesto Sauce

1 c. fresh basil leaves
¼ c. olive oil
2-3 cloves garlic
¼ c. pine nuts, walnuts or sunflower seeds
salt to taste
½-1 c. grated Parmesan cheese

Combine all ingredients (except the cheese) in a blender or food processor until well blended. Toss over hot pasta and add cheese to your own taste. This makes enough pesto sauce for 1 lb. of pasta.

Parsley Pesto

2 c. lightly packed parsley leaves, Italian, preferred
¾ c. olive oil
½ c. toasted pine nuts
¾ t. dried thyme leaves
1 clove garlic
½ c. Parmesan cheese
salt and pepper to taste

Combine all ingredients in blender or food processor except cheese and salt and pepper. Add cheese in on and off pulses. Salt and pepper to taste. Toss with about 12-oz. pasta, cooked. You can keep the sauce several days in the fridge or you can freeze the sauce for up to 1 month.

Ratatouille Sauce

1 large onion, chopped
2 cloves minced garlic
3 T. oil
1 medium eggplant, peeled and diced
1 (28 oz. can) diced tomatoes, undrained
2 small zucchini, trimmed and diced
2 sweet peppers, any color, seeded and chopped
1 T. Italian seasoning
salt and pepper to taste

Sauté onion and garlic in oil over medium low heat until vegetables are lightly browned but not burned. Add eggplant, cover pot and cook 10 minutes longer. Add remaining vegetables and simmer, covered, stirring often until squash are tender. Add seasonings, cover and simmer 10 minutes more. Serve over hot pasta and add grated Parmesan cheese, if desired. Makes about 6 cups of sauce, enough for 4-6 servings.

Chicken Cacciatore Sauce

1 onion, chopped
1 T. oil
3 c. spaghetti sauce
3 c. cubed cooked chicken
2 T. fresh chopped basil
fresh grated Parmesan cheese

Sauté onion in oil until tender. Stir in all but the cheese and heat through. Serve over hot pasta and garnish liberally with the cheese. Serves 3-4.

Asian Pasta Sauce

1 onion, chopped
2 T. oil
2 ribs celery, diced
½ c. sliced carrots
2 c. shredded cabbage or shredded Chinese cabbage
1 c. chicken stock
8 oz. sliced mushrooms
2 c. pea pods, trimmed and cut in half
2 t. grated ginger
1-2 T. soy sauce
½ c. chicken stock or water
2-3 T. cornstarch
sash red pepper flakes

Cook onion in oil until golden. Add celery, carrots and cabbage and cook 5 minutes. Add stock, cover and simmer about 10 minutes, or until carrots are tender. Add mushrooms, pea pods, ginger and soy sauce and cook 5 minutes longer. Add cornstarch to remaining stock in a small bowl and stir until smooth. Add the vegetables and cook until thickened and bubbly. Add pepper flakes, if desired, and serve over angel hair or ramen type pasta. Serves 3-4.

Red Wine Sauce with Chicken

2 T. butter
4 oz. mushrooms, sliced
½ c. chopped onion
2 cloves of garlic, minced
1 whole boneless chicken breast, about 1 lb.
2 T. flour
1½ c. red wine, any table wine is O.K., but not a dessert wine
2/3 c. chicken stock
1 bay leaf
1 sprig fresh parsley
½ t. dried thyme
salt and pepper to taste

In skillet or pot brown the onion and mushrooms in oil. Add garlic and chicken and cook over high heat 5 minutes, turning chicken once. Remove chicken pieces and set aside. Add flour to pot and toss to coat vegetables. Add wine, stock and herbs and simmer, cover and simmer about 15 minutes. Meanwhile dice chicken into bite sized pieces. Add chicken to sauce, heat through and remove bay leaf. Serve over hot pasta or rice. Serves 4.

White Clam Sauce

2 T. butter or margarine
2 T. flour
1 c. milk
1 10 oz. can clams, undrained
2 T. fresh chopped parsley
salt and pepper to taste

Melt butter in saucepan and stir in flour, stirring to blend well. Pour in milk and stirring constantly, cook over medium heat until thickened. Stir in remaining ingredients and heat through.

Marinara Sauce

2 T. olive oil
2 onions, chopped
2 cloves garlic, minced
1 (28 oz. can) canned tomatoes, broken up slightly
1 t. dried oregano
1 t. sugar
½ t. dried basil
salt and pepper to taste

Sauté onions in oil until tender. Add remaining ingredients and cook over medium low heat, stirring occasionally, for 1 hour or until sauce is thickened. This is a nice basic tomato sauce and can be made in larger batches for freezing.

Variations

Spaghetti Sauce

To basic marinara sauce add 1 lb. lean ground beef, chicken or turkey that has been browned and drained. Or add meatballs, sausage etc.

Red Clam Sauce

To basic marinara sauce one or two (10 oz. can) canned clams. For a stronger clam flavor include the liquid in the canned clams. Simmer long enough for clam liquid to evaporate and sauce to thicken.

Mushroom and Tomato Sauce

2 T. butter or oil
½ c. minced onion
½ c. minced carrot
3 c. sliced mushrooms
½ c. chicken broth
1 (28 oz. can) whole tomatoes
1 t. thyme
½ t. oregano
salt and pepper to taste
¼ c. Parmesan cheese
¼ c. chopped fresh parsley

Sauté onion and carrot in butter or oil until tender. Add mushrooms and broth and cook until mushrooms have wilted, about 5 minutes. Add tomatoes and thyme and stir, breaking up tomato pieces. Reduce heat and simmer, stirring occasionally for 30 minutes. Season with salt and pepper. Toss sauce with hot cooked pasta, cheese and parsley.

Zucchini, Tomato and Basil Sauce

2 T. olive oil
½ c. minced onion
2 small zucchini, sliced thin
½ c. chicken broth
1 (14-16 oz. can) tomatoes
¼ c. julienne basil
salt and pepper to taste
Parmesan cheese

Cook onion in oil until tender. Add zucchini, broth and tomatoes and cook, stirring occasionally until sauce has thickened. Stir in basil and season with salt and pepper, if desired. Add cheese to sauce after it is tossed with pasta.

Sun-Dried Tomato Pesto

½ c. sun-dried tomatoes
½ c. warm water
1/3 c. olive oil
1/3 c. pine nuts
1 T. minced garlic
1 t. thyme
salt and pepper to taste
2-4 T. grated Parmesan cheese

Soak tomatoes in warm water for 20-30 minutes. Drain and combine in blender or processor with oil, pine nuts and garlic. Blend until smooth. Add seasonings and cheese. When ready to toss on hot pasta add ½ c. of the hot pasta cooking water to the tomato Pesto. Add sauce to hot pasta and toss to blend evenly.

Chick Pea and Rosemary

1 T. olive oil
1 c. chopped onion
3 cloves minced garlic
½ t. rosemary
1 (28 oz. can) tomatoes
salt and pepper to taste
1 (19 oz. can) chick peas, drained
2-3 slices bacon, cooked crisp and crumbled

Sauté onion in oil until tender. Stir in remaining ingredients, except peas and bacon and cook, stirring occasionally until thickened. Stir in chick peas and cook about 5 minutes. Then stir in bacon and toss with hot pasta.

Herbed Fish Sauce

1 c. parsley
3 T. olive oil
1 T. fresh lemon juice
2 t. capers
1 t. salt
½ t. pepper
1 lb. mild fish

In blender combine all ingredients but the fish and blend until smooth. Set aside. Bake or broil fish until flesh is opaque. Flake fish into sauce and toss with hot cooked pasta.

Indonesian Peanut Sauce

1/3 c. peanut butter
1/3 c. milk
1/3 c. chicken or vegetable broth
½ t. crushed red pepper
1-2 cloves garlic
1 t. fresh grated ginger
1 t. soy sauce
dash hot red pepper sauce
salt and pepper to taste

Combine all ingredients in a blender or food processor until smooth. Toss with hot pasta.

Almost Alfredo Sauce

This is a lighter version of the original, which contained nearly a whole stick of butter and a cup of cream.

2 T. butter or margarine
1 c. evaporated skim milk
½ c. grated Parmesan cheese
½ t. garlic powder
salt and pepper to taste
seasonings of your choice: Italian seasoning, basil, marjoram, nutmeg, mint, parsley, cilantro, poppy seeds, red pepper flakes, chives, fennel seeds, taco seasoning etc.

Melt butter in saucepan and stir in milk. Bring to a simmer and stir in the cheese. Add remaining ingredients and seasonings of your choice.

Mushroom Sauce

1 large onion, sliced
2 T. oil
2 ribs celery, diced
1 lb. fresh mushrooms, sliced
2 c. milk
4 T. flour
salt and pepper to taste
fresh chopped parsley

Sauté onion in oil until tender. Add celery and cook until celery is tender. Add mushroom s and cook 5 minutes over medium high heat. In a jar with a tight fitting lid combine flour and milk and shake until smooth. Add to mushroom mixture, stirring until sauce returns to the boil. Reduce heat and simmer 2 minutes. Adjust seasonings and add parsley. Toss over hot pasta.

Ethiopian Vegetable Sauce

1 T. oil
2 large onions, chopped
1 c. diced carrots
1 c. diced celery
2 c. tomato sauce
1 (14-15 oz. can) canned tomatoes, any type
1 T. paprika
1 t. minced garlic
1 t. ginger
1 t. cumin
½ t. cinnamon
¼ t. allspice
cayenne pepper to taste
salt to taste

Sauté onion in oil until just browning. Add carrots and celery and sauté 10 minutes more. Stir in remaining ingredients, bring to a simmer and cook, covered, until vegetables are very soft. Process sauce in batches and return to pan. Adjust seasonings and cook longer to thicken, if you like. Serve with meats, rice, and pasta.

Artichoke Sauce

2 T. oil
1 large onion, chopped
3-4 T. flour, more for thicker sauce
1 (14 oz. can) artichokes, drained and chopped
2 c. chicken or vegetable stock
1 c. milk
salt and pepper to taste
fresh lemon zest

In large skillet sauté onion in oil until tender. Stir in flour. Add artichokes and stock and stir until smooth. Add milk and bring to a boil over medium heat, stirring often. Simmer 1-2 minutes then toss with hot pasta. Season to taste and add lemon zest just before serving. Makes enough for 1 lb. of pasta.

Fresh Tomato Sauce

This is a great sauce to make with fresh garden tomatoes on a summer evening.

3 T. oil
1 large onion, chopped
1 clove garlic, minced
1½ lbs. fresh tomatoes, peeled and chopped
½ c. chopped ripe olives
2 T. capers
generous handful of fresh chopped herbs including at least 2 of these:
parsley, basil, thyme, marjoram and oregano
salt and fresh ground pepper to taste

In large skillet sauté onion in oil until tender. Add garlic and cook 1 minute more. Add tomatoes and cook until tomatoes and softened and sauce has thickened a little, about 10-15 minutes. Add olives, capers and herbs and just heat through. Season to taste with salt and pepper. Toss over fresh, hot pasta and garnish with fresh shaved Parmesan cheese. Makes enough for 1 lb. of fresh pasta.

Note: To peel tomatoes just drop them in a pot of boiling water for 1 minute and remove. Allow them to cool a little so you can handle them. Core the tomato and use a knife to slip off the skins.

Beef and Mushroom Sauce

1 T. oil
1 large onion, sliced thin
8 oz. sliced mushrooms
1 lb. beef, cut in thin strips (sirloin works well)
2 T. flour
1 c. beef broth
½ c. red wine
fresh chopped parsley
salt and pepper to taste

In skillet sauté onion in oil until tender. Add mushrooms and sauté until tender. Remove vegetables and set aside. Add beef to skillet and stir-fry over high heat until no pink is visible. Remove to dish with the vegetables. Add flour to skillet and stir around in pan drippings. Stir in broth and wine and bring to a boil. Cook until sauce is thick and bubbly. Strain sauce and return to pan along with beef and veggies. Heat through and season to taste with salt, pepper and parsley. Makes enough for 1 lb. of pasta.

Chapter 10:
One Pot Meals

Cooking in a Crock Pot

Do's

Use inexpensive cuts of meat that benefit from long, slow cooking. Some good cuts include:

> **Beef, chuck or rump roast, chuck shoulder steak, bottom round, arm pot roast, tip roast, beef ribs, brisket, corned beef brisket, shanks, stew meat**
>
> **Pork, Boston Butt roast, shoulder roast, shoulder pieces, country style ribs, spare ribs, sausage**
>
> **Lamb, Shoulder, shank, stew meat, riblets**
>
> **Poultry, dark meat preferred in turkey or chicken. Breasts should never cook longer than 4-5 hours. Duck works great, but trim off as much fat as possible**
>
> **Game, All good choices, since they tend to be tough if not cooked with moist heat**

Use a quick-read thermometer to test for doneness. Beef should register at 155 degrees, pork at least 160 degrees, lamb at 155 degrees and poultry at 170 degrees.

USDA recommends that all meat dishes be started in a slow cooker at high for an hour before turning it down to low. You don't have to, though.

Trim off excess fat to minimize fat in the final dish.

Use lean meats to start with.

Skim off fat from the top of the dish before serving or thickening.

Browning meats before cooking will reduce fat in the final dish as long as you drain it off before transferring the meat to the crock-pot.

Don'ts

Cook whole chicken or other poultry as it takes too long to reach a safe internal temperature. Always use pieces.

Meatloaf takes too long to get to a safe internal temperature and ground meat is potentially higher in contamination so always pre-cook ground meat before using it in a crock pot.

Frozen or partially frozen meat takes too long to reach a safe temperature so use thawed meat.

Easy Rice Casserole

1 lb. ground meat, beef, chicken or turkey
2 ribs celery, chopped
1 small onion, chopped
¼ c. soy sauce
2 c. cooked rice, white or brown
1 can cream of mushroom soup

In skillet cook meat and vegetables until meat is cooked, about 10 minutes. Drain off fat. Combine meat mixture with remaining ingredients in casserole. Mix well. Bake in a 350 degree oven for 40 minutes. Serves 4.

Chicken and Asparagus Casserole

2 lbs. fresh cooked asparagus
12 slices cooked chicken
2 cans cream of mushroom soup
1 c. evaporated milk
¼ t. curry powder
4 drops Tabasco
4 T. chopped pimento or red sweet pepper
4 T. Parmesan cheese

Place asparagus in bottom of 12-inch casserole dish. Place chicken slices over asparagus. Combine remaining ingredients and pour over chicken layer. Bake uncovered in 400 degree oven for 20 minutes. Brown under broiler and serve. Serves 6.

Sage and Rosemary Pork Stew

2 lb. boneless pork, cubed
1 T. oil
4 c. chicken stock
2 carrots, peeled and cubed
½ c. sliced green onions
1 T. fresh minced rosemary, or 1 t. dried
½-1 t, fresh minced sage, or a dash of dry sage
salt and pepper to taste
2 lbs. cubed unpeeled potatoes
½ lb. green beans, cut up
1/3 c. flour
2/3 c. half and half or evaporated milk (regular or skim)

In Dutch oven, brown pork cubes in oil over medium heat. Add stock, carrots, onions and simmer, uncovered for 20 minutes. Add seasonings, potatoes and beans and cook 15-20 minutes, or until potatoes are tender. Combine flour with half-and-half or milk and stir until smooth. Gradually stir into stew and cook until thickened. Serves 6.

Note: This recipe can be made with beef (2 lb. cubed) or chicken pieces (3 lb. cut into pieces, skinned if desired).

New England Corn Chowder

¼ c. butter
1 onion, diced
¼ c. flour
¼ t. basil leaves
salt and pepper to taste
2 c. chicken broth
2 c. cubed potatoes
1 c. chopped carrots
1½ c. fresh or frozen corn
1½ c. (8 oz.) cubed Canadian bacon
2 c. half and half or evaporated milk (regular or skim)
1 T. fresh chopped parsley

In Dutch oven cook onion in butter until tender. Stir in flour until smooth. Add seasonings, broth, potatoes and carrots and simmer, covered, until potatoes are tender (about 15 minutes). Uncover and stir in remaining ingredients, cooking until very hot, not boiling. Makes 6 servings.

Boston Boiled Dinner

6-7 lb. smoked pork picnic roast
water
1 T. pickling spice
1 T. dried minced onion
6-8 carrots, peeled, cut in 2-inch pieces
6 potatoes, halved
1 small cabbage, cut in wedges
1 green pepper, seeded, cut in strips

Sauce:
1 c. sour cream or strained yogurt
2-3 T. Dijon mustard
1 T. honey
1 t. dry mustard
1 t. dried minced onion

Mix together sauce ingredients and chill until ready to use. In large kettle place pork roast and cover with cold water. Add seasonings and bring to a simmer. Cook, covered, 3-4 hours, or until meat is tender. Add carrots and potatoes and cook, covered 20 minutes. Add cabbage and peppers and cook 15 minutes. Spoon vegetables out carefully when serving. Serves 12.

For crock-pot: Cook on high 4-5 hours or on low 8-10 hours.

Ham with Fruit Chutney

3 lb. fully cooked ham, boneless
¼ t. pepper
2 (6 oz. jars) each, fruit chutney
1 c. dried mixed fruit
1 c. frozen small whole onions
1 T. balsamic vinegar

Place ham in slow cooker and sprinkle with the pepper. Combine remaining ingredients and pour over the ham. Cover and cook on low 6-8 hours. Serves 8.

Joe's Special

½ lb. ground beef or turkey
4 green onions, chopped
1 medium tomato, chopped
½ t. seasoned salt
1 t. garlic salt
1 t. Italian seasoning
1 10 oz. package spinach, thawed and squeezed dry
1 (4 oz. can) mushrooms, drained
¼ c. grated Parmesan cheese
3 eggs, slightly beaten

Brown meat in skillet. Drain off fat and add remaining ingredients (except cheese and eggs). Cook until tomatoes are tender, stirring occasionally. Beat cheese and eggs together and add to skillet, cooking until eggs are set. Serves 4.

Ham and Cheese Strata

12 slices bread, crusts removed if desired
6 slices American cheese
¼ c. diced green onions
½ c. chopped green pepper
2 c. diced cooked ham or turkey ham
3 eggs
2 c. milk
1 t. salt
1/8 t. pepper

Place six slices of bread on bottom of 2-quart oblong casserole. Top each slice of bread with a slice of cheese. Top cheese with the onions, peppers and ham. Top with remaining bread and cut each "sandwich" in half diagonally. Combine remaining ingredients and pour over sandwiches. Cover dish and let stand several hours or overnight in the fridge. Bake uncovered in a 350 degree oven for 40-45 minutes, or until puffed and set. Serves 6.

Chicken and Dumplings

1 T. oil
1 (3 lb.) broiler, cut into pieces
salt and pepper
flour for dredging
1 medium onion, chopped
2 carrots, peeled and sliced
3-4 potatoes, cut into chunks
2-3 c. chicken stock
2 t. poultry seasoning
1 c. buttermilk baking mix
1/3 c. milk

Season chicken pieces with salt and pepper and dredge pieces in flour. Heat oil in large skillet and brown chicken pieces on all sides. Remove chicken pieces and sauté onion until tender. Add carrots, potatoes, broth and chicken to skillet and cook, covered, 20 minutes. Sprinkle herbs over the chicken. Combine baking mix with milk and spoon batter in skillet in 8 mounds. Cover and cook over low heat 20 more minutes. Serves 4.

Ethiopian Chicken

1 chicken, 3-4 lbs. cut into pieces
1 T. paprika
1 t. each cayenne pepper, cumin, garlic powder, salt and ginger
½ t. allspice
¼ t. cinnamon
½ c. flour
3 T. oil
2 large onions, sliced thin
1 c. tomato sauce
1 c. chicken stock

Combine spices with flour in a plastic bag. Add the chicken a few pieces at a time and shake to coat. Set aside. Add onion to hot oil in large skillet and cook until onions are browned. Remove onions and brown chicken pieces on all sides. Return onions to pan and add tomato sauce and stock. Cover and simmer 35 minutes, adding water if sauce gets too thick. Serve with a cooked grain such as rice, millet, quinoa, wheat berries etc. This dish is also good served with lentils and cooked greens. Serves 4.

Tuna Noodle Combo

1 can cream of celery or cream of mushroom soup
½ c. sour cream or strained yogurt
1 can tuna, drained and flaked
2 T. each chopped parsley and chopped red pepper or pimento
2 c. cooked noodles, I like broken up spaghetti
salt and pepper to taste
2 T. bread crumbs

In 1½-quart casserole combine all ingredients except the breadcrumbs. Bake in a 400 degree oven for 25 minutes. Stir then top with breadcrumbs and return to oven for 5 minutes more. Makes 4 cups.

Tortilla Soup

1 onion, sliced thin
1 T. oil
6 c. chicken stock
½-¾ c. salsa
2 T. chopped cilantro
½ t. cumin
2 c. diced cooked chicken
8 small or 4 large tortillas

Heat oil in soup pot and cook onion until tender. Add stock, salsa and seasonings and simmer, covered 10 minutes. Add chicken and heat through. Meanwhile roll tortillas up tightly one at a time and cut cross wise into ½-inch wide strips. Divide strips among 4 bowls and ladle in the soup in the bowls. Serves 4.

Parmesan Chicken

¼ c. bread crumbs
4 T. grated Parmesan
½ t. oregano
dash each onion powder and pepper
4 boneless skinless chicken breasts halves
1 can cream of chicken or cream of mushroom soup
½ c. milk
paprika

Combine crumbs and 2 T. of the cheese in plastic bag. Place breasts 2 at a time in the bag and shake to coat. Place breasts in shallow baking dish and bake at 400 degrees for 20 minutes, turning once during cooking. Meanwhile combine soup and milk and pour over the chicken. Sprinkle with the remaining cheese and paprika. Return to oven and bake 15 minutes longer. Serves 4.

Whole Wheat Baking Mix

5 c. flour
3 c. whole wheat pastry flour
1 c. whole wheat flour
1/3 c. baking powder
1 c. powdered milk, not non-fat
2 t. salt
3½ sticks light margarine

Mix dry ingredients together well, then cut in margarine. Store in fridge for up to 3 months and can be frozen for up to a year. Makes about 12 cups.

Garden Skillet

1 large onion, sliced
2 small zucchini, sliced
1 T. oil or butter
1 t. dried basil
1 (15-16 oz. can) tomatoes, chopped, undrained
4 c. cooked macaroni
½ c. milk
2 c. shredded cheddar cheese
1 t. spicy mustard

In large skillet cook onion and zucchini in oil or butter until tender. Add remaining ingredients and cook over medium heat until heated through and cheese has melted. Serves 3-4.

Slow Cooker Stew

3 lbs. beef for stew, cut into cubes
1 lb. bag carrots, cut into 1½-inch chunks
1 large onion, sliced
¼ c. each flour and water
1 T. salt or beef flavored soup base
½ t. marjoram
¼ t. pepper
10 oz. frozen lima beans, thawed

In 5-quart slow cooker combine all ingredients, except lima beans and cook on low for 11½ hours or on high for about 5 hours. Meat should be fork tender. Stir in lima beans and cook 30 minutes longer. Skim off fat and serve. Makes 12 servings.

Brown Rice Casserole

¼ c. oil, butter or margarine
1 c. chopped onion
1 clove garlic, minced
12 oz. sliced mushrooms
¼ t. savory or thyme
1 c. brown rice
1 c. sliced carrots
2 c. broth or water
salt to taste
½ c. shredded Swiss cheese
2 c. zucchini, julienne
½ c. toasted pumpkin or sunflower seeds

In skillet heat oil or butter and cook until onion is tender. Add garlic, mushrooms and savory and cook 2 minutes more. In casserole add rice, carrots, liquid, salt and onion mixture. Cover and bake in a 350 degree oven for 40 minutes. Remove from oven and stir in cheese and zucchini. Cover and return to oven for 30 minutes more. Sprinkle on seeds and serve. Makes 6 servings.

Beef Stew Milanese

oil
2 lbs. stew beef, cubed
1 large onion, diced
1 large carrot, diced
2 large celery ribs, diced
1 clove garlic, minced
1/3 c. dry wine
1 (16-oz. can) diced tomatoes
½ t. basil
salt and pepper to taste
1 T. chopped parsley
1½ t. grated lemon or orange peel

Heat about 2 T. oil in Dutch oven and brown meat. Add vegetables and cook 5 minutes longer, stirring as needed. Add remaining ingredients, except parsley and citrus peel and cook, covered, over medium heat until meat is fork tender, about 1½ hours. Ladle into bowls and sprinkle with parsley and lemon peel. Makes 6-8 servings.

For crock-pot: Combine all ingredients, except parsley and peel and cook on high 1 hour. Reduce to low and cook 7-9 hours longer.

Hearty Cassoulet

2 T. oil
2 lbs. beef short ribs
2 medium onions, sliced
1 garlic clove, minced
1 c. wine
1 (8 oz.) can tomato sauce
3 cans cooked beans
2 ribs celery, sliced
water
¼ c. chopped parsley
½ t. thyme
salt and pepper to taste
1 lb. kielbasa, cut into 1-inch slices
1 lb. peeled baby carrots

Heat oil in large Dutch oven. Brown meat and onions until well browned. Add remaining ingredients, except sausage and carrots, adding enough water to just come to top of ingredients. Cover and simmer until meat is tender, about 1½ hours. Stir occasionally. Add sausage and carrots and cook 30 minutes longer. Skim off fat from cassoulet before serving. Serves 12.

Versatile Vegetable Soup

1 onion, chopped
1 T. oil
8 c. chicken or vegetable stock
½ c. rice, white, brown or wild
1 c. chopped celery
1 lb. frozen mixed vegetables
1 can beans, any type, drained
2 c. cubed cooked meat such as chicken, turkey, sausage, meatballs etc. **use whatever is on hand**

Cook onion in oil until tender. Add stock, rice and celery and cook, covered, until rice is almost cooked (15 minutes for white, 35 minutes for brown, 45 minutes for wild). Add remaining ingredients and cook, covered, 10 more minutes. Makes 8 servings.

Turkey and Wild Rice Casserole

1 c. wild rice
2 c. cooked turkey
½ lb. sliced mushrooms
1 can evaporated milk (regular or skim)
2½ c. turkey stock, heated up
2 T. chopped onion
salt and pepper to taste
½ c. grated cheddar cheese
1 T. butter

Soak wild rice in cold water for 1 hour. Drain and rinse. Combine rice with remaining ingredients, except cheese and butter in a buttered casserole dish. Bake covered in a 350 degree oven for 1 hour. Stir, sprinkle with cheese and butter, cover and bake 25 minutes longer. Serves 4-6.

For crock-pot: Cook on low 4 hours.

Skillet Pork and Rice

1 T. oil
2 large onions, chopped
2 lbs. boneless western style pork ribs, cut in chunks
2 c. rice (uncooked)
4 c. stock or water
2 c. peeled and sliced carrots
1 c. chopped celery
1 green pepper, seeded and chopped
1 red pepper, seeded and chopped
½ t. sage
salt and pepper to taste

Heat oil in large skillet or Dutch oven and sauté onions until tender. Add pork and brown. Add 2 cups water to pan and cook pork, covered, until pork gets tender, about 45 minutes. Add rice, stock carrots and celery and cook until rice is nearly cooked (15 minutes for white rice and 35 minutes for brown). Add remaining ingredients and cook, uncovered for 10-15 minutes, or until liquid is used up and vegetables are tender. Serves 8.

Variations

Tex/Mex: Add a 28 oz. can of diced tomatoes and 1 package of taco seasoning mix. Omit carrots and sage.

Mushroom: Add 2 cans of cream of mushroom soup and 1 lb. of sliced mushrooms. Omit peppers.

Harvest: Add 6 oz. can of frozen apple juice concentrate, 4 peeled, sliced apples. Omit peppers.

Fruitful: Add 8 dried apricots, snipped and 20 oz. can of pineapple in juice, undrained. Add fresh grated ginger (1-2 t.) and omit sage.

Note: You can also use chicken, turkey or beef in place of the pork. This dish can also be cooked in an oven safe pan in the oven at 350 degree oven.

Cheesy Italian Tortellini

½ lb. ground meat
½ lb. bulk Italian sausage
2 c. marinara sauce
1 c. sliced mushrooms
1 (15 oz. can) diced tomatoes with Italian seasoning
9 oz. refrigerated cheese tortellini
1 c. shredded mozzarella cheese

Cook beef and sausage in skillet until done. Drain off any fat. Place in a crock-pot that has been sprayed with non-stick coating. Add remaining ingredients, except tortellini and cheese and cover, cooking on low 7-8 hours. Add tortellini and cover. Continue cooking about 15 minutes or until tortellini are tender and heated through. Serve with shredded cheese. Serves 4-6.

Spring Vegetable Stew with Pesto

5 c. vegetable stock
1 c. fresh or frozen lima beans
2 c. broccoli florets
1 lb. asparagus spears, cut into 2-inch pieces
1 c. diced celery
1 plum tomatoes, canned or fresh, peeled and diced
1 yellow squash, sliced thin
12 oz. spinach leaves, chopped
½ c. frozen peas
salt and pepper to taste
fresh chopped parsley
½ c. pesto sauce, homemade or store-bought

Heat stock in pot and add Lima beans, broccoli, asparagus, celery, tomatoes and squash. Cook 5-7 minutes. Add spinach and peas and cook 3 more minutes. Don't overcook. Adjust seasonings. After ladling soup into individual bowls, sprinkle with parsley and add a dollop of pesto sauce. Serves 6.

Fiesta Chicken Chili

2 lbs. boneless skinless chicken thighs
1 (28 oz. can) diced tomatoes, undrained
1 (15 oz. can) tomato sauce
1 (15 oz. can) black beans, drained and rinsed
1 (15 oz. can) garbanzo beans, rinsed and drained
1 (4 oz. can) green chilies, diced
1 T, chili powder, or to taste
1-2 t. cumin
1 t. hot sauce, or to taste
salt to taste

Place all ingredients in slow cooker, cover and cook on high 1 hour. Turn down to low and cook an additional 7-8 hours. Check chicken for doneness. Adjust seasonings. Serve with sour cream and shredded cheese, if desired. Serves 6.

Cream of Wild Rice Soup

½ c. wild rice
2-2½ c. chicken or vegetable broth
¼ c. chopped onion
¼ c. diced carrot
1 small bay leaf
½ t. dried basil
1 c. sliced mushrooms
¼ c. snipped parsley
2 c. light cream, milk or evaporated skim milk
1 T. flour

Rinse rice. Combine in saucepan with broth, vegetables and herbs. Bring to boil, reduce to a simmer, cook, covered, 45 minutes. Remove bay leaf. Add mushrooms and parsley. Combine cream or milk with flour until smooth and add to rice mixture. Bring to a simmer and cook, stirring often for 5 minutes, or until mushrooms are cooked and soup is thickened. Add pepper if desired. Serves 4.

For crock-pot: Cook on high 3 hours before adding flour mixture. Cover and cook 30 minutes more.

Two Grain Vegetable Casserole

2 medium carrots, halved lengthwise and sliced thin
1 c. quartered mushrooms
1 c. canned black beans, drained and rinsed
1 c. corn, fresh frozen or canned
1 c. vegetable broth
½ c. barley
1/3 c. snipped parsley
¼ c. bulgur
¼ c. chopped onions
¼ t. garlic salt
½ c. shredded cheddar cheese

In 1½ qt. casserole combine all ingredients except the cheese and bake in a 350 degree oven about 1 hour, or until grains are tender, stirring once during the cooking. Sprinkle with the cheese, let stand 5 minutes and serve. Makes 6 side or 4 main dish servings.

Quick Veggie Chill with Cheese

1 (28-oz. can) crushed tomatoes
2 (15 oz. can) each, pinto beans, undrained
1 (15 oz. can) red kidney beans, undrained
1 (15 oz. can) garbanzo beans, drained
1 (15 oz. can) corn, drained
1(15 oz. can) tomato sauce
1 (4-oz. can) diced green chilies, drained
2 medium onions, chopped
2 medium zucchini, sliced
1-2 T. chili powder
1 t. cumin
1 t. garlic powder or dried diced garlic
½ t. sugar
4-8 oz. shredded Monterey Jack cheese

In Dutch oven combine all ingredients, except the cheese and heat to boiling. Reduce heat and simmer, covered 30-45 minutes. Remove from heat and stir in desired amount of cheese. Add salt if desired, as well. Serves 8.

For crock-pot: Cook on high 3-4 hours or on low for 7-8 hours.

Barley and Cheese Strata

1 c. barley
1 c. cottage cheese
2 T. chopped pimento or sweet red pepper
1 egg, beaten
salt to taste
½ c. sliced celery
½ c. sliced onion
2 T. butter, margarine or oil
2 c. shredded cheddar cheese
chili powder
tomato wedges and pepper slices for garnish, optional

Cook barley according to package directions. Combine cooked barley with cottage cheese, pimento, egg and salt. Cook onion and celery in butter or oil until tender and stir into barley mixture. Spoon ½ of the barley mixture into a casserole and top with ½ the cheese. Repeat with remaining barley and cheese then sprinkle lightly with chili powder. Cover and bake in a 350 degree oven until hot, about 30 minutes. Serve with vegetables if desired. Makes 5-6 servings.

Crab Potage

1 can cream of celery or cream of mushroom soup
3½ c. milk
¼ t. dried thyme
dash pepper
salt to taste
2 c. loose pack frozen vegetables such as green beans, carrots, peas, mixed etc.
2 (5-6 oz. can) crab meat, drained
½ c. instant mashed potatoes

Heat together soup, milk and seasonings, whisking smooth. Add remaining ingredients and cook over low heat until vegetables are tender and soup is hot. Can be served as is or ladled over hot cooked pasta or rice.

Lentil and Barley Soup

¾ chopped onion
¾ chopped celery
1 clove garlic, minced
¼ c. margarine, butter or oil
6 c. water
1 (28 oz. can) of tomatoes, cut up
¾ c. lentils, rinsed and drained
¾ c. pearl barley
6 vegetable bouillon cubes
½ t. each dried oregano and rosemary
pepper to taste
1 c. thinly sliced carrots
1 c. shredded Swiss cheese

In Dutch oven cook onion, celery and garlic in butter or oil until tender. Add remaining ingredients, except carrots and cheese and simmer, covered for 45 minutes. Add carrots and cook 15 minutes longer. Ladle into soup bowls and top with cheese. Makes 5 servings.

For crock-pot: Combine all ingredients but the carrots and cheese and cook on low 8-10 hours. Add carrots and cook 1 hour longer.

Chapter 11:
Vegetarian Cooking

Definitions

Vegetarian: A vegetarian is any person who does not eat meat. Well, that's the simple definition and it is true, but not all vegetarians are created equal. Some say that "if it had a face, don't eat it" or "if it had a mom don't eat it". For some clarifications read on.

Vegan: This person eats no meat or any animal derived products including eggs, dairy and even honey. Strictest of the vegetarians.

Ova-Vegetarian: Person who eats no meat, but does eat eggs.

Lacto-Vegetarian: Vegetarian who eats no meat but does eat dairy.

In an effort to include more people under the umbrella of "vegetarian" there are also now…..

Pollo-Vegetarian: Person who eats no other meat except chicken.

Paska-Vegetarian: Person who eats no other meat except seafood and fish.

If you don't eat red meat you can now be an ova-lacto-pollo-paska vegetarian. I find it easier to just say I don't eat mammals.

People are vegetarians for different reasons. Some are motivated by religion, politics, health or social conscience. It can also be fun to be creative when you cook. Perhaps once a week make a dinner that is animal-free and see if you can come up with something the family will eat.

Protein Pairing

If you don't eat any meat, you have to be sure to get enough protein. All animal sources are complete proteins in that they contain all the amino acids that make up protein. With 2 exceptions*, all plant sources of protein are incomplete. It's like an alphabet. You need all the letters to spell all the words. If you consume milk, cheese and eggs you are getting all the amino acids you need.

You can also pair up foods to provide all the amino acids, or a complete protein. Adding dairy to a meal that includes dried beans, peas or other legumes** will give you complete protein. Some examples would be bean and cheese burritos, Bean soup with a glass of milk or cheese with bean dip.

You can also get complete protein by pairing up any legume with any cereal grain***. Some pairings could include Red beans with rice, baked beans with cornbread, Bean tacos, peanut butter sandwich or lentil soup with crackers.

* Both soybeans and a grain called quinoa (pronounced "keen-wah") are complete proteins.
** Legumes include dried beans, dried peas, lentils and peanuts.
*** Cereal grains include wheat, corn, rice, barley, quinoa, rye and oats to name a few.

How much do I need to eat To get enough protein?

To get the same amount of protein that you would from a 4-oz.(raw weight) burger (about 22 grams) you would need to eat (legumes, nuts, seeds, & grains):

1½ c. great northern beans
1 1/3 c. navy beans
1½ c. kidney beans
1 1/3 c. Lima beans
1¼ c. split peas
1 c. soybeans
3 c. soybeans sprouts, raw or cooked
1 c. black beans
1 c. chick peas
1½ c. black-eyed peas
7/8 c. pinto beans
4½ T. peanut butter
½ c. peanuts
½ c. pumpkin seeds
½ c. sunflower seeds, hulled
4 c. corn
2/3 c. cornmeal

An average man needs about 56 grams of protein each day and an average woman needs about 46 grams.

Don't forget that you get protein in other foods including eggs, dairy, spinach, mushrooms, rice, bread and pasta. These are smaller amounts than in meats, but all of these amounts end up at the end of the day.

Just a couple of things to keep in mind. Besides the protein you get in legumes and cereal grains you also get fiber. Fiber is only found in plants. Unlike the fats found in meats, plant fats are always cholesterol free. Cholesterol is only found in animal sources of food.

If you or someone you know is a vegan, be sure to eat a diet rich in legumes and whole grains. Fruits and green salads are important parts of a healthy diet, but are lacking the protein needed for good health. You also need to eat plenty of leafy greens for calcium and may want to drink calcium fortified orange juice. If the vegan is child or teen, consult with a nutritionist or dietician for nutrition information. You don't need to eat meat to be healthy, but you do need protein as part of a healthy diet.

Basic Bean Burgers

2 c. cooked beans, drained and mashed
1 c. cooked rice
1 medium onion, chopped
2 eggs or egg substitute
½ c. breadcrumbs, plus extra for coating
salt and pepper to taste
oil for frying

Combine all ingredients, except oil, in a bowl and mix well. Add more breadcrumbs, if needed, to make the mixture thick enough to shape into patties. Shape into patties and roll in extra crumbs. Heat small amount of oil in skillet and cook until browned on both sides and cooked through. Eat as you would any meat burger. Makes 6-8, depending on the size.

Variations: Just start with the recipe above

Chili Bean Burgers: Use kidney beans or black beans and season with chili powder and oregano, maybe even cilantro. You can also roll them in cornmeal, rather than the breadcrumbs. Top with salsa.

Veggie Burgers: Add 1 or 2 grated carrots, 1 chopped and seeded sweet pepper and 2 ribs of celery, minced. You'll likely need extra breadcrumbs. Add some herbs for extra flavor or some hot sauce.

Taco Bean Burgers: Use pinto beans or kidney beans, season with taco seasoning and add a small can of diced green chilies, drained. You can also add minced black olives, if you like. Mix flour and cornmeal together for coating.

Mushroom Burgers: Add 1 c. fine chopped fresh mushrooms that have been sautéed a little and drained. Increase bread crumbs a little and season with parsley and basil.

Mexican Bean Dip

2 c. cooked beans (pinto, black or kidney preferred)
1 c. cottage cheese
2 T. sour cream or strained yogurt
salt and pepper sauce to taste
1 t. each chili powder and cumin
½ t. each paprika and oregano

Combine all ingredients in a blender or processor until smooth. Adjust seasonings. Chill. Serve with taco chips or fresh veggies. Makes 3 cups.

Note: You can also spread on tortillas and top with salsa, cheese, peppers and olives for Mexican pizza. Just heat and eat.

Mexican Bean Salad

1 envelope taco seasoning mix
½ c. oil
½ c. cider or red wine vinegar
2 t. sugar
3 c. green beans, cut in 1-inch pieces and cooked 5 minutes, drained
1 can black beans, drained
1 can kidney beans, drained
1 sweet pepper, any color, seeded and chopped
1 small onion, diced
tomato wedges

Combine seasoning mix with oil, vinegar and sugar and mix well. Combine remaining ingredients (except tomatoes) in a large bowl and toss with the dressing. Cover and chill before serving. Garnish with tomatoes when serving. Makes 6 servings.

Chili Bean Spoon Bread

½ lb. lentils
pinch of ground cloves
2 c. milk
½ t. salt
2/3 c. cornmeal
4 T. butter or margarine
4 eggs or egg substitute
4 T. oil
2 large onions, chopped
1 clove minced garlic
1 T. chopped parsley or 1 t. parsley flakes
1 T. chili powder
1 t. ground cumin
1 (14 oz. can) diced tomatoes, undrained
salt and pepper to taste

In saucepan cover lentils with about 2 c. water and add cloves. Bring to a boil, turn down to a simmer and cook, covered, until lentils are tender, about 20 minutes. You may need to add a little more water. Meanwhile in another saucepan heat milk and salt almost to boiling. Stir in cornmeal and continue cooking, stirring constantly until thickened. Remove from heat. Stir in butter and eggs and set aside. In oil sauté onions and garlic until tender. Add seasonings, tomatoes and lentils and heat until bubbly. Adjust seasonings. Pour lentil mixture into greased 2-quart casserole dish. Spoon over the cornmeal mixture. Set casserole dish in larger pan and add 1-inch of hot water to larger pan. Bake in a 350 degree oven for 30-40 minutes, or until bread is firm and golden. Serves 4-6.

Hummus

1 can garbanzo beans, drained
¼ c. olive oil
2 T. lemon juice
2 T. tahini (sesame seed paste)
2 cloves garlic
salt and hot pepper sauce to taste

Combine all ingredients in a blender or food processor until smooth. Adjust seasonings. Chill. Serve with pita bread, crackers or fresh vegetables. Also nice spread in a pita bread with sliced tomatoes, cucumbers and lettuce. Freezes well.

Black-eyed Pea Salad

1 lb. dried black-eyed peas
1 large onion, chopped fine
1 sweet pepper, seeded and chopped
¼ c. olive oil
¼ c. red wine vinegar
¼ c. chopped fresh parsley
½ t. dried thyme
salt and pepper to taste

Cover beans with cold water in saucepan and bring to a boil. Boil 5 minutes. Turn off heat and allow to stand 1 hour. Drain and rinse beans. Return to saucepan and cover with cold water. Simmer beans until tender, about 1½ hours. Drain. Place cooked beans in a bowl and cover with remaining ingredients. Toss to coat, cover and chill. Serve as a main dish or on the side. Also tasty served over salad greens or stuffed in a hollowed out tomato. Serves 6-8.

Almond Tabbouleh

1 c. bulgur (cracked wheat)
1 c. chopped tomatoes
½ c. toasted almonds, chopped or slivered
½ c. chopped parsley
1/3 c. lemon or lime juice
¼ c. chopped fresh mint
¼ c. olive oil
salt and pepper to taste

Place bulgur in a bowl and cover with cold water and let stand for 30 minutes. Drain and combine with remaining ingredients, except lettuce. Toss to coat evenly and chill. Serve over lettuce leaves, if desired or stuff in pita bread. Makes 4-6 servings.

Note: I also sometimes cook quinoa and use it as a substitute for the bulgur.

Spinach Lasagna

15 oz. ricotta cheese
1½ c. shredded mozzarella cheese
1 egg
1 (10 oz. package) frozen spinach, thawed and drained
1 t. salt
1 t. oregano
1/8 t. pepper
28-30 oz. spaghetti sauce
8 oz. lasagna noodles, uncooked
1 c. water

In medium bowl combine ricotta, 1 c. of the mozzarella, egg, spinach and seasonings. In a greased 13x9-inch baking dish layer ½ c. of the sauce, 1/3 of the noodles and half of the cheese mixture. Repeat. Top with the remaining noodles, then the sauce then the remaining mozzarella. Pour water in pan around edges. Cover tightly with foil. Bake in a 350 degree oven for about 1 hour and 15 minutes. Let stand 15 minutes before serving. Serves 8.

Eggplant Parmesan

2 large eggplants
salt
flour
2 eggs
bread crumbs
oil
1 (15 oz. container) ricotta cheese or cottage cheese
1 T. Italian seasoning or pizza seasoning
2-3 c. tomato sauce or marinara sauce
12 oz. mozzarella cheese
Parmesan cheese

Peel and slice eggplant about 1-inch thick. Place in a bowl and salt lightly. Allow eggplant to stand 30 minutes, then rinse and drain. Beat eggs in a bowl with a little water. Place bread crumbs in a shallow bowl. Dredge eggplant slices in flour and then dip in egg mixture and then in the crumbs. Sauté eggplant in oil until browned and tender. Note: If you prefer you can place eggplant slices on a baking sheet coated with oil and bake in a 400 degree oven, turning once until browned and tender, about 20 minutes. Drain. Place a small amount of sauce in the bottom of a casserole dish. Add a layer of eggplant slices. Combine ricotta with seasoning and spread over the eggplant. Top cheese with a little more sauce and another layer of eggplant. Top with mozzarella, remaining eggplant and remaining sauce. Sprinkle generously with Parmesan cheese and bake, uncovered in a 350 degree oven for about 40 minutes, or until bubbly and browned around the edges. Serves 6-8.

Curried Black Bean Soup

2 c. black beans (dry)
water
4 medium onions, chopped
5 cloves minced garlic
2 T. oil
1 green pepper, seeded and chopped
1 sweet red pepper, seeded and chopped
3 T. lemon juice
2 t. curry powder
2 bay leaves
3 T. soy sauce or tamari sauce
1 t. cumin
½ t. each chili powder, ginger, cloves
cayenne to taste
½ c. chopped parsley
1 c. raisins or chopped apples
1 lb. tofu, cubed
1 c. peanuts

Cover beans with water and bring to a boil. Simmer 5 minutes and turn off heat. Cover and let stand 1 hour. Drain beans and cover with 5 c. water. Bring to a boil and simmer, covered, until beans are tender, about 1½ hours. Drain beans and set aside. In large pot cook onions and garlic in oil until tender. Add peppers and cook a couple of minutes longer. Add beans, 6 c. of fresh water and remaining ingredients, except the parsley, raisins or apples, tofu and peanuts. Cover and simmer 45 minutes. Add parsley, tofu and raisins and cook 15 minutes longer. Add salt, if needed. Ladle into bowls and top with peanuts. Serves 8.

Easy Frittata

3 T. butter, margarine or oil
2 medium zucchini, diced
1 c. sliced mushrooms
2 green onions, sliced
1 ripe avocado, seeded, peeled and sliced
½ t. dried basil
salt and pepper to taste
4 eggs or egg substitute beaten together with ¼ c. water
4 oz. grated cheese (I like Swiss or Monterey Jack)

Sauté zucchini, mushrooms and onions in butter or oil until tender. Top with avocado, basil and salt and pepper. Pour over the egg mixture and cook over medium heat, using a spatula to lift up cooked egg and allow uncooked egg to flow underneath. Once eggs are cooked, sprinkle on the cheese and cover, cooking over low heat until cheese is melted. Serve immediately. Serves 3-4.

Quinoa with Mushrooms

1 c. quinoa
2 c. water
3 T. oil
½ lb. sliced mushrooms
4 green onions, sliced
1 T. lemon juice
¼ c. parsley or cilantro, chopped
salt and pepper to taste

Rinse quinoa and combine with water in saucepan. Bring to a boil and turn down heat. Simmer, covered until water is absorbed, about 10 minutes. Meanwhile, sauté mushrooms and onions in oil until tender. Season to taste. Add lemon juice and parsley or cilantro and add to quinoa. Stir and adjust seasonings. Serves 4-6.

Basque Soup

1 c. chopped onions
1½ c. chopped celery
¼ c. oil
¼ c. flour
3 c. milk or soy milk
1 (14 oz. can) diced tomatoes, undrained
1 can whole kernel corn, undrained
3-4 cans butter beans, drained and rinsed
3-4 c. water and 1T. paste-type vegetable soup base or 3-4 c. vegetable broth
pepper to taste
hot pepper sauce to taste
shredded mild cheese, optional

Sauté onions and celery in oil until tender. Stir in flour until smooth and add milk, stirring to keep lumps from forming. Stir over medium heat until milk has thickened and begins to boil. Stir constantly as mixture simmers for an additional minute or two. Add remaining ingredients, except cheese and bring up to a simmer. Adjust seasonings. Ladle into bowls and top with cheese, if desired. Serves 8-10.

Vegetarian Tacos

2 T. oil
1 large onion, chopped
1 can (about 15 oz.) kidney beans, drained and rinsed
1½ c. cooked brown or white rice
1 envelope taco seasoning (about 1½ oz.)
12 corn taco shells
2 c. chopped tomatoes
1½ c. chopped sweet pepper, any color
½ c. chopped onion
1½ c. chopped lettuce, I like Romaine
2 c. shredded cheese, optional

Heat oil in skillet and cook onions until tender. Add beans, rice and seasoning mix and heat until browned. Warm taco shells in a 350 degree oven for about 3 minutes. Spoon in a little of the bean mixture in a warmed shell and add whatever toppings you like. Makes 12, serving 4-6.

Note: You can also use fresh tortillas in place of the taco shells and make into warm wraps.

Hint: When cooking with dried beans always drain and rinse them of their cooking liquid, whether fresh cooked or canned. The beans will taste fresher, will retain most of their nutrients and will be easier to digest.

Pecan Cheese Balls

2 c. cracker crumbs
1 c. shredded mild cheese
1 c. finely ground pecans
½ c. minced onion
6 eggs (you can use egg substitute)
2 garlic cloves, minced
1 T. wheat germ
1 t. dried basil
2 T. oil
3-4 c. spaghetti sauce, bottled or home-made

Combine all ingredients in bowl, except oil and sauce and mix well. Form into 1½-inch balls. Brown in skillet in oil and place in shallow baking dish. Pour over sauce and bake, covered in a 350 degree oven for about 1 hour. Dish should be bubbly. Serves 4-6.

Scrambled Egg Casserole

2-3 T. oil
1 onion, chopped
1 stalk celery, chopped
1 sweet pepper, seeded and chopped
1 c. sliced mushrooms
3 c. chopped vegetables using any combination of the following: cabbage, broccoli, zucchini, tomatoes, carrots, cauliflower, Chinese cabbage, pea pods, green beans, water chestnuts or baby corn
3 c. cooked brown or white rice
2-3 T. soy sauce
5 eggs
6 oz. sliced Swiss cheese

Sauté all vegetables in oil until tender. Add rice and heat through, stirring often. Add soy sauce to taste. Transfer mixture to 3-quart casserole dish. In skillet scramble eggs, adding a little more oil if necessary and place on top of the rice mixture. Top with the cheese and place in a 400 degree oven for 15 minutes, or until cheese melts. Serves 4-6.

Chapter 12:
Great Grains

Grain Terminology

Bran: Partially ground husk or outer covering of a kernel of grain

Endosperm: The outside covering of a grain's germ. Contains both starch and gluten forming proteins

Flour: Any finely ground grain. May or may not contain the germ and bran. Any grain can be flour when ground fine.

Germ: Embryo of the grain, rich in oil, stores vitamins and minerals

Groats: Whole kernel of any grain, most often used referring to buckwheat and barley

Grits: Hulled and coarsely ground grain, usually corn or buckwheat

Grind: Refers to the size of the grind, goes from coarse to fine

Husk: Sometimes called the hull it is the inedible outer covering on a kernel of grain

Kernel: Whole grain seed

Meal: Coarse powdered grind of grain

Whole Grain: Refers to any grain that still contains its germ and bran

Types of Grains

There are dozens of grains out there. Here are some of the ones you can find in your local grocery stores, specialty stores and health-food stores. Don't be afraid to try something new. Keep in mind that if you are baking breads all grains do not contain enough gluten to make good bread. These grains may need to work in combination with wheat or other flours containing gluten.

Barley: A staple on soups and casserole. Barley is normally found as pearl barley which means it has been husked and polished which makes it cook faster.
Wheat berries- Just refers to wheat kernels before being ground or cracked. These take a long time to get tender when cooking and are helped by presoaking.

Bulgur Wheat: Wheat-berries are steamed and dried before being cracked. This makes them quicker cooking

Cracked Wheat: Wheat berries that are cracked so as to speed up cooking. They are not steamed like bulgur wheat.

Triticale Flour: Made from finely ground triticale kernels. This grain is a cross between rye and wheat. It is lower in gluten than wheat and should be combined with wheat in breads

Steel-Cut Oats: Also called Irish oatmeal and are made by coarsely chopping whole oats. Rolled oats are made by rolling whole oats between a series of warm rollers.

Rice: Probably the most widely consumed grain in the world. Go beyond white rice and try brown, red, black and even green. Long grain rice is best for eating on the side. Short grain rices are available for specialized uses like risotto (Arborio rice) and sushi (sticky or sweet rice). Whole grain rice takes longer to cook.

Millet: Yes, the same grain in that bag of birdseed. Millet is quick cooking for a whole grain and has a mild flavor.

Kasha: Sometimes called buckwheat groats. Kasha is buckwheat kernels that have been toasted for a different flavor.

Amaranth: Grown by Aztecs this grain is very nutritious. It contains no gluten so must be mixed with other grains in breads but can be used alone in pastas and pancakes. It can be cooked as porridge, popped or ground into flour.

Quinoa: This protein packed grain resembles both millet and mustard seeds. Unless the package says quinoa has been pre-washed it must be rinsed before cooking to avoid a soapy taste. It is higher in protein than other grains and is a complete protein. It can be cooked like rice and used the same way. It cooks quickly, 10-15 minutes making it great for quick meals. It can also be used as a breakfast cereal and is also found in flour form.

Spelt: Similar to wheat in its uses it is easier to digest than wheat and has been used for thousands of years. It is higher in protein and fiber than wheat flour. In most recipes you will need less liquid if using spelt flour. In recipes using little liquid like cookies increase the amount of spelt flour by ¼ cup for each cup of wheat flour used.

Teff: This tiny grain has been a staple in North Africa for years and is used to make the Ethiopian bread Injera. It can be cooked as a cereal or toasted and added to other foods like cereals, breads and muffins. It is also available in flour form and can be used to make pancakes, crepes and other flatbreads.

Rye: Used in baking rye does not rise well on its own so should be combined with wheat flour when making bread. Rye adds nice flavor and color to breads and crackers as well.

Buckwheat: This grain is more widely used in Russia than almost anywhere else. It is used in flour form to make blini, pancakes and soba noodles. It has a nutty flavor and is used in both its whole grain form, often toasted and in flour form as well.

Kamut: This grain originated in Egypt and is related to wheat. It has much larger kernels so takes longer to cook. It is found in both flour form and as kamut berries. It has more protein than other wheat flours and works well in all types of bread products.

Corn: This grain was a staple in the Americas and once spread throughout the world helped people to live in areas once too forbidding. The ancient corn is not like the sweet corn we enjoy so much now. Closer to popcorn and field corn the kernels were dried and ground for use as a flour in many staples. Dried kernels are also used popped. From tortilla to polenta and grits corn is still a staple in diets throughout the world.

Couscous: Originally couscous was a small grain type of wheat that was just chopped small and cooked. Now most couscous is very tiny pasta although you can find traditional couscous in health food stores and in specialty markets. It comes in whole grain, white and multi-color. To prepare just bring liquid to a boil, add the couscous off heat and wait 5 minutes. Fluff with a fork and serve. Israeli couscous is bigger, a round pasta about the size of a lentil.

Basic Quinoa

2 c. water
1 c. quinoa

Rinse quinoa well. Place in saucepan with water and bring to a boil. Reduce to a simmer and cook, covered until water is absorbed and quinoa has become somewhat transparent. Cooking time is about 15 minutes. Makes 3 cups.

Quinoa Vegetable Soup

4 c. water
¼ c. quinoa
1 small potato, diced
1 small carrot, diced
1 rib celery, diced
¼ c. chopped onion
½ green pepper, diced
2 cloves minced garlic
1 T. oil
½ c. tomatoes, chopped
½ c. chopped cabbage
1 t. salt, or to taste
fresh chopped parsley

Rinse quinoa well. Heat oil in saucepan and sauté quinoa, potato, carrot, celery, onion, pepper and garlic until golden brown. Add remaining ingredients, except salt and parsley and simmer, covered until vegetables are tender, about 20 minutes. Add salt to taste and garnish with parsley. Serves 4-6.

Storing Grains

Whole grains should be stored in a cool, dry place and used within six months of purchase. Whole grains keep longer than ground. For longer storage store all whole grains and whole grain flours refrigerated or frozen to maintain freshness.

Quinoa Pilaf

3 c. water, chicken or vegetable broth
2 c. quinoa
1 T. oil
salt and pepper to taste
¼ c. sliced green onions
2 T. fresh chopped parsley

Bring water or broth to a boil. Rinse quinoa thoroughly in a fine sieve. Heat skillet over medium heat and add quinoa, heating until quinoa starts to crackle, 5-10 minutes. Add oil and stir to coat grains. Add hot water or broth and turn down to simmer. Cook, covered, until liquid is absorbed, about 20 minutes. Stir in green onions and season to taste. Serves 4-6.

Quinoa and Garbanzo Salad

1 can garbanzo beans, rinsed and drained
2 c. cooked quinoa
1 sweet red or green pepper, seeded and chopped
2 green onions, sliced
1 rib celery, diced
8 oz. Italian dressing

Combine all ingredients and toss well to coat evenly. Chill before serving. Serves 4.

Quinoa and Chicken Salad

2 c. cooked chicken
2 c. cooked quinoa
1 c. diced celery
¼ c. chopped walnuts
½-1 c. mayonnaise
salt to taste
paprika

Combine chicken, quinoa, celery, walnut and mayo. Season to taste. Dust with paprika for color. Serves 4.

Quinoa Paella

1½ c. quinoa, rinsed
2 c. cooked chicken
3 c. chicken stock
2 T. olive oil
2 cloves minced garlic
1 onion, chopped
1 can black olives
1 c. peas
2 sweet red peppers, seeded and sliced in strips
pinch of saffron
salt to taste
½ lb. chorizo sausage or any sausage
¼ lb. raw shrimp
12 fresh clams, shells scrubbed

In skillet sauté onion and garlic until tender. Add chicken and sausage and cook until lightly browned. Add remaining ingredients (except peppers and seafood and mix well. If skillet is too small transfer mixture to a casserole. Cover and bake in a 350 degree oven until liquid is absorbed, about 45 minutes. Add shrimp, clams and peppers and bake, covered an additional 10 minutes. Serves 5-6.

Wild Rice Salad with Basil and Tomatoes

2 c. cooked wild rice
3-4 T. fresh basil, chopped
3-4 green onions, chopped
3 large tomatoes, peeled, seeded and chopped,
salt to taste
2-3 oz. Italian or Russian dressing
lettuce leaves
croutons

Combine all but the lettuce and croutons and toss well. Let stand 30 minutes before serving. Serve on lettuce leaves and sprinkle with croutons. Serves 3-4.

California Stir Fry

½ c. wild rice
2 c. water
2 c. pea pods (or 6 oz. package frozen pea pods)
¼ c. sliced green onion
1 small minced garlic clove
2 T. oil
salt and pepper to taste

Rinse rice. Combine with water in saucepan and simmer, covered until water is absorbed, about 45 minutes. In skillet or wok stir fry pea pods, onions and garlic until pea pods are tender. Add rice and mix well. Cook until rice is heated through. Serves 3-4.

Three Rice Stir Fry

½ c. wild rice
1 c. brown rice
1 c. white rice
5-6 c. vegetable broth or water
soy sauce to taste
oil
1 onion, chopped
1 carrot, peeled and sliced
1 rib celery, diced
2 small zucchini, sliced
2 c. broccoli florets
12 oz. sliced mushrooms
2 sweet peppers seeded and cut into strips
1 can Asian baby corn
1 c. pea pods
2 green onions, chopped
2 c. vegetable or chicken stock
1-2 T. soy sauce, or to taste
1 t. dried minced garlic
2 t. fresh grated ginger
pinch of red pepper flakes
¼ c. hoisin sauce
2 T. cornstarch
3 T. water

Heat the broth and add the wild rice. Simmer, covered 10 minutes and stir in the brown rice. Continue cooking 20 minutes more. Stir in white rice, cook 10 minutes more. Turn off heat and let rice mixture stand 10 more minutes. Meanwhile prepare veggies. Heat oil in large skillet or wok and add onions and carrot and stir fry 3 minutes. Add celery, zucchini, broccoli and mushrooms and fry 4- 5 minutes longer. Add remaining vegetables and stir fry until pea pods are tender-crisp, about 2 minutes. Add broth, soy, garlic, ginger, red pepper flakes, hoisin sauce and cornstarch mixed with water. Heat until sauce thickens. Adjust seasonings, serve veggies over rice. Serves 8-10.

Red Beans with Rice

1 c. brown or white rice
2 c. water or broth
1 can kidney beans, drained and rinsed
1 T. oil
½ c. chopped onion
¼ c. chopped parsley or cilantro
salt and pepper to taste

Simmer rice, covered until tender (40 minutes for brown, 15 minutes for white rice). Meanwhile heat oil in skillet and cook onions until tender. Add beans, cooked rice, and seasonings. Stir until heated through. Serves 4.

Italian Rice

3 c. cooked rice, any type
1 packet dry Italian dressing mix
2 T. fresh basil leaves
1 T. oil or melted butter or margarine

Place hot cooked rice in a bowl. Combine ½ of the dressing mix with the remaining ingredients and toss with rice. Add additional dressing mix according to your taste. Serve as is or with grilled meat or fish. Makes 3 cups.

Cream of Rice

2 c. white or brown rice

In small batches grind rice in blender, food processor or grain mill until quite fine. Sift to remove any big pieces. When all the rice is powdered place it in a large heavy skillet and warm over low heat, stirring often until rice feels warm to the touch, taking care not to brown the rice. (This removes excess moisture from the rice). Allow to cool and store in an airtight jar. To use, cook as you would regular Cream of Rice. Store in a cool, dry place.

Dirty Rice

1 c. long grain rice
¼ lb. bacon, diced
½ lb. chicken livers, quartered
½ c. chopped onion
½ c. chopped celery
1 garlic clove, minced
salt and pepper to taste

Cook rice according to package directions. Meanwhile cook bacon until crisp. Set bacon aside and cook livers in drippings until just cooked. Set aside and sauté onions and celery in same drippings. Combine all ingredients, tossing well to mix thoroughly. Adjust seasonings. Makes 5 cups

Brown Rice Salad with Mint

2 c. brown rice
¼ c. fresh lime juice
½ t. sugar
½ t. salt
½ t. freshly ground pepper
3 T. oil
1 c. frozen peas, thawed
1 c. diced celery
¾ c. fresh mint leaves, chopped
½ c. chopped fresh parsley
¼ c. sliced green onions

Cook rice in 4 c. water for 45 minutes, or until tender. In salads, rice can be a little under cooked. Combine lime juice with sugar salt and pepper. Add oil and place in jar with tight fitting lid. Shake well to blend. Place cooked rice in large bowl and add remaining ingredients, stirring to mix well. Add dressing and toss. Chill 30 minutes. Serves 8.

Spanish Rice

1-½ c. long grain rice
2 T. oil
1 onion, chopped
1 sweet green pepper, seeded and chopped
1 sweet red pepper, seeded and chopped
2 c. chicken stock, vegetable stock or water
1 (16 oz. can) whole tomatoes, cut up
salt and pepper to taste

Heat oil in skillet. Add rice and onion, cooking until onions are tender. Add remaining ingredients and simmer, covered until rice is cooked, about 20 minutes. Makes 5 cups.

For crock-pot: Combine all ingredients and cook on high 3 hours or on low for 6 hours.

Tropical Rice Salad

1¾ c. water
¾ c. brown rice
1 t. salt
1 large red apple, unpeeled, cored and diced
2 t. lemon juice
¼ c. chopped green onions
2 mangoes, peeled, seeded and chopped
½ c. shredded coconut, toasted

Dressing
¼ c. plain yogurt
2 T. lime juice
1 t. fresh grated ginger
½ t. curry powder
dash of salt
pepper to taste

Cook rice in salted water until tender, about 40 minutes. Cool 15 minutes. Toss apple with lemon juice. Add warm rice, onions, coconut and toss. Add mangoes and toss gently. Combine dressing ingredients in a small bowl and pour over the rice mixture. Toss and serve with additional mango slices for garnish, if desired. Can also be served on lettuce leaves. Makes 6 servings.

Barley with Zucchini and Peanuts

3 c. water
3 T. vegetable soup base
1 c. barley
4 medium zucchini, julienned
3 T. butter, margarine or oil
1½ c. salted blanched peanuts, chopped coarse
salt and pepper to taste

Cook barley in water with cubes for 45 minutes, or until tender. Sauté zucchini in butter or oil until tender. Stir in peanuts and season to taste. Serve over the hot cooked barley. Makes 4 servings.

Fried Rice

4 c. cooked rice
1 lb. pork, diced, chicken, diced or small raw shrimp, peeled
1 T. dry sherry
1 T. soy sauce
1 t. cornstarch
salt to taste
2 eggs
1 (10 oz. package) frozen spinach, thawed and squeezed dry
½ c. frozen peas, thawed
½ c. chopped green onions
oil

In small bowl combine pork, chicken or shrimp with sherry, soy and cornstarch. Add about ½ t. salt. Set aside. In small bowl beat eggs with ½ t. salt and 2 T. water. Heat oil in skillet until very hot and add half the egg mixture, tipping pan to coat bottom. Cook until eggs are set and turn over to cook top. Remove from pan and repeat with remaining eggs. Roll cooked eggs and cut crosswise into strips. Set aside. Heat oil in skillet and add meat or shrimp, frying until just cooked. Add spinach, peas and green onion and stir fry 1 minute. Add rice and continue cooking until rice is heated through. Add eggs, stir to combine and serve. Makes 6 servings.

Rice Stuffed Peppers

1 large onion, minced
2 T. olive oil
2 T. pine nuts
1¼ c. rice (preferably short grained)
2 T. currants or raisins
1 (16 oz. can) whole tomatoes, diced
4 green onions, chopped
1 t. sugar
2 c. water
1 c. fresh chopped mixed herbs such as parsley, basil, and dill
6 large green peppers

In large heavy saucepan cook the onion in oil until tender. Add pine nuts, and rice and cook 3-4 minutes longer. Stir in the currants, tomatoes, green onions, sugar and 1 cup of the water. Add salt and pepper to taste and simmer, covered until liquid is absorbed, about 15 minutes. Fluff the rice with a fork and stir in the herbs. Cut the top ½-inch from the peppers and reserve these caps. Seed the peppers, removing any of the ribs inside as well. Divide the rice mixture between the peppers and arrange in a 15x11-inch baking dish. Replace caps and pour remaining cup of water into bottom of baking dish. Cover with foil and bake in 375 degree oven for 40 minutes. Remove foil and bake 20 minutes more. Serves 6.

Kasha Pilaf

1 egg
1 c. medium kasha (buckwheat groats)
3 T. oil
1 Medium onion, diced
3½ c. boiling water
½ c. rice
2 chicken or vegetable bouillon cubes
1 c. frozen peas

Combine egg and kasha and set aside. In skillet cook onion in oil until tender. Add kasha and cook until dry and browned. Add remaining ingredients, except peas and cook, covered 10 minutes. Add peas and cook 5 minutes more. Add salt and pepper if needed. Makes 6 main dish servings

Tabbouleh

1 c. bulgur
boiling water
1 c. diced fresh tomatoes
2/3 c. chopped green onions
½ c. chopped parsley
2 T. chopped fresh mint
1/3 c. lemon or lime juice
¼ c. olive oil
salt and pepper to taste
lettuce leaves

Place bulgur in large bowl and pour over enough boiling water to just cover. Let stand 30 minutes, draining off any remaining water. Add remaining ingredients, except lettuce, cover and chill several hours or overnight. Serve on lettuce leaves. Makes 6 servings.

Note: You may prefer to rinse the bulgur in cold water and refrigerate several hours instead of using the boiling water. It will take longer to soften, but it will eventually get tender. Also, tabbouleh is also good served as a pita filling as is or with thin sliced cucumbers.

Whole Grain Vegetable Pilaf

2 c. water
2 t. vegetable soup base
½ c. barley
½ c. brown rice
½ t. crushed, dried oregano
1/8 t. black pepper
1 (10 oz. package) frozen Lima beans
1 medium carrot, sliced thin
1 rib celery, sliced
1 medium onion, chopped
1 c. shredded Mozzarella or Provolone or Monterey Jack cheese
paprika

Cook water, cubes, barley, rice, oregano and pepper at a simmer, covered for 45 minutes or until grains are tender. In another sauce pan combine remaining ingredients, except cheese and paprika, with ½ c. water and cook 10 minutes, or until vegetables are tender. Spoon barley mixture into a casserole and press firmly to create a well in the center. Drain excess water from lima bean mixture and spoon into the well. Cover and bake 350 degree oven for 15 minutes. Uncover, sprinkle with cheese and bake 5 minutes longer, or until cheese melts. Sprinkle with paprika and serve. Makes 6-8 servings.

Amaranth Date Nut Bread

1 c. chopped dates
½ c. amaranth
1 c. boiling water
2 eggs or egg substitute
½ c. honey
¼ c. butter, melted
2 c. whole wheat flour (pastry preferred)
2 t. baking powder
1 c. chopped nuts
1 t. vanilla

Soak dates and amaranth in boiling water. Beat eggs well and add honey and butter, beating well. Stir in remaining ingredients and mix well. Pour batter into oiled 9x5-inch loaf pan and bake in a 350 degree oven for 1 hour 15 minutes. Yields 1 loaf.

Mandarin Millet

2 c. water
1 c. millet
½ t. salt
2 ribs celery, sliced
4 green onions, sliced
1 T. sesame or cooking oil
1 (8 oz. can) water chestnuts, drained and chopped
2 T. soy sauce
1 (11 oz. can) mandarin oranges, drained
2 T. sliced almonds

In medium saucepan heat together water, millet and salt. Simmer gently, covered until liquid is absorbed, about 10-15 minutes. Remove from heat and let stand 10 minutes. Meanwhile gently cook the vegetables in oil until tender. Stir in soy and water chestnuts and heat through. Stir in cooked millet, and then gently fold in oranges. Sprinkle with almonds and serve. Makes 6 side servings, 3-4 main dish.

Amaranth Hot Cereal

1 c. amaranth
3 c. water

Simmer water and amaranth together, covered, about 25 minutes. Cereal will absorb water and bind together. Makes 3-4 servings.

Three Grain Salad with Pesto Vinaigrette

4 c. water
½ c. wheat berries
½ c. quinoa
¼ c. millet
1 (15-16 oz. can) garbanzo beans, rinsed and drained
1 c. chopped sweet peppers, any color
1 c. diced celery
½ c. currants or raisins
salt and pepper to taste
cut up fresh fruit or veggies as garnish and lettuce leaves

Pesto Vinaigrette
1 c. fresh basil leaves
¼ c. olive oil
½ c. red wine vinegar
pinch salt
1 t. dried minced garlic

Cook wheat berries in water, covered for 40 minutes. Rinse quinoa and add along with millet. Cover and simmer 15 minutes longer. Drain any excess water off and add garbanzos. Mix dressing ingredients in blender or processor until smooth and toss with grains. Chill several hours or overnight. Add remaining ingredients up to an hour before serving. Can be served on lettuce leaves or with fruits and veggies. Serves 4-6.

Super Salad

1 c. water
½ c. wheat berries
2/3 c. plain yogurt
½ t. dried dill weed
hot pepper sauce to taste
1 (3¾ oz. can) salmon, drained, skin and bones removed, flaked
¼ c. chopped celery
2 T. sliced almonds
2 small heads butter head or bibb lettuce
½ c. finely shredded carrot
6 radishes, shredded
celery and carrot sticks for garnish, optional
croutons, optional

Simmer the wheat berries in the water, covered for 1 hour. Drain off any remaining water, cool. For dressing combine the yogurt, dill and hot sauce in small bowl. Combine wheat berries, salmon celery and almonds with half the dressing. Cover and chill. Chill remaining dressing as well. To serve, remove center leaves of lettuce to form a bowl. Reserve removed leaves for another use. Rinse lettuce bowls gently and invert on paper toweling to drain. Place lettuce bowls on individual serving plates. Arrange half the wheat berry mixture, carrots and radishes in each. Arrange celery and carrot sticks around lettuce bowls if desired. Sprinkle on croutons and serve with extra dressing on the side. Makes 2 main-dish servings.

Granola

3 c. oats
½ c. wheat germ
1 c. mixed seeds and nuts, choose from pumpkin, sunflower, almonds, walnuts, peanuts etc.
¼ c. sesame seeds
½ c. raisins
¼ c. oil
¼ c. honey
1 t. vanilla

Toss together all but honey, oil and vanilla. Heat oil, honey and vanilla together and toss over oat mixture. Spread into a large shallow baking pan and bake at 325 degrees for 15 to 20 minutes, or until lightly toasted. Stir halfway through baking to prevent edges from getting too brown. Yields about 2 lbs.

Wheat Berry Salad

1 c. wheat berries
½ t. salt
2 T. soy sauce
2 T. sesame oil
2 t. red wine or rice vinegar
2 t. sugar
2 scallions, chopped
¾ c. diced seeded cucumber
2/3 c. each diced red and yellow sweet peppers
½ c. chopped onion

Combine wheat berries with 4½ c. water. Simmer, covered, until wheat berries are tender and water is absorbed, about 1 hour. Meanwhile make dressing by combining the salt, oil, soy sauce, vinegar and sugar in small saucepan. Toss warm dressing over warm cooked wheat berries and allow to cool to room temperature. Toss in remaining ingredients and chill 1 hour before serving. 4 Servings.

Couscous Salad

2 c. broth
2 T. butter
1½ c. couscous
2 c. chopped pecans, lightly toasted
½ c. currants
1 T. freshly grated orange zest
½ c. chopped parsley
2 c. drained mandarin oranges, about 2 (11 oz. cans)
1/3 c. fresh orange juice
3 T. fresh lemon juice
1/3 c. olive oil

Bring broth and butter to a boil. Add couscous and remove from heat. Let stand 5 minutes. Meanwhile combine remaining ingredients in a small bowl. Pour nut mixture over the couscous and toss gently to mix. Serves 6-8.

Couscous Salad with Shrimp and Dill

½ c. olive oil
¼ c. fresh lemon juice
1 clove minced garlic
1 t. celery seed
2 c. couscous, about 10 oz.
2¼ c. boiling water
1 lb. peeled cooked shrimp
1½ c. chopped seeded tomatoes
1 c. diced celery
½ c. chopped green onions
2 T. fresh dill weed or 2 t. dried

Whisk first 4 ingredients together for dressing. Place couscous in heat proof bowl and pour over the boiling water. Let stand until water is absorbed, about 10 minutes. Fluff with a fork and add remaining ingredients, stirring to mix well. Pour over dressing and toss to coat. Chill at least 30 minutes or up to 2 hours. 6 Servings.

Herbed Couscous with Vegetables

1 c. sliced mushrooms
1 T. butter or margarine
1 c. water
1 T. snipped parsley
½ t. each dried basil and oregano
salt and pepper to taste
2/3 c. couscous
1 medium tomato, peeled, seeded and diced

Cook mushrooms in butter until tender. Add seasonings water and bring to a boil. Remove from heat and stir in couscous. Let stand 10 minutes. Stir in tomatoes. 4 Servings.

Barleycorn Salad

½ c. pearl barley
salt
3 T. cider or white wine vinegar
1 t. Dijon mustard
fresh ground pepper
3 T. olive oil
½ t. dried oregano
3 c. cooked corn, from six ears
1 c. cooked fresh or frozen peas
1 c. sliced radishes
¼ c. sliced green onions

Combine barley, 2 c. water and ½ t. salt in saucepan and simmer, covered until barley is tender, about 50 minutes. Drain and rinse under cold water. Combine remaining ingredients and toss with barley in large bowl. Makes 6 servings.

Venetian Cornmeal Cookies

¾ c. raisins
6 T. rum
½ c. plus 3 T. butter, at room temperature
½ c. plus 1½ t. sugar
2 eggs, at room temperature
1½ c. plus 1½ T. flour
1 c. plus 3 T. yellow cornmeal
2 t. baking powder
¾ t. salt

Soak raisins in rum 30 minutes or more. Drain. Beat butter and sugar until light and fluffy. Beat in eggs one at a time. Sift together the 1½ c. flour, cornmeal, baking powder and salt. Stir into batter. Mix raisins with remaining 1½ T. flour and stir into dough. Shape dough into an 18-inch log. Slice 3/8-inch thick and shape slices into ovals. Place 2 inches apart on greased baking sheet and bake in a preheated 375 degree oven for about 15 minutes. Cool a little before moving cookies to cooling rack. Makes 4 dozen.

Chapter 13:
It's Soy Wonderful -
Cooking with Soy
and Soy Products

Soy Products

Soy nuts are soaked then roasted uncooked soybeans. You can buy ready-made, or make your own. To make soak 1 or 2 cups of dry soy beans in water for 3 hours. Drain and place on an oiled cookie sheet. Roast at 350 degrees, stirring often, until browned.

Soy flour is ground soybeans and can replace some of the wheat flour in recipes, but it contains no gluten, so will not rise. Replace no more than ¼ of the regular flour in a recipe.

Pressed liquid from soaked soybeans makes **soymilk**. It comes plain and in flavors and can be used interchangeably in recipes with cow's milk.

Soy protein isolates a mild flavored protein powder is made from de-fatted soy flakes. Small amounts can be blended into fruit shakes, soups, puddings and baked goods.

Textured Vegetable Protein or **T.V.P.** is a fat free granulated product made from defatted soy flakes. When re-hydrated it has the texture of ground meat. Use in spaghetti sauce, chili, sloppy Joes, etc. Soak in water then replace in equal amounts for the meat.

Tempeh is a cultured soy food made from cooked soybeans combined with a grain like barley or rice. It has a dense chewy texture and smoky flavor that absorbs the flavors around it.

Combining soybeans with a grain such as barley or rice, salt and a mold makes **Miso**. Sort of like making cheese. It is aged in cedar vats for up to 3 years. Small amounts (¼ c. to a quart of water) can be used to make a savory broth. Used a lot in

Japanese cooking. Miso can also be used full strength to replace soy sauce in recipes.

Curdling soymilk with a salt makes **tofu**. Its bland taste and porous texture enable it to absorb the flavors around it. Firm tofu is used in stir frying in to sauté or barbecue. Soft tofu is used in desserts, dips, custards, cream soups and pudding.

Working with tofu can help you use it in more dishes. Freezing tofu changes its texture, becoming chewier. Just freeze tofu for several hours or up to 3 months. Thaw in fridge overnight then press out the water and grate tofu or chop in a food processor. It will be very chewy and should be crumbled to the size of coarse crumbs.

You can also press tofu to make its texture firmer. Just place tofu on a baking sheet and top with another baking sheet. Add a weight (I use a can) and look at the tofu. It should be bulging, but not splitting. Let stand 30 minutes, then drain off water and use in your recipe. If it is going to be used uncooked in your recipe, boil it in water for up to 5 minutes after pressing to improve texture and to make it more digestible.

Only use organic soy products!

Some easy ways
To get more soy in your diet

1) Use soymilk in cooked and cold cereals, custards, cream soups, coffee, sauces and baked goods calling for cow's milk

2) Replace up to ¼ of the wheat flour (all-purpose or whole wheat) with soy flour. This will work in most recipes without any noticeable change in the end product.

3) Mash a little tofu into mild cheeses like cottage or ricotta. The texture will not be affected very much and you can gradually increase the amount of tofu as your palate changes. I really like adding tofu to ricotta in lasagna. No one ever knows.

4) Dice tofu into vegetable soups during the last few minutes of cooking. It will absorb some of the flavors and boost the protein, too.

5) Add diced tofu to stews and chili. In spicy dishes tofu really picks up flavors. T.V.P. really has the texture of ground meat once moistened. Add a little to chili, sloppy Joes, spaghetti sauce, and stuffed peppers. Well, you get the idea. It will pick up the tastes around it and can be purchased in an imitation beef flavor. Still, don't try to add tons of it to your cooking without warning your family. T.V.P. is very high in fiber and can cause digestive upsets to someone on a low fiber diet. Still, we all need more fiber and T.V.P. Can be a part of getting both fiber, soy and protein in our diets in a nearly fat-free package.

6) Marinade tofu before cooking. Salad dressings, barbecue sauce, Asian sauces or whatever you like can be poured over sliced or cubed tofu. Then you can bake or sauté it or even crumble it over a salad.

7) Add a spoonful or two of miso to your soups to add flavor. Try a little at a time or just add to a little of the broth to see if you like it.

8) Mash a little soft tofu and add to your favorite custard recipe.

9) Add a little moistened T.V.P. To your favorite meatloaf to add fiber and stretch the meat.

10) Add some cubed tofu to a skillet and sauté until heated through. Add beaten eggs for a lower cholesterol scrambled egg or omelet.

Using Tofu

Pressing Tofu

Pressing tofu makes it more absorbent. Many recipes call for tofu to be pressed. Just place the cake of tofu on a baking sheet and top with another baking sheet. Weigh down with a large can or a bowl of water. Tofu should bulge a little but not split. Let stand for 20 minutes or so and then use in your recipe.

Blanching Tofu

If you are using the tofu uncooked in a recipe you can cube it and cook it in boiling water for 3-4 minutes. Drain then use. It will be firmer and more digestible.

Freezing Tofu

Freezing tofu makes it chewier and more meat-like in texture. Freeze solid and then defrost in the fridge for a day. Press and then grate or crumble to use. The package may tell you not to freeze it, but don't worry, it works.

Soy "No Milk" Shake

2-3 scoops Tofutti or other tofu frozen product
1 c. soymilk, vanilla or chocolate

Place Tofutti in blender and pour over the soymilk. Blend until smooth. Serves 1.

Soy Orange Smoothie

1/3 c. frozen orange juice concentrate
½ c. cold water
¼ c. sugar or equivalent in sugar substitute
5-6 ice cubes
½ c. soymilk
½ t. vanilla

Combine all ingredients in blender and process until smooth. Serves 2.

Berry Good Tofu Smoothie

½ package chilled tofu, drained
½ c. soy milk, plain or vanilla
1 c. frozen blueberries
1 pear, cored, unpeeled
4-6 ice cubes
sugar or honey to taste
2 scoops vanilla frozen yogurt, ice cream or Tofutti

Place first six ingredients in blender and process until smooth. Taste and add more sweetener, if needed. Add yogurt, ice cream or Tofutti and blend until smooth. Serves 2.

Note: You can use frozen strawberries or raspberries instead of the blueberries and about any ripe fruit for the pear. Bananas, peaches, nectarines or additional berries work well.

Soy Tortoni

8 oz. tofu, drained
1 c. corn syrup
1 c. milk, regular or soy
1 c. macaroons, broken
½ c. chopped nuts
1 t. vanilla
¼ t. almond extract

Mix all ingredients until smooth. Freeze until firm enough to scoop. Spoon mixture into paper baking cups set in muffin tins and freeze until firm. Garnish with maraschino cherries, if desired when serving.

Stir-Fried Vegetables with Tofu

2 T. oil
1 large onion, sliced or chopped
1 t. minced garlic
½ c. sliced carrots
2 ribs celery, sliced
1 sweet pepper, any color, seeded and sliced
1-2 c. slice mushrooms
2 cakes tofu, diced
½ c. vegetable broth
¼ c. dry sherry
1 T. soy sauce
2 t. grated fresh ginger
2 t. sesame oil
2-3 t. cornstarch
hot cooked rice or chow-mein noodles

In skillet or wok heat oil and cook onions until tender and a little browned. Add carrots and celery and stir-fry 4 minutes. Add peppers and mushrooms and cook 2 minutes more. Add tofu and cook 2 more minutes. Combine remaining ingredients (except rice or noodles) and stir to dissolve cornstarch. Add to vegetables and cook until thickened and bubbly. Serve over rice or noodles. Serves 4.

Hot and Sour Soup

2 c. chicken or vegetable broth
1 c. raw chicken or pork sliced in thin strips, optional
1 T. soy sauce
4 Chinese black mushrooms, soaked 30 minutes and sliced or 1 can straw mushrooms, drained
½ c. sliced bamboo shoots
10 oz. tofu, cubed
¼ t. white pepper
2 T. rice or cider vinegar
2 T. cornstarch mixed with ¼ c. water
1 beaten egg
Sesame oil
1 green onion, sliced thin

Combine broth with meat soy sauce, mushrooms and bamboo shoots in pot and simmer 10 minutes. Add tofu, pepper, vinegar and cornstarch mixture and bring to a boil. As soup thickens and clears pour egg in slowly. Remove from heat; stir in a little oil and onions and serve. Serves 2.

Types of Tofu

Not all tofu is created equal. There are different degrees of firmness. Generally firmer types are used in main dishes and softer types are used in desserts and custards. However, there is more to the tofu story. Regular tofu is found in the refrigerated section of the grocery in a water bath. It is sometimes grainy in texture and appearance and is made is a process similar to that of making cheese. Silken tofu is usually found in the produce section of the store or on the shelf. It is made in a process more like the making of yogurt and is therefore smoother, softer and wetter. You may have to try several different brands before you find the one that best serves your needs. Usually silken tofu is pressed to extract excess water and to make it firmer. All tofu is made from soymilk and ranges in firmness from the soft to extra firm.

Nutty Coleslaw Spring Rolls

¼ c. soy sauce
2 T. rice or regular vinegar
½ t. sesame oil
¼ t. sesame seeds
2 c. coleslaw mix (shredded cabbage and carrots)
1 (10 oz. package) firm tofu, drained and diced
1/3 c. toasted chopped nuts
1/3 c. sweet and sour sauce
8 dried rice papers (available in Asian markets)
fresh cilantro leaves, optional
4 (10-inch long) green onion tops

Make dipping sauce by combining soy, vinegar, oil and sesame seeds. Set aside. Then make filling by combining coleslaw mix, tofu and nuts. Toss with sweet and sour sauce and set aside. Pour warm water into large shallow dish and dip rice papers into water. Place papers between damp cotton dish towels and let stand 10 minutes. Papers will become translucent. In the center of each paper place 1 cilantro leaf, if desired. Top with about 1/3 c. of the filling. Fold one edge over the filling then fold in the sides. Roll up. Split green onion tops in half lengthwise and wrap on of the strips around the spring roll twice tucking underneath on the serving plate. Repeat with remaining papers, makes 8 no-cook rolls, serving 4.

Soy Chili

2 c. T.V.P. (textured vegetable protein) available in health food stores, I like to use the type that is the size of lentils.
3 c. tomato juice or water
2 T. olive oil
2 large onions, chopped
1 sweet pepper, seeded and diced
1 rib celery, chopped
1 large carrot, peeled and diced
2 t. dried minced garlic
¼ c. chili powder, or to taste
1 T. dried oregano
1 t. cumin
1 t. red pepper sauce
salt and pepper to taste
1 c. tomato sauce
1 (28 oz. can) diced tomatoes
1 (15 oz. can) kidney beans, drained
Shredded cheese, chopped onions, sour cream or yogurt as toppings.

Heat tomato juice or water and pour over T.V.P. soaking 5 minutes. Heat oil in large kettle and cook onions until tender. Add remaining ingredients, except toppings and simmer, covered for 1-2 hours, stirring occasionally. Serves with toppings on the side. Makes 6-8 servings.

Easy Tofu Dip

2 (10 oz. carton), each, soft tofu
1 package ranch dressing mix

In a bowl mash the tofu and stir in the dressing mix. Chill and serve with veggies and chips for a low calorie dip.

Tofu Italiano

1 cake tofu, crumbled
¼ c. Italian dressing, regular or fat free
1 T. oil
1 large onion, chopped
1 c. sliced mushrooms, optional
1 (28 oz. can) diced tomatoes, undrained
2 t. Italian seasoning
salt to taste
hot cooked pasta
grated parmesan cheese, optional

Place tofu in shallow dish and toss with the dressing. Set aside. Heat oil in skillet and cook onion until lightly browned. Add tofu and continue cooking until tofu has browned a little. Add mushrooms, if desired, tomatoes and seasonings and simmer, stirring occasionally until sauce has thickened. Stir in pasta or place pasta on serving dish and spoon over the sauce. Top with grated Parmesan cheese, if desired. Serves 4.

Squash and Tofu Balls

2 c. grated summer squash
1 T. minced garlic
2 T. oil
½ c. minced celery
1-2 T. pizza seasoning
1 t. salt
2 blocks tofu, pressed (See earlier section on pressing tofu)
2-3 T. flour
sweet and sour or barbecue sauce

Cook squash and garlic in oil until tender and most of the liquid has evaporated. Stir in celery and seasonings and cook 2 more minutes. Crumble tofu and add flour in medium bowl. Add squash mixture and mix well. Form into walnut-sized balls and place on an oiled baking sheet. Bake at 350 degrees for 25-30minutes. Makes about 2 dozen. Serve with dipping sauce or on rice with sauce.

Tempeh Stir Fry

4 oz. tempeh, cut in ½-inch pieces
2 T. soy sauce
2 T. hoisin sauce
2 T. balsamic vinegar
2 t. grated ginger
1 t. minced garlic
dash of hot sauce
2 T. water
1 t. honey
1 t. cornstarch
1 T. oil
1 sweet onion, sliced
2-3 c. broccoli flowerets
1 sweet red or yellow pepper, seeded and cut into thin strips
½ c. cashews, optional
hot cooked rice or pasta

Place tempeh in shallow dish. Combine next 6 ingredients and pour over the tempeh. Marinate 1 hour at room temperature. Drain marinade off tempeh and combine liquid with the water, honey and cornstarch, stirring until smooth. Heat oil in skillet and cook onion until tender. Add broccoli and stir-fry 3 minutes more. Add tempeh and stir-fry 3 more minutes. Add pepper and cook 2 minutes more then add the reserved sauce and heat until thickened and bubbly. Serve over rice or pasta. Serves 2-3.

Miso Soup

2 T. oil
1 c. chopped onions
1–2 t. minced garlic
2 carrots, sliced
2 t. ginger, minced
½ c. chopped sweet peppers
4 c. vegetable or chicken stock
1 bunch spinach, chopped
soy sauce
2 T. miso
¼ c. chopped cilantro
cooked Asian noodles

Sauté onion in oil until browned. Add garlic and carrots and cook 4 minutes more. Add ginger and peppers and sauté 2 more minutes. Add stock and heat to a simmer. Cook until vegetable are tender then stir in spinach. Cook until spinach is wilted. Add soy sauce to taste and miso, stirring until miso dissolves. Add cilantro and heat to a simmer but do not boil. Ladle over hot cooked noodles. Serves 4-6.

Miso Vinaigrette

2 T. miso
1 T. Dijon mustard
2-3 T. rice vinegar
1 T. water
1 ½ t. grated gingerroot
1 clove garlic
2 T. minced green onions
1/3 c. oil
salt to taste

In blender combine first 4 ingredients until smooth. Add next 3 ingredients and blend until smooth. With blender running add oil in a slow stream until dressing thickens (emulsifies). Add salt to taste. Makes about 2/3 cup.

Lentil and Tofu Soup

2 T. oil
2 c. chopped onion
1-1½ c. lentils, rinsed and drained
2 c. chopped carrots
2 c. chopped celery
1 c. chopped cabbage, bok choy or Chinese cabbage
1 (29 oz. can) diced tomatoes, seasoned if available, undrained
8-10 c. vegetable stock
1 lb. firm tofu, drained and cubed
salt and pepper to taste
hot sauce to taste
fresh chopped parsley or chives, optional

Heat oil in kettle and cook onions until tender. Add remaining ingredients, except tofu and seasonings and simmer, covered until lentils and vegetables are tender, about 25 minutes. Stir in tofu and simmer at least 10 minutes more. Adjust seasonings, adding more stock or water if soup is too thick. Serves 8.

Rice and Tofu Salad

10 oz. firm tofu pressed (See earlier section on pressing tofu)
4½ c. cooked brown rice, about 1½ c. uncooked
½ lb. green beans, trimmed and cut in 1–inch pieces, cooked 2 minutes.
1 sweet pepper, seeded and julienned
oil
vinegar and oil dressing or miso vinaigrette, recipe below
4 hard-cooked eggs, peeled and cut into wedges
lettuce leaves

Press tofu. Combine rice with beans and peppers and chill. Cube tofu. Heat oil in skillet and brown tofu until golden. Drain on paper towels and season with salt and pepper. Toss rice mixture with dressing and season with salt and pepper, if you like. Place lettuce leaves on serving platter. Top with the rice mixture, the tofu and the eggs. Serve with extra dressing on the side, if you like. Serves 4-6.

Fried Tofu Bites

1 package tofu, drained and cubed
2 T. balsamic vinegar
2 T. soy sauce
1 T. brown sugar
2 cloves garlic, minced
2 t. grated ginger
½ t. red pepper flakes
½ c. sesame seeds
¼ c. each flour and cornmeal
oil

Place tofu in shallow dish. Combine vinegar and soy sauce with garlic, ginger and pepper and toss over tofu. Allow to marinade 1-2 hours. Combine dry ingredients in bag and toss in cubed tofu to coat. Heat ¼-inch of oil in skillet and cook tofu cubes until golden and crispy. Drain and serve with dipping sauce, honey mustard etc.

Orange Oat Muffins

1¼ c. all-purpose flour or whole wheat pastry flour
½ c. quick oats
1/3 c. soy flour
2 t. baking powder
1 t. baking soda
¼ t. *each* salt and cinnamon
1 egg
2/3 c. soymilk, regular or vanilla
½ c. orange juice
1 t. grated orange zest
¼ c. maple syrup
2 T. oil

Combine dry ingredients in medium bowl and stir to mix well. In small bowl beat together liquid ingredients and fold into dry ingredients. Divide batter among 12 greased or paper-lined muffin cups. Bake in a preheated 400 degree oven for 20 minutes or until light golden on the top. Makes 12.

Portobello Mushroom Pizza

8 Portobello mushroom caps
1 sweet onion, diced
1 T. oil
1-1½ c. T.V.P.
1 T. pizza seasoning
1 c. water or vegetable broth
1-2 c. tomato sauce or bottled marinara sauce
1-2 c. shredded mozzarella cheese

Stem mushrooms and scrape out a little of the dark gills. Brush with oil and bake, rounded side down in a preheated 350 degree oven for 10 minutes. Meanwhile, sauté onion in oil until tender. Add T.V.P. seasoning, water or broth, and sauce. Simmer 15-20 minutes or until sauce has thickened. Divide mixture among mushroom caps, top with cheese and return to oven. Bake until cheese is melted and bubbly, about 10-15 minutes. Brown under broiler, if desired. Makes 8.

Soybean and Cabbage Salad

¾ c. dry soybeans
water
½ c. vinegar
2 T. honey
½ t. salt
½ t. dry mustard
½ t. paprika
½ c. oil
2 c. shredded cabbage
1 carrot, shredded
1 c. shredded cheese, any type
1 rib celery, diced
1 sweet pepper, seeded and diced

Place beans in saucepan and cover with cold water. Bring to a boil and cook 5 minutes. Turn off heat and let beans stand 1 hour. Drain beans, cover with fresh cold water and simmer until tender, about 2-2½ hours. Drain beans, rinse under cold water and set aside. In blender combine vinegar with honey and seasonings until smooth. With blender running pour oil in slowly until dressing thickens. Pour over prepared beans and toss to coat. Chill at least 1 hour. Add remaining ingredients and toss to coat. Serves 3-4.

Sweet and Sour Tofu

1-2 lbs. tofu, drained
1 egg
1 t. cornstarch
¼ t. salt
1 t. soy sauce
additional cornstarch for dredging
2 T. oil
1 medium onion, chopped
1 medium carrot, peeled and sliced thin
1 sweet green pepper, seeded and chopped
1 sweet red or yellow pepper, seeded and chopped
1 (20 oz. can) pineapple chunks, drained, reserving juice for sauce
sweet and sour sauce, see recipe under Saucy Sauces

Cut tofu into cubes and place in bowl. Combine egg, 1 t. cornstarch, salt and soy sauce and pour over the tofu, stirring to coat. Allow to marinade at least 1 hour in fridge. When ready to cook, heat 1T. Oil in large skillet or wok. Sauté onions on high until tender. Add carrots and stir fry 3 minutes. Add peppers and sauté 3 minutes more. Remove to bowl and stir in pineapple. Dredge the tofu in additional cornstarch and sauté in remaining oil until browned and crispy.

Meanwhile, combine sauce ingredients in a saucepan and heat to boiling. Return vegetables to pan with pork and pour over sauce to desired amount. Serve over rice, makes 4-6 servings.

Note: If you make the sweet and sour sauce ahead of time it will get runny when reheated if made with regular cornstarch. Either use modified cornstarch (Clear Gel A) or make sauce just when you are ready to use it.

Easy Vegetarian Lasagna

1 (16 oz. box) lasagna noodles, uncooked
16 oz. tofu, drained and crumbled
2 small zucchini, sliced
8 oz. tomato sauce
14 oz. diced tomatoes, undrained
2-3 c. shredded mozzarella cheese
1 T. pizza or Italian seasoning
½ c. water

In a 9x13-inch baking dish place a layer of the noodles. Top with the tofu, spreading to smooth. Add another layer of the noodles then top with the sliced zucchini, the diced tomatoes and 1 T. of the seasoning. Add another layer of the noodles and top with the mozzarella cheese. Then place remaining noodles on top. Combine sauce with remaining seasoning and water and pour over the top. Seal casserole tightly with foil and refrigerate several hours or overnight. To bake, let lasagna sit at room temperature 30 minutes before baking in a 350 degree oven for 1½ hours. Remove foil and let lasagna sit 10 minutes before cutting.

Szechwan Spicy Tofu

2 T. oil
2 T. green onion
1 T. chopped fresh ginger
1 clove garlic, minced
1½ T. hot bean paste, available in Asian markets
1 lb. diced raw chicken, optional
2 T. dry sherry
1 T. soy sauce
water
1 lb. tofu, drained and cubed
2 T. cornstarch
hot pepper flakes to taste
1 t. sesame oil
1 green onion cut up for garnish
hot cooked rice

Heat oil in skillet and cook onion, ginger and garlic. Stir fry 30 seconds. Add bean paste and stir fry 30 seconds more. Add chicken, stir one minute and add sherry and soy sauce. Add 1 c. of water and bring to a boil. Add tofu and cover, simmering 10 minutes. Mix cornstarch with 2 T. water and add to tofu mixture stirring until thickened and bubbly. Add pepper to taste and sesame oil. Serve over rice and sprinkle with onions. Makes 4-6 servings.

Chapter 14:
Soup's On

Homemade Soup Stock

For chicken:
3-4 lbs. chicken backs, necks, wings etc. or 4 lbs. chicken legs or a 4 lb. soup chicken
2 onions, peeled and chopped
2 ribs celery, with leaves, chopped
3 carrots, sliced
3½ qt. cold water
2 small tomatoes, fresh or canned, halved
1 cabbage core or a few outer leaves
1 clove garlic
1 bay leaf
½ t thyme, crumbled
pinch of sage
½ t. whole peppercorns or ½ t. coarse ground pepper
½ c. fresh parsley or 3 T. dried parsley
salt or chicken flavored soup base to taste

In large stock pot brown chicken, in batches. Return all chicken to pot and add onions, cooking until they are browned. Add celery and carrots and brown 5 minutes longer. Add remaining ingredients, except parsley and salt and bring to a boil. Cover and simmer 2½ hours. Add parsley and cook 30 minutes more. Strain through a fine sieve, discard vegetables and remove any meat from the bones you wish to use. Return soup to kettle, add salt or soup base to taste and de-fat or chill and refrigerate to remove fat later. Makes about 12 cups.

For Beef:
Follow the same directions, but use 4 lbs. Beef bones or soup cuts like beef ribs, oxtails, neck bones, shank or knuckle bones, sliced into 1-inch thick slices. Use beef flavored soup base instead of chicken and cook for about 4 hours.

For Vegetable:
Use all the same ingredients as for the chicken stock but eliminate meat and meat flavored soup base and use vegetable soup base. Use a little oil to brown the vegetables. Add 2 leeks, ½ lb. mushrooms, a handful of green beans and a seeded and chopped sweet red pepper. You can also add extra celery or carrots and any leftover vegetables you may have on hand. Canned beans such as kidney or butter beans can also add a nice flavor. Some also like to add ¼ c. of lentils (uncooked). Cook for about 2 hours.

Stock can be frozen, but try to use a little less salt than usual, as they will freeze better. They can be frozen for up to 3 months for freshest flavor, longer and they will be safe, but not as tasty.

To de-fat stock you can chill it and remove the fat the next day, but sometimes you can't wait. To remove fat quickly you can use a de-fatting cup, found in many housewares stores. They are like measuring cups with a spout that comes up from the bottom. This way as you pour stock out of the cup it pours from the bottom, leaving the fat behind.

You can also use a turkey baster to remove fat from the top, or to get stock up from the bottom of the pot. Effective, but a little slow.

You can also remove fat by freezing it off. Skim as much fat as you can from the strained stock. It can be warm, but should be removed from the heat. Dump in a tray or two of ice cubes and gently stir them about the top of the soup with a slotted spoon. The fat will freeze and congeal around the ice. Remove with the slotted spoon and discard. Very easy.

Stock Options

For recipes calling for stock or broth you have several choices. Homemade of course, would be the best choice and recipes follow, but for those times when you don't have the time or the inclination here are some alternatives.

Canned broth can be found in natural strength and concentrated. There are also low salt varieties, for those looking to reduce their sodium intake. Chicken and beef are the most readily available.

Bouillon cubes and granules are found in most supermarkets, but tend to be salty. Use sparingly, and only as a substitute for the salt in a recipe. By itself the flavor lacks a lot.

Paste types soup bases are also in most stores, though brands and quality vary. Some are just a step above bouillon in flavor and others are quite good. They come in jars and are sometimes found in the soup aisle with the other broth makers. Other varieties are in the freezer section or refrigerated in the meat section. Come in chicken, beef, vegetable and ham flavors among others. My personal favorites are the Stouffer's and Minor's brands found in Heinen's and Giant Eagle markets. Tone's bases are also nice and you may know of other brands. These can be used in place of stock by diluting with water, or for a richer flavor, use these bases in place of the salt in homemade recipes.

Mock Wonton Soup

4 c. chicken stock
1 c. uncooked baby shrimp
1 c. cooked roast pork, cut in thin strips
2 c. bok choy cut in thin strips
6 oz. wide egg noodles
2 T. chopped green onions

In medium saucepan bring stock to the boil. Add next three ingredients and simmer about 5 minutes. Stir in noodles and heat through. Ladle into bowls and sprinkle with onions. Serves 3-4.

Acorn Squash Soup

2 lb. acorn squash, halved and seeded
2 T. butter
2 large leeks, white part only, cleaned and chopped
5-6 c. chicken stock
1 T. tomato paste
1 sprig thyme or ½ t. dried and crumbled
salt and pepper to taste
¼ c. whipping cream
snipped chives for garnish, optional

Arrange squash; cut side down, in a baking dish with ½-inch of water and bake at 350 degrees until soft, about 30 minutes. Meanwhile, cook leeks in butter until soft. Scoop out squash pulp and add to leeks with stock, paste and seasonings. Cover and simmer 20 minutes. Puree soup and stir in cream. Do not boil. Ladle into bowls and garnish with chives, if desired. Serves 4-6.

Broccoli Soup

1 lb. broccoli
2 leeks, trimmed, washed and cut in 1-inch pieces
1 T. butter
1 clove minced garlic
1/8 t. red pepper flakes
3 medium potatoes, peeled and diced
6 c. chicken or vegetable stock
¼ t. nutmeg
salt and pepper to taste

Peel broccoli stems and cut into 1-inch strips. Cut flowerets into small pieces. Cook leeks in butter 4 minutes. Add garlic and cook 3 minutes. Add remaining ingredients and simmer, covered 20 minutes. Adjust seasonings and serve. Serves 4-6.

Cream of Chicken Soup

4 c. chicken broth
2 c. fine chopped celery
1 clove garlic, minced
¾ c. half and half or evaporated milk
salt and pepper to taste
2 c. minced cooked chicken
½ c. grated Parmesan cheese

Cook celery and garlic in broth until tender. Pour into blender or food processor and puree until smooth. Add half-and-half and heat almost to the boil. Season to taste. Stir in chicken and cheese and cook until cheese melts. Serves 6-8.

Crab Bisque

1 medium onion, diced
½ sweet pepper, seeded and diced
2 T. butter or margarine
½ lb. Sliced mushrooms
2 tomatoes, diced
1 lb. crabmeat, lump preferred but canned is O.K.
1 t. salt
dash of cayenne
1½ c. cream or evaporated milk
1 T. minced parsley

In saucepan sauté onion and pepper until tender. Add mushrooms and cook 3 minutes. Add tomatoes and cook 3 more minutes. Add remaining ingredients and heat almost to the boil. Sprinkle with a little parsley. 4-6 servings.

Leftover Turkey Soup

1 turkey carcass, broken into small pieces
2 qts. Water
1 carrot, chopped
1 rib celery, chopped
1 turnip, chopped
1 onion, chopped
1 bay leaf
1 sprig parsley
1 c. canned tomatoes
salt and pepper to taste

Cover turkey and vegetables with the water and cook, covered for 2 hours. Add seasonings and tomatoes and cook 30 minutes longer. Strain and skim fat. Makes 1½-2 quarts stock.

Sweet Potato and Leek Soup

2 onions, chopped
2 cloves garlic, minced
1 t. peppercorns
3 whole cloves
¼ c. olive oil
6 leeks, washed, trimmed and cut into 1-inch pieces
1 red sweet pepper, seeded and chopped
½ c. dry white wine
4 large sweet potatoes, peeled and cubed
3 white potatoes, peeled and cubed
1 lb. mushrooms, sliced
6 c. stock
1 c. apples juice or cider
1/8 t. ground allspice
½ c. chopped parsley

Cook first 5 ingredients until onions are tender. Add leeks and pepper and cook2 minutes. Add wine and simmer until mixture is reduced by half. Discard peppercorns and cloves and add all but the parsley. Cover and cook 40 minutes. Whisk soup until it is smooth. Add parsley. Serves 10-12.

Zucchini Soup

1 medium onion, chopped
1 T. butter
4-6 medium zucchini, sliced
1 large potato, peeled and diced
¼ t. each thyme, rosemary, basil and sage
salt and pepper to taste
6 c, chicken broth
1 c. skim milk

In Dutch oven cook onions in butter until tender. Add vegetables and seasonings and cook until hot. Add broth, heat to a simmer and cook 15 minutes. Puree mixture in blender in batches and return to pot. Add milk and heat through. Serve hot or cold. Serves 6-8.

White Gazpacho

2 c. chicken broth
1½ c. watercress, chopped
2 medium cucumbers, peeled and sliced
1 sweet pepper, seeded and chopped
3 T. fresh dill, or 1 T. dried
2 T. chopped green onion
3 T. each mayonnaise, sour cream and white wine vinegar
2 T. sugar
1 t. salt
½ t. pepper

Place all ingredients in a blender and process in batches until smooth. Chill at least 3 hours before serving. Serve in chilled bowls. Serves4-6.

Easy Corn and Chicken Chowder

1 can cream style corn
2 c. milk
2 c. diced chicken
1 baked potato, diced
salt and pepper to taste
1 T. butter or margarine

Combine all ingredients in a saucepan and heat over medium heat until mixture almost boils. Serves 3-4.

Avocado Soup

2 ripe avocados, pitted and peeled
1 t. lemon juice
1 c. cold chicken or vegetable stock
1 c. light cream or evaporated milk
½ c. yogurt
½ c. dry white wine
salt and pepper to taste

Set a few thin slices of avocado aside and brush with lemon juice to prevent discoloring. Combine remaining ingredients in blender until smooth and chill until ready to use. Garnish with reserved avocado slices. 4 cups.

Bean and Barley Soup

8 oz. dry pinto beans, rinsed
1 T. oil
1 onion, chopped
2 cloves garlic, minced
2 carrots chopped fine
2 ribs celery, chopped fine
1 lb. spare ribs or 1 lb. turkey drumstick or thigh
1 lb. ham hock or 1 lb. smoked turkey drumstick or wing
1 qt. chicken stock
2 qts. vegetable stock or water
1 c. barley
½ lb. green beans, cut
salt and pepper to taste
1 T. parsley

Place beans in saucepan with water and boil 5 minutes. Set aside to soak 1 hour. Drain. Meanwhile cook vegetables and garlic in oil in large kettle. Add meats and stocks and bring to a boil. Stir in pinto beans. Cover and simmer on top of the stove for 1 hour. Or if pan is ovenproof place in 350 degree oven and cook 1 hour. Stir in barley and beans and cook 1 hour more. Remove from heat and remove meat. Remove any meat from bones, shred and return to soup. Stir in parsley and adjust seasonings. Serves 8-10.

Pumpkin Soup

2 T. butter
¼ c. chopped onion
½ t. ginger
1 T. flour
2 c. cooked pumpkin
2 c. chicken broth
2 c. milk
salt and pepper to taste

Sauté butter, onion and ginger. Stir in flour. Add pumpkin and cook 5 minutes. Add broth and milk and stir often until heated through. Adjust seasonings. Serves 4-6.

Hot and Sour Soup

3 c. chicken broth
½ lb. raw pork or chicken, cut in strips
4 Chinese black mushrooms, soaked 30 minutes and sliced
2 oz. extra firm tofu, cut into matchstick pieces
2 T. dry sherry
1 t. salt
½ t. pepper
2 T. rice or cider vinegar
1 T. cornstarch dissolved in 2 T. water

Bring broth to a boil. Add meat, mushrooms and tofu and cook about 8 minutes, or until meat is cooked. Add remaining ingredients and cook until thickened. Makes 3-4 servings.

Aunt Josie's Clam Chowder

2 T. butter
1 onion, chopped
1 rib celery, chopped
2-3 small potatoes, cubed
1 c. water or stock
2 (10 oz. can) clams, undrained
2 t. butter
2 T. flour
2 c. milk
salt and pepper to taste

Sauté onions and celery in butter until tender, but not browned. Add potatoes and water or stock and cook, covered until potatoes are tender. Stir in clams and set aside. In another saucepan, combine butter and flour over low heat and stir in milk, stirring to make a white sauce. Add to clam mixture and adjust seasonings. Serves 4.

Yellow Split Pea Soup

1½ c. yellow split peas
6 c. water
1½-2 lbs. meaty ham bones or smoked turkey pieces
2 medium onions, chopped
1 T. paste type soup base
1 T. grated ginger-root or 1 t. ground ginger
pepper to taste
1 medium carrot, peeled and diced
1 sweet pepper, seeded and diced

Rinse peas. Place all ingredients, except carrots and peppers in soup pot and simmer, covered, for 1 hour, stirring occasionally. Add carrots and simmer 15 minutes. Add pepper and simmer 5-10 minutes longer. Remove bone. Cut up and return any meat to soup, if desired. Adjust seasonings and serve. 6-8 servings.

Aunt Josie's Cabbage Soup

1 T. oil
1 c. chopped onion
1 clove minced garlic
1½ lbs. cooked smoked sausage, sliced or diced, **I use turkey sausage**
3 carrots, peeled and cubed
8 c. coarsely chopped cabbage, a small head
1 sweet pepper, seeded and chopped
1 c. tomato sauce
2 qts. Water
1 t. salt or paste type soup base
pepper to taste
3 medium potatoes, cubed
2 T. oil
1/3 c. flour
1 t. paprika

Sauté onion in oil until browned. Add garlic and sausage and cook until sausage is browned. Add vegetables, sauce water and seasonings and cook, covered 15 minutes. Add potatoes and cook, covered, 15 minutes more. In bowl combine oil, flour and paprika and stir until smooth. Ladle some hot soup into flour mixture and whisk until smooth. Repeat a few more times, until flour forms a paste. Pour this mixture into soup and simmer 2 minutes, until thickened. Serves 10-12.

Turkey Soup with Herbs

2 T. butter or oil
1 medium zucchini, sliced
2 medium carrots, peeled and chopped
1 small onion, chopped
1 rib celery, chopped
5-6 c. Turkey or chicken stock
1 c. sliced mushrooms
2-4 c. cubed cooked turkey
1 T. chopped parsley
1 T. chopped basil
1 t. thyme, crumbled
salt and pepper to taste

Cook first 5 ingredients together, over low heat, covered, until vegetables are tender. Add broth and mushrooms and cook, covered, 10 minutes. Stir in remaining ingredients and heat through. Serve immediately. Makes 4-6 servings.

This is a great way to use leftover turkey, but you can also use chicken or even leftover cooked pork or beef roast. Versatile and fast.

Tomato Bisque Soup

2 T. oil
1 c. chopped onion
1 (28-29 oz. can) whole tomatoes, cut up or diced tomatoes, undrained
1 qt. beef or chicken or vegetable stock
½ c. raw rice
1 c. sour cream

Cook onions in oil until tender. Add tomatoes and stock and bring to the boil. Add rice, cover and simmer until rice is tender, about 20 minutes. Place sour cream in bowl and stir in a cup of the hot soup, stirring until smooth. Add another cup of the soup and then add this mixture to the pot. Heat through, but do not boil. Makes 6-8 servings.

Variations: Brown or wild rice can be added instead, but cooking times will be longer, about 45-50 minutes. Barley can also be added instead of the rice, but allow 45 minutes to cook.

Seafood: Once rice is tender, but before adding sour cream you can add any one of the following; ½-1 pound raw diced fish (mild white fish are good or even salmon for a special treat), ½-¾ pound salad size raw shrimp, 2 cans crabmeat, 2 (10 oz. can) clams, drained.

Rita's Vegetable Soup

4 T. oil
1 turnip, peeled and chopped
8 carrots, peeled and chopped
8 ribs celery, chopped
5-6 medium onions, chopped
2 T. sugar
2 T. poultry seasoning
1½ T. parsley flakes
pepper to taste
2 T. paste style soup base, any flavor
1 (28 oz. can) diced tomatoes

Sauté vegetables in oil until browned, about 10-15 minutes. Add remaining ingredients and enough water to cover and simmer, covered, until vegetables are tender, about 20 minutes. Serves 10-12.

Variation: You can add diced, cooked, chicken or leftover turkey. You can also make mini meatballs and add during the last 15 minutes of cooking.

Chapter 15: Totally Terrific Tomatoes - Cooking and Canning Tomatoes

Tomato Relish

12 large tomatoes, peeled, seeded and chopped
1 c. diced celery
3-4 medium onions, peeled and sliced thin
1 green sweet pepper, seeded and chopped
3 red or yellow sweet peppers, seeded and chopped
3 T. canning salt (or non-iodized)
1-2 T. prepared horseradish
1¼ c. sugar
1-2 T. whole mustard seed
1 t. ground cinnamon
½ t. fresh grated ginger
½ t. fresh ground pepper
¼ t. ground cloves
1 c. cider vinegar

Combine vegetables with salt and horseradish in a stainless steel or ceramic container. Cover and refrigerate overnight. Remove from fridge and drain off all liquids in a colander. Discard juices. Return tomato mixture to bowl and add remaining ingredients, stirring to dissolve sugar. Chill several hours before serving. Adjust seasonings to suit your taste. Repackage in sterile canning jars for easier storage in refrigerator, or for gift giving. Keeps for several weeks in the fridge.

Stuffed Tomatoes

medium to large tomatoes, allow 1 per serving
cold salad for stuffing (allow ½-1 c. per serving)
fresh chopped parsley, chives, or cilantro for garnish

Slice top off tomatoes and scoop out seeds and ribs. Lightly salt inside of tomatoes and invert 30 minutes on paper towels. Spoon in filling, mounding slightly and garnish with herbs, if desired. Chill until ready to serve, or serve immediately. Some fillings could include ham, chicken, tuna or bean salad. If tomatoes are small you can just use two per serving, or even stuff lots of cherry tomatoes for an easy appetizer. You can also stuff sweet peppers instead of the tomatoes.

Cream of Fresh Tomato Soup

3 medium-sized ripe tomatoes
1 small onion, chopped fine
1 rib celery, chopped fine
pinch of sugar, optional
3 whole cloves
1 small bay leaf
3 T. butter
3 T. flour
1 t. salt
3 c. milk

Peel and chop tomatoes. Place tomatoes in saucepan with onion, celery, sugar (if adding), cloves and bay leaf. Bring mixture to a boil; reduce heat and cover, simmering 15 minutes. Melt butter in a large saucepan then stir in flour and salt. Cook mixture until bubbly. Add milk and cook until thickened stirring constantly. Puree tomato mixture through strainer, food mill or in a blender or processor. Add to milk mixture and heat through. Serves 6.

Chicken Tomato Sauce

2 T. oil
4 chicken breast halves
salt and pepper
2 T. butter
3 large leeks, trimmed, washed and chopped
2-3 garlic cloves, minced
1 (28 oz. can) diced tomatoes, drained
2 T. Marsala wine or dry Vermouth
1 lb. hot cooked pasta
1 c. Parmesan cheese, grated
¼ c. chopped fresh herbs, parsley, chives, basil, lovage etc. (optional)

Heat oil and sauté chicken until just cooked through. Season with salt and pepper while cooking. Remove and allow to cool a little, cut chicken into strips. Heat butter in same skillet and add leeks and garlic, cooking over medium heat until leeks are tender. Add tomatoes, wine and ½ c. of the Parmesan cheese and heat through. Toss chicken in pasta, toss in sauce and add herbs, if desired. Serve with extra cheese on the side.

Ratatouille

1 large onion, sliced in thin wedges
2 cloves garlic, minced
3 T. oil
1 (15-16 oz. can) tomatoes, cut up
1½ t. dried thyme
1 t. salt
½ t. pepper
1 bay leaf
1 medium eggplant, peeled and cubed
2 medium zucchini, cut in chunks
1 sweet green pepper, seeded and chopped
1 sweet red pepper, seeded and chopped

Heat oil in Dutch oven and cook onion and garlic until tender. Add remaining ingredients, except peppers and cook until vegetables are tender and sauce is thickened, about 30 minutes. If stew is too runny, remove lid and cook 10 minutes longer. Add peppers and cook, covered 15 minutes. Remove bay leaf. Serves 8-10. In crock-pot combine all ingredients and cook on low 6-8 hours.

Chopped Arabic Salad

1 lemon
¾ t. salt
¼ t. black pepper
3 T. olive oil
1 seedless cucumber cut into ¼-inch dice
1 lb. tomatoes, cut into ½-inch dice
1 c. finely chopped red onion or 1 c. chopped green onions
1 c. fine chopped fresh parsley
½ c. fine chopped fresh mint

Cut lemon in half. Scoop or cut out the flesh from one half and chop fine. Squeeze the juice out of the second half and combine with seasonings and oil. Blend well. Toss with remaining ingredients and chill until ready to serve. Serves 4-6.

Tomato and Herb Dressing

1 c. tomatoes, peeled and seeded, fresh or canned
½ c. chopped parsley
2 green onions, chopped
2 T. fresh celery or lovage leaves
2 t. basil leaves. Dried
½ t. each salt and garlic powder
½ c. olive oil
dash hot pepper sauce

Combine all ingredients in blender until smooth. Makes 1½ cups.

Cornbread Salad

4 c. crumbled cornbread or corn muffins
1 c. shredded mild cheese
1 sweet red pepper seeded and diced
1 c. diced celery
½ c. diced green onion
4 hard-cooked eggs, peeled and chopped
¼ c. chopped parsley
1-1½ c. mayonnaise or salad dressing, sometimes I use potato salad dressing or even slaw dressing
2 c. diced fresh tomatoes
1 c. toasted pecans
paprika for sprinkling on the top, optional

Place cornbread and next 6 ingredients in a medium bowl. Stir in dressing until desired moistness is achieved. Chill and stir in tomato and nut just before serving. Sprinkle with paprika if you like. Serves 6.

Note: You can add whole kernel corn also if you like.

Vegetables in Lemon-Herb Dressing

8 oz. fresh pea pods or 6 oz. package frozen pea pods, thawed and drained
1 (14 oz. can) artichoke hearts, drained
½ of a 14 oz. can baby corn, drained
8 mushrooms, quartered
2 medium tomatoes, seeded and chopped
¼ c. olive oil
¼ c. salad oil
¼ red wine or herbal vinegar
2 t. lemon zest
1 T. lemon juice
1 t. sugar
1 t. basil

If using fresh pea pods blanch in boiling water for 2-4 minutes. Place in cold water to stop cooking. If using frozen pea pods do not cook. Combine all vegetables in bowl and set aside. Combine remaining ingredients to make dressing and shake well to mix. Toss over vegetables and chill several hours before serving. Serves 8.

Marinated Tomato Salad

3 large tomatoes, cut in wedges, or 2 pints cherry tomatoes, halved
1 T. olive oil
1 clove garlic, minced
2-3 basil leaves, cut into thin strips
2 T. balsamic vinegar
salt and pepper to taste

Combine ingredients and serve at room temperature. Serves 4-6.

Tomato Baby Bites

1-2 pints cherry tomatoes
1 (8 oz. package) cream cheese, softened
2 green onions, minced
¼ c. minced celery
dash Tabasco
1 T. chopped dates
1 T. chopped parsley

Wash tomatoes and slice a little off the bottom of the tomatoes so they will stand up. Cut off the cap from the tomatoes and scoop out the seeds. Combine remaining ingredients and spoon into empty tomatoes. Chill until ready to serve.

Italian Bread Salad

1 lb.loaf, day old crusty bread, cut into 1-inch cubes
5-6 plum tomatoes, sliced
½ English cucumber, sliced
1 c. sliced sweet onion
2/3 c. olive oil
1/3 c. red wine vinegar
3 T. balsamic vinegar
¼ c. fresh basil leaves, cut into thin strips
2 t. Italian seasoning

In large bowl toss together bread cubes and vegetables. Combine remaining ingredients in a smaller bowl and pour over the bread mixture, tossing to coat well. Be sure that all the bread gets coated. Serves 6-8.

Pizza Zucchini

1 T. oil
½ c. chopped onion
1 sweet pepper, seeded and chopped
1 c. sliced mushrooms, optional
3-4 c. sliced zucchini or other summer squash, trimmed and sliced
1-2 c. tomato sauce, or 3 c. diced fresh tomatoes
1-2 t. pizza seasoning, or to taste
8 oz. Mozzarella cheese

Sauté onion in oil until tender add pepper and mushrooms and sauté 2 minutes more. Add squash and cook until tender. Add sauce or tomatoes, seasonings and salt if desired. Heat through, turn down heat and add cheese. Cover and allow to cook on low until cheese melts. Serve as is, over rice or pasta or in pita bread. Serves 3-4.

Warm Pasta Salad

1 lb. plum tomatoes, chopped
1 medium onion, chopped
4 oz. fresh mushrooms, sliced
2 cloves garlic, minced
¼ c. fresh parsley, chopped
1 T. dried basil
1 t. dried oregano
½ c. olive oil
¼ c. red wine vinegar
3 T. balsamic vinegar
dash of hot red pepper flakes
salt to taste
1 lb. uncooked pasta

Combine all ingredients, except pasta and chill overnight. Cook pasta, drain and toss with tomato mixture. Mixture should be served right away. Serves 6.

Caponata

2 small eggplants, unpeeled and cut into ½-inch pieces, about 5-6 c.
1 large onion, chopped
½ c. olive oil, or a little more
4 celery ribs, sliced
2 sweet peppers, seeded and chopped
1 heaping T. chopped garlic
3 tomatoes, chopped
1 c. sliced black olives
3-4 T. red wine vinegar
salt and pepper to taste.

Soak eggplant in salted water for at least 15 minutes. Rinse, drain and pat dry. Set aside. Meanwhile in skillet cook onion in 2 T. of the oil until tender. Add the celery and cook until the celery is tender-crisp. Place mixture in a mixing bowl and set aside. Heat 2 T. more of the oil and cook the peppers until tender. Add garlic and cook 1 minute longer. Add the tomatoes and cook 1 minute longer. Add this mixture to onion mixture and return skillet to the heat. Add remaining oil to skillet and cook eggplant until golden brown and tender. You may have to do this in 2 batches. Add remaining ingredients to bowl while eggplant is cooking. When eggplant is done add it to the bowl and mix well. Season to taste. Serve with crusty breads cold, hot or at room temperature. Serves 10-12.

Greek Salad

8 c. mixed salad greens
3-4 tomatoes, seeded and diced
1 roasted sweet pepper, seeded and diced
2 c. sliced cucumber
½ sweet onion, sliced thin
½-¾ c. sliced olives
4 oz. crumbled feta cheese

Dressing
Juice of 2 lemons
2-3 cloves garlic
1 t. sea salt
½ t. oregano
¼ t. crushed red pepper
½-2/3 c. olive oil

In large bowl combine vegetables. In blender combine lemon juice with garlic, salt, oregano and pepper and blend until smooth. With machine running add oil in a slow steady stream until it becomes emulsified. Adjust seasonings. Toss with vegetables and top with olives and cheese before serving. Serves 4-6.

Zucchini and Tomato Casserole

6 c. sliced zucchini
6 c. sliced tomatoes
4-6 c. thin sliced onion
4 T. butter
1 c. bread crumbs
2 c. shredded mild cheese
salt and pepper to taste

Place tomato slices in a colander and allow to drain. In 9x13-inch casserole dish layer half of the zucchini and top with a layer of half the tomatoes and then a layer of half the onion. Sprinkle with salt and pepper and repeat with the remaining vegetables. Season with salt and pepper and dot with butter. Sprinkle on the bread crumbs and bake, uncovered, in a 375 degree oven for 45-55 minutes or until vegetables are tender. If a lot of liquid had accumulated in the pan use a baster to remove most of it. Sprinkle on the cheese and return casserole to oven for 10 minutes longer or until cheese is melted and bubbly. Great as is or spooned over hot pasta or rice. Serves 4-6.

Tip: To peel tomatoes place clean tomatoes in boiling water a few at a time and remove in a minute or so. Cool in cold water and then core the tomatoes. Skins should slip right off.

To seed tomatoes cut them in half and then squeeze. Most of the seeds will just get "squished" out.

Canning Basics

Before canning there are some basics you should know. There are general guidelines that need to be followed and some equipment that will make the job easier.

The USDA recommends that all jams and jellies be processed in a boiling water bath, unless it is a recipe that is frozen or unless all the preserves are to be kept refrigerated. Sealing jars with paraffin is no longer considered to be a safe way to preserve jams and jellies. Other high acid foods, like tomatoes (when acidified) and fruits and fruit products or pickled foods can also be canned in a hot water bath. Low acid foods, like vegetables and meats must always be processed in a pressure canner.

Since the jars are sterilized in the canning process there is no need to sterilize jars as a rule. They should be freshly washed in hot, soapy water, rinsed and kept warm in a pot of hot water or in a low oven until ready to use. You can also run them through the dishwasher and keep them in there until ready to fill. Because jams and jellies are packed when hot, cold jars might crack. Before starting make sure the jars are free of nicks and cracks, being extra careful to check the rims.

Note: The only time you must sterilize a jar is if it contained food that had spoiled. When I get jars second-hand I also sterilize them before use. To sterilize jars submerge them in boiling water for twenty minutes.

To prepare water bath have a canner (large kettle with a wire rack) filled with enough water to cover the jars by 1-2 inches and have it boiling when the jars are added. Timing begins when the water comes back to the boil (usually only a minute or two when hot jelly-filled jars are added). I get the water in the canner boiling first and turn it down to a high simmer until just before it is needed. Keep it covered to heat up faster and to prevent evaporation. If you do not have a canner and kettle deep enough to accommodate the jars can be used but you must cover the bottom with a towel. Jars that touch the bottom of the pan directly will break during processing. Also the lid of the kettle is left on during processing. Timing starts when water returns to the boil.

To prepare a pressure canner add several inches of hot water in the bottom of the canner. The canner will usually come with specific directions or a fill line. After jars are added to the canner the lid is secured and the heat is turned on. When proper pressure is attained timing begins. When the time is up the canner is removed from the heat and allowed to cool down before removing the lid. It is like a pressure cooker. If you remove the lid too soon, the lid will fly off and you'll likely get burned. Besides, the cooling down time is part of the canning time. Don't hurry the cooling down process by placing the canner in cold water or outdoors on a chilly day.

Prepare foods for canning in enamel, non-stick or stainless steel pans. Never use aluminum or copper, or enamel cookware that has chips.

Today, lids are two pieces consisting of the ring and a flat lid with a rubber ridge. Lids should be prepared according to the manufacturer's instructions. Some ask you to boil them, others may just ask you to wash them and hold in warm water until ready to use. The rings can be used over and over, but the flat lids should only be used once. They may fail to seal if processed a second time.

Jar-lifters can be a handy tool to have. They allow you to place and remove the jars easily, with little risk of dropping them. They are available at many grocery stores and in cookware and department stores as well. A wide-mouth funnel (or canning funnel) is also real handy when trying to ladle hot liquids into jars. Be sure to wipe off jar rims before putting the lid on to prevent food from causing the jars not to seal.

Screw the ring on firmly, but not too tight, or the jars will not seal properly.

Jars removed from the water bath should be placed on a wire rack or on a towel to cool. Keep them away from drafts until cooled down. When completely cooled check to make sure that the jars have sealed. Press down on the middle. If the lid make a "plink" noise it is not sealed. After jars have sealed and cooled remove outer ring, wipe with a damp cloth and store in cupboard until ready to use.

Always start with top quality produce. Bruises and blemishes will lead to spoilage. Small blemishes can be cut off but be sure to remove all areas of spoilage.
If you are canning tomatoes and have a lot of imperfect fruit you are better off trimming off any bad spots and using this produce in recipes that will be frozen rather than canned.

When canning always use non-iodized salt, or preferably canning salt. Iodine will cause an off-flavor in canned foods.

When using older books always check with your local Extension Office or the USDA for most current information and canning times. Periodically times are changed or ingredients are adjusted for maximum safety. If you have old family recipes also check with your local Extension Office to find out if the recipe is still considered safe.

Never can in an oven or in a steam canner. Both of these methods are not USDA approved.

Nothing beats planning. When getting ready to can read the recipe all the way through and get all your equipment out. It is often easier and more fun to can with a friend or two. The extra hands always come in handy and when time is critical the extra help will make errors less likely.

In tomato based products herbs can be added for flavor but do not randomly start adding other vegetables (like onion, peppers etc.) They will reduce the acidity and may make the product unsafe to can in a water bath.

Green Tomato Sweet Pickles

1 gallon green tomatoes (16 c. sliced)
¼ c. salt
½ T. powdered alum
3 c. vinegar (5% acidity)
1 c. water
4 c. sugar
1 T. mixed spices
½ t. cinnamon
1 T. celery seed
½ t. allspice
1 T. mustard seed

Slice tomatoes. Sprinkle with salt and allow to stand overnight. Next morning, drain and pour 2 quarts of boiling water with ½ T. of powdered alum over the tomatoes and let stand 20 minutes. Drain and cover with cold water, drain. Combine vinegar, water, sugar and spices (tie spices loosely in a bag) and bring to a boil. Pour this over the tomatoes. Let stand in this solution overnight. Then drain and bring solution to boil and pour over tomatoes. Let stand overnight. On the third morning bring the pickles and solution to a boil. Pack into sterilized canning jars to within ½-inch of top. Put on cap, screw band firmly tight. Process in boiling water bath for ten minutes. Yields 8 pints

Acidity and Tomatoes

Tomatoes must be acidified before canning. When canning either whole, crushed or juiced tomatoes you must add either 2 T. bottled lemon juice per quart or ½ t. citric acid. For pint use 1 T. lemon juice or ¼ t. citric acid. You can also use 4 T. (5%) vinegar per quart, but it will alter the flavor and is not recommended. You can add a little sugar to offset the flavor, if you like.

Canning Tomatoes

Certainly one of the most popular products to can each year here are a couple of recipes to start you off.

Crushed Tomatoes

Peel and core tomatoes, trim off any bad spots and quarter. Place about ¼ of your prepared tomatoes in the kettle and cook, stirring constantly over high heat. Use a potato masher to crush tomatoes and extract juices. Once they are boiling add remaining tomatoes, stirring constantly. You don't need to crush these tomatoes. Bring to a boil and boil for 5 minutes. In clean, hot jars add needed acidity (see above). You can also add 1 t. of canning salt per quart if desired. Ladle in hot tomatoes, leaving ½-inch headspace. Wipe jar rims clean and adjust lids. Process in boiling water bath. Pints 35 minutes, quarts, 45 minutes. 1,000-3000 ft. over sea level add 5 minutes. Twenty-two lbs. of tomatoes will yield about 7 quarts of tomatoes.

Whole Tomatoes in Juice

Use any extra tomatoes to make juice. I use tomatoes that are too big to can whole, or those that have blemishes that need to be trimmed. Cut up clean, unpeeled tomatoes in a kettle and cook, stirring often until tomatoes are mushy. Strain mixture, pressing on solids or run through a food mill or tomato juice extractor. Set aside. Place peeled, whole tomatoes in kettle and add enough tomato juice to cover them. Heat to a simmer and simmer gently 5 minutes. Add lemon juice or citric acid to jars, using guide under *Canning Basics*. Add salt, if desired. Add tomatoes and cover with hot juice, leaving ½-inch headspace. Wipe rims and adjust lids. Process both pints and quarts 85 minutes in a boiling water bath.

Whole or Halved Tomatoes with no added Juice
Add lemon juice or citric acid to jars and add salt, if desired. Place whole or halved peeled raw tomatoes in jars, pressing to remove any gaps and air bubbles. Leave ½-inch headspace. Wipe rims and adjust lids. Process in a boiling water bath 85 minutes for pints or quarts. Add 5 minutes at 1,001-3,000 ft. above sea level.

Tomato Juice
Wash, stem and trim bruises off tomatoes. Cut into chunks. Add about 1 lb. of tomatoes to kettle and bring to a boil while crushing. Continue to add additional cut up tomatoes slowly, keeping mixture boiling. This will keep the juice from separating later. Simmer an additional 5 minutes once the tomatoes have all been added. Press mixture through a strainer, sieve or food mill to remove seeds and skins. Add lemon juice or citric acid to jars using guide under *Canning Basics*. Add salt if desired. Return juice to boil and add to prepared jars leaving ½-inch headspace. Wipe rims and adjust lids. Process in a boiling water bath pints 35 minutes and quarts 40 minutes.

Tomato Sauce

Prepare as for juice. After juice is made return to pot and start cooking down to desired thickness. You'll lose about 1/3 of the volume for thin sauce and ½ of the volume for thick. Add lemon juice or citric acid to prepared jars using guide under *Canning Basics*. Add salt if desired. Add boiling sauce leaving ¼-inch headspace. Wipe rims and adjust lids. Process in a boiling water bath 35 minutes for pints and 40 minutes for quarts. Add five minutes at 1,001-3,000 ft. elevation.

Freezer Tomato Catsup

1 stick, cinnamon, broken
1 t. whole cloves
1 t. mustard seed
1 t. celery seed
1 c. vinegar
8 lbs. tomatoes
1 c. chopped onion
¼ t. cayenne pepper
1 c. sugar
1 T. salt

Combine cinnamon with cloves, mustard seed and celery seed in a large tea ball or tie up in cheesecloth. Add to vinegar in a saucepan and bring to a boil. Remove from heat at let stand. Core and cut up tomatoes and combine in a saucepan with onions and pepper. Simmer until vegetables are soft and press through a strainer or food mill. Combine sugar with tomato pulp and salt in saucepan and simmer until reduced by half. Remove spices from vinegar and add vinegar to tomato mixture. Simmer, stirring often until desired consistency is reached, about 30 minutes. Cool. Ladle catsup into freezer containers leaving ½-inch headspace. Seal, label and freeze. Makes about 5 half-pints

Salsa

12 lbs. tomatoes, peeled, seeded and chopped)
1 T. olive oil
4 large onions, chopped
4-5 cloves garlic, minced
4-5 chopped sweet red, yellow or green peppers
1-2 T. cumin, or to taste
1 T. chili powder
salt to taste
chopped hot peppers to taste, or hot pepper flakes or hot sauce
1½ c. chopped fresh cilantro
¼-½ c. clear-gel or corn starch

Place oil in heavy saucepan and add onion, cooking until onions are translucent. Add tomatoes and garlic and cook until tomatoes are softened, about 20-30 minutes. Add peppers and seasonings and cook until peppers just start to soften. Adjust seasonings. Combine Clear-Gel with a little water or tomato juice and pour into simmering salsa until mixture thickens. Don't add all at once because the amount of moisture in your vegetables may vary. Mixture will thicken as it cools. Cool salsa and divide among freezer containers. Label and freeze. Makes about 12-16 cups. Great with chips, tacos and as a side dressing for grilled meats, poultry and seafood.

Freezing Tomatoes

You can always save some tomatoes by freezing them. Just drop the tomatoes in boiling water for a minute or so to loosen the skins. Cool in ice water and slip off skins. Just chop and bag tem up. Note: Tomatoes have a very high water content and fall apart once frozen. They are only good for adding to sauces and soups or even chili.

Chapter 16:
Awash in Squash-
Cooking with
Summer and Winter Squash

About Squash

This chapter of the book is about enjoying and using both summer and winter squashes. Summer squash includes zucchini, yellow summer squash, crookneck squash, patty pan squash and dozens of others. They are used when the skin is still tender and the seeds have not fully developed. They are used quickly after harvesting.

Winter squashes are the hard-shell fully matured squash with developed seeds and sweet flesh. They include butternut, acorn, buttercup, turban, pumpkin, delicata and dozens of others. These store well and can easily be kept throughout winter stored in a basement or even at room temperature.

Choosing Summer Squash

When picking zucchini and other summer squash bigger is not better. Small to medium squash are the best, when the skin is tender and the seeds have not yet begun to mature. You should be able to easily pierce the skin of a summer squash with your fingernail. If you do grow a few that get away and get really big, don't toss them, but peel them and use the flesh shredded in dishes like cakes, breads and pancakes discarding seeds.

Choosing Winter Squash

Look for squash with hard, unblemished shells and no soft spots. On dark colored squash you should see a circle of yellow or even orange. This is a good thing as it indicates that the squash has been in contact with the ground long enough to have changed color and it shows ripeness. Store winter squash in a cool place like a cellar and keep them in a single layer, if possible to slow down decay. They can lasts for months when properly stored, but keep an eye on them. Better to cook them up and freeze them than to let them go bad.

Zucchini Bake

This can be served as a main dish or as a side.

2 c. baking mix, like Bisquick or Jiffy
3 c. shredded zucchini
½ c. shredded Parmesan cheese
1 c. finely chopped onion
¼ c. chopped fresh parsley
¼ t. pepper
1 clove minced garlic
2 T. oil
½ c. milk
4 eggs, lightly beaten

Mix together baking mix, zucchini, cheese, onion, parsley, pepper and garlic. Beat together the oil, milk and eggs and pour mixture into zucchini mixture. Spread mixture in a greased 13x9-inch baking dish. Bake in a 350 degree oven for 45 minutes or until brown. Serves 4-6 main dish servings, more as a side.

Fried Squash Blossoms

12 squash blossoms, rinsed and dried
1 egg, beaten
salt and pepper
1 t. chopped parsley
1 t. paprika
3 T. water
1 c. bread crumbs (or a little more)
oil for frying

Pull pistils out of blossoms. Beat together the egg, seasonings and water. Dip in blossoms allowing excess to drip off and dip in crumbs, coating evenly. Continue until you have coated all the blossoms. Heat 2-inches oil in a deep skillet to 375 degrees. Cook blossoms, a few at a time until golden brown. Makes 12, serves 3-4.

Summer Squash Strata

2 medium yellow summer squash, sliced thin
2 medium zucchini, sliced thin
3 large tomatoes, sliced
2 medium onions, sliced thin
salt and pepper
4 T. olive oil
½ c. shredded cheese
½ c. bread crumbs

In a greased 13x9-inch baking dish layer slices of the vegetables adding salt and pepper to taste. Use up all the veggies. Drizzle with the oil and sprinkle the cheese and bread crumbs over the top. Bake in a 350 degree oven for 30 minutes, or until vegetable are tender. Serves 6.

Zucchini Bread

3 c. flour
3 eggs
2 c. sugar
2 c. shredded zucchini
1 c. oil
1 c. chopped nuts or raisins
½ c. sour cream or strained yogurt
1 t. each vanilla, cinnamon, baking powder, salt and baking soda

Preheat oven to 350 degrees and grease 2 (9x5-inch) loaf pans. Set aside. Place flour in large bowl. Beat eggs and add with remaining ingredients to flour, mixing well and scraping bowl. Pour batter into prepared pans and bake 1 hour and 20 minutes, or until browned and toothpick in center emerges clean. Cool in pans on wire rack. Freezes well. Makes 2.

Zucchini Carrot Cake

2 eggs
1 c. sugar
2/3 c. oil
1¼ c. flour
1 t. baking powder
1 t. baking soda
1 t. cinnamon
½ t. salt
1 c, grated carrot
1 c. grated zucchini, squeezed dry and packed tightly
½ c. chopped nuts

Beat eggs with sugar until frothy. Beat in oil then add dry ingredients. Beat on high for 4 minutes. Stir in veggies and nuts. Pour batter into a greased 9-inch square baking pan. Bake in a 350 degree oven for about 35 minutes or until top springs back when lightly touched. Cool and frost

Frosting
4 oz. cream cheese, softened
3 T. butter or margarine, softened
1 t. vanilla
2 c. powdered sugar

Beat together cream cheese and margarine or butter until smooth. Beat in vanilla and sugar. Spread over cooled cake.

Quick Corn and Zucchini Sauté

2 sweet peppers, seeded and cut into strips
2 medium zucchini, sliced
oil
2 c. corn kernels cut from cobs, about 4 ears
1 t. garlic salt
½ t. Italian seasoning

In oil cook peppers and zucchini until crisp tender, about 5 minutes. Add remaining ingredients and cook 4 more minutes, or until heated through. Serves 6-8.

Zucchini Potato Pancakes

4 medium potatoes
2 medium zucchini
2 eggs, lightly beaten
2 T. flour
¼ t. baking powder
1 t. salt or to taste
pepper to taste
2 T. grated onion, I used dried chopped onion
½ c. oil

Peel and grate potatoes. Place them in cold water and set aside. Trim zucchini and grate coarsely. Place in large bowl. Drain potatoes and squeeze dry. Place between towels to get out excess moisture and place in bowl with the zucchini. Add the rest of the ingredients, except the oil and stir to combine. Heat oil in a skillet. Drop rounded tablespoonfuls of the potato batter into the skillet. Cook several minutes per side or until golden and crispy. Drain on paper towels and serve. Serves 6-8.

Easy Zucchini Pie

1 (8 oz. can) refrigerator crescent rolls
3 medium zucchini, sliced thin
3 T. butter
1 clove crushed garlic
¼ t. salt
¼ t. celery seed
pepper to taste
2 eggs, beaten
1 c, cubed Monterey Jack cheese
1 T. chopped fresh parsley

Remove rolls from package, unroll and press them into a 10-inch pie pan to form a crust. Sauté zucchini slices in butter until tender. Stir in garlic and seasonings and pour over crust. Pour eggs over the zucchini. Top with the cheese and parsley. Bake at 325 degrees for 45-50 minutes or until edges are golden brown. Serves 6-8.

Baked Zucchini with Mushrooms

2 T. butter or margarine
8 oz. sliced mushrooms
½ t. salt
1 clove minced garlic
pepper to taste
½ t. Italian seasoning
4 medium zucchini, about 1 lb., shredded
¼ c. bread crumbs
4 T. fresh grated Parmesan or Romano cheese
4 eggs, slightly beaten

In a skillet heat butter or margarine and sauté mushrooms until tender and liquid is evaporated, about 5 minutes. Place mushroom mixture in mixing bowl and add the zucchini, seasonings, bread crumbs and half of the cheese. Combine ingredients and spoon them into a greased 8-inch square baking dish. Pour over the eggs and bake at 325 for 35-40 minutes or until custard is set. Sprinkle with remaining cheese and return to oven for 5 minutes. Serves 4-6.

Fresh Summer Squash Relish

2 c. shredded summer squash, any type, peeled if desired
1 c. finely diced sweet onion
¼-½ c. bottled Italian dressing or other vinaigrette

Combine all ingredients and chill until ready to use. Nice on cold and hot sandwiches and in tuna salad. Keeps in fridge for a couple of weeks.

Vegetable Pizza

Crust
2/3 c. milk
¼ c. oil
1¼ c. flour
¾ c. cornmeal
1 t. baking powder
1 t. salt

Topping
8 oz. pizza sauce or 8 oz. tomato sauce with 1 t. pizza seasoning
1 medium sweet pepper, seeded and cut in strips
1 medium onion, sliced thin and separated into rings
1 medium zucchini, sliced thin
2½ c. shredded Mozzarella or Provolone cheese

To make crust combine all ingredients in a bowl and stir until a soft ball forms. Let rest 3-4 minutes. Press dough into a greased 12-inch pizza pan shape edges into a rim. Bake in a 425 degree oven for 15 minutes. Remove from oven and spread with the sauce, toppings and cheese. Return to oven and bake at 425 for 15-20 minutes or until golden brown.

Zucchini Drop Cookies

1 c. grated zucchini
1 t. baking soda
1 c. sugar
½ c. shortening
1 egg, beaten
2 c. flour
1 t. cinnamon
½ t. each cloves and salt
1 c. chopped nuts
1 c. raisins

In medium bowl cream together zucchini, baking soda, sugar, shortening and egg. Mix dry ingredients together and add to zucchini mixture. Stir in nuts and raisins. Drop by rounded teaspoonfuls onto greased cookie sheet. Bake at 375 degrees for 12-15 minutes. Makes about 36.

Orange Zucchini Cake

1 c. butter or margarine, softened
1 T. grated orange peel
1 t. cinnamon
½ t. nutmeg
2 c. brown sugar
4 eggs
3 c. flour
1 T. baking powder
½ t. salt
1/3 c. orange juice
1 c. shredded zucchini
Glaze, recipe follows

In large mixing bowl cream together first 5 ingredients until light and fluffy. Beat in eggs one at a time. Mix together dry ingredients and mix into creamed mixture alternately with the orange juice. Stir in zucchini. Pour batter into a greased 10-inch tube or Bundt pan. Bake in a 350 degree oven for 55-65 minutes or until toothpick inserted in cake comes out clean. Cool in pan on a rack for 10 minutes then remove from pan to cool completely. Spread top with glaze once cool. Serves 12-16.

Glaze
1½ c. powdered sugar
1 T. butter or margarine, softened
1 t. vanilla
2-3 T. milk

Mix all together until smooth and use to glaze the cake.

Multi-Grain Squash Bread

1¼ c. whole wheat pastry flour
1 c. wheat germ
½ c. sunflower seeds or chopped nuts
1 T. baking powder
½ t. salt
¾ c. shredded summer squash
1/3 c. honey
¾ c. milk
1 egg

Grease a 9-inch cake pan and preheat oven to 375 degrees. Combine dry ingredients and set aside. In medium bowl combine remaining ingredients and stir in flour mixture. Pour batter into prepared pan and bake 30-35 minutes or until toothpick inserted into middle comes out clean. Cool in pan ten minutes then remove from pan and cool on a rack.

Pumpkin Chiffon

½ c. applesauce
1 c. pumpkin or squash
¾ c. brown sugar
1 t. cinnamon
½ t. salt
½ t. nutmeg
1/8 t. cloves
4 eggs, well beaten
1 c. light cream or evaporated milk

Stir together first seven ingredients. Beat in eggs and stir in milk. Place mixture in 1½ quart casserole and bake in a 350 degree oven for 1 hour and 15 minutes. Serve alone or with cookies. Serves 6-8.

Zucchini Wraps

1 T. vegetable oil
1 t. mustard seed (optional)
1 t. cumin seeds
1 small red onion, thinly sliced
1 T. grated fresh ginger
4 c. grated zucchini
½ t. chili powder
¼ t. ground black pepper
¼ t. ground cloves
¼ t. ground cinnamon
salt to taste
4 (10-inch) flour tortillas
4 fresh chives
½ c. sour cream (optional)

In a medium size wok or sauté pan, heat the oil over medium-high heat. Add mustard and cumin seeds. As they begin to pop, lower the heat and add the onion and ginger. Sauté until onions are soft and light pink in color.

Add the shredded zucchini, increase the heat slightly. Stir frequently until the zucchini gets soft and well-cooked, approximately 5 to 10 minutes. Stir in the chili powder, pepper, clove, cinnamon and salt.

Warm the tortillas and place the tortillas on a flat surface. Place ¼ of the zucchini filling in the center of each tortilla. Roll up each tortilla and tie it closed with a chive. You can serve the wrap with a dollop of sour cream on the side; it makes for a well-rounded wrap!

Curried Pumpkin Soup

1 (7-8 lb.) pumpkin
5-6 c. chicken or vegetable stock
2 baking apples, peeled and coarsely chopped
1 carrot, chopped
2 t. grated gingerroot
1 t. curry powder
1 t. cumin
1½ c. evaporated milk
1 c. diced ham or turkey ham
½ c. diced onion
2 T. sugar
1 c. croutons

Cut top fourth of pumpkin off and set aside. Scoop out seeds and stringy pulp. Replace top and place on a jelly roll pan. Bake in a preheated 375 degree oven for 1 hour. Remove from oven cool. When cool enough to handle, carefully scrape flesh out from sides of pumpkin, leaving about ¾-inch of flesh on sides. Do not remove pulp from bottom. You should have about 4 c. Place pumpkin, stock, apples, carrot and seasonings in saucepan and cook until vegetables are tender. Puree soup in batches in blender or processor until smooth and stir in milk. Add salt and pepper to taste. Place pumpkin in a 3-quart casserole dish. You can leave the pumpkin in the casserole to serve, but if you want to take it out of the casserole to serve, then line the casserole dish with foil to make the pumpkin easier to move. Pour soup into pumpkin shell and return to oven for 20 minutes. Note: Cooking the pumpkin too long can make it soft and cause it to split. Do not overcook. Meanwhile sauté the ham and onion in a skillet until onion is tender. Stir in sugar and cook 2 minutes longer. Add croutons and toss to coat. Sprinkle ham mixture over soup in pumpkin and serve. Serves 8.

Note: You can also dollop with sour cream.

Pumpkin Crunch

1 box yellow cake mix
1 (15 oz. can), solid pack pumpkin or 2 c. cooked squash or pumpkin
1 (12 oz. can), evaporated milk
3 large eggs
1½ c. sugar
1 t. sugar
½ t. sugar
½ c. chopped pecans
1 c. butter
Whipped topping

Preheat oven to 350 degrees. Grease bottom of 13x9-inch pan. Combine pumpkin, milk, eggs, sugar, cinnamon and salt and pour into prepared pan. Sprinkle dry cake mix over batter and top with nuts. Melt butter and pour over. Bake 50-55 minutes or until golden brown. Cool, serve chilled with topping.

Pumpkin Bread

1¾ c. flour
1½ c. sugar
1 t. baking soda
¾ t. salt
½ t. each cinnamon and nutmeg
½ c. shortening
2 eggs, beaten
1 c. pumpkin
1/3 c. water

Mix dry ingredients and set aside. Beat together shortening and eggs until fluffy. Beat in pumpkin and water until smooth. Stir in dry ingredients until smooth. Pour into a greased 9x5-inch loaf pan. Bake in a preheated 350 degree oven for 60-65 minutes. Cool in pan 10 minutes before removing from pan and placing on cooling rack. Wrap in plastic, best served the next day. Freezes well. Makes 1 loaf.

Pumpkin Squares

1 c. sugar
½ c. oil
1 (16 oz. can) pumpkin
4 eggs, beaten
2 c. biscuit mix (homemade or Bisquick or Jiffy Mix)
2 t. cinnamon
½ c. raisins

Grease a jelly roll pan and set aside. Preheat oven to 350 degrees. Beat first 4 ingredients for 1 minute. Stir in mix, cinnamon and raisins. Pour in prepared pan and bake 25-30 minutes. Test for doneness with a toothpick. Cool and frost. Frosted cake must be kept refrigerated between servings.

Frosting
6 oz. cream cheese
2/3 c. margarine
2 T. milk
2 t. vanilla
3 c. powdered sugar, or more

Beat together until smooth.

Cooking Winter Squash

Winter squash can be baked, steamed or boiled. Wash squash and set on cutting board. Since winter squash are so hard they can slip and you can easily cut yourself. Either place the squash on a towel for additional stability or trim a little off one side so the squash will lie flat. Cut in half and scoop out the seeds. Place squash halves cut side down in a baking dish and pour 1-inch of water around them. Bake at 350 degrees until tender - 45 minutes for little squash and longer for bigger squash. Use a fork to test for tenderness. In the microwave the cooking time is much less. Or you can place squash pieces, peeled in a steamer and cook until tender. Once cooked puree or mash. For larger pumpkins and squash you might want to place in a strainer to drain. Use or freeze to use later.

Pizza Butternut Squash Sauté

3 c. diced fresh butternut squash
1 T. oil
1 medium onion, sliced
coarse sea salt
1 sweet red pepper, seeded and chopped
1-2 t. pizza seasoning
½ c. Shredded cheddar cheese, any type you like

Place squash in microwave steamer and cook 6 minutes or steam on stovetop for 6 minutes over boiling water. Heat oil in pan and sauté onion and salt until onions are wilted and getting a little brown. Add squash and sauté for 4-5 minutes more or until squash is getting color. Add peppers and seasoning and sauté 3 minutes more or until peppers are heated through, but still a little crisp. Adjust seasoning, if needed. Spoon mixture into serving bowls and top with a little sprinkle of cheese. Serves 4.

Note: For a little more protein you can add a handful of cashews, peanuts or almonds when you add the peppers.

Pumpkin Cheesecake

Crust
1½ c. finely ground gingersnap cookies
¾ c. ground hazelnuts
3 T. brown sugar
6 T. unsalted butter, melted and cooled

Filling
1½ lb. cream cheese, at room temperature
1 c. brown sugar
1½ c. canned solid pack pumpkin
½ c. whipping cream or evaporated milk
1/3 c. pure maple syrup
1 T. vanilla
¾ t. cinnamon
¼ t. allspice
4 eggs

For crust combine all ingredients and press in the bottom and 2-inches up the sides of a 9-inch spring form pan. Bake in a preheated 325 degree oven for 8 minutes. Cool.

Prepare filling by beating cheese and brown sugar until fluffy. Beat in all but the eggs and mix until smooth. Beat in the eggs one at a time just until mixed. Pour into prepared crust and return to oven. Bake until cake puffs up and center is set, about 1½ hours. Cool completely. Use knife to loosen cake from edges of pan. Store cake in fridge. Serves 10-12.

Pumpkin Roll

6 eggs, separated, at room temperature
1 c. sugar, divided
1 c. flour
1 c. canned pumpkin
2 t. cinnamon
1 t. baking powder
1 t. ginger
½ t. nutmeg
½ t. salt
about 4 c. powdered sugar
1 lb. cream cheese, softened
1 t. vanilla
1 c. chopped nuts

Preheat oven to 375 degrees. Grease 2 jellyroll pans and line with wax paper. Grease and flour paper and set aside. In large bowl beat egg whites until soft peaks form. While beating add ½ c. of the sugar, 2 tablespoons at a time. Beat until peaks are firm and glossy. In small bowl on low speed mix together flour, pumpkin, spices, baking powder, salt, remaining sugar and egg yolks. Gently fold flour mixture into egg whites. Divide batter between prepared pans and bake one 12 minutes or until cake springs back when touched lightly. Meanwhile, prepare a tea towel by laying on a clean surface and dusting generously with powdered sugar. When cake is done immediately turn onto prepared towel and remove wax paper. Starting at narrow end roll up cake in the towel and allow to cool. Repeat with second cake.

Prepare filling by beating together 3 c. of powdered sugar with the cream cheese and vanilla. Add additional sugar, if needed. Stir in nuts.

To finish cakes, carefully unroll and remove towel. Spread half of the filling on one cake and re-roll. Repeat with second cake. Chill. Makes 20 servings and can be frozen.

Chocolate Zucchini Cake

2½ c. flour
¼ c. cocoa
2 t. cinnamon
1 t. baking powder
1t. baking soda
½ t. salt
1 c. brown sugar
½ c. sugar
½ c. butter or margarine, softened
½ c. oil
3 eggs
1¾ c. shredded zucchini, squeezed dry
1 t. vanilla
½ c. buttermilk
½ c. chocolate chips

Combine dry ingredients and set aside. Beat together sugars and margarine or butter until fluffy. Beat in oil and eggs until well mixed and stir in vanilla and zucchini. Beat in half of the flour mixture until smooth and then add the buttermilk, beating until smooth. Add remaining flour mixture and just mix in. Pour batter into a greased 9x13-inch baking dish. Sprinkle chocolate chips over the top. Bake at 325 degrees for about 45 minutes or until toothpick inserted in center comes out clean. Cool in pan. Serves 12.

Zucchini Rice Casserole

1 c. water or broth
½ c. raw rice
salt and pepper to taste
2 T. oil
1 medium onion, chopped
1 lb. small to medium zucchini, about 3-4, sliced
1 sweet pepper, seeded and diced
8 oz. tomato sauce
1 c. shredded cheese, any type you like
¼ c. freshly shredded Parmesan cheese

Bring water or broth to a simmer and stir in rice. Cover and cook over low heat until rice is tender, about 20 minutes for white rice and 40 minutes for brown. Season with salt and pepper to taste, using less salt if cooking in broth. Meanwhile heat oil in a skillet and cook onion until wilted and tender. Add zucchini and pepper and cook until both are tender. Season with salt and pepper to taste. Combine vegetable mixture with the rice and tomato sauce and pour into 1½ quart casserole. Sprinkle with cheeses and bake in a 350 degree oven until heated through and cheese is bubbly, about 20 minutes. Serves 6.

Chapter 17: Cooking With Apples and Pears

Cooking With Apples and Pears

Although apples and pears are available throughout the year they are at their peak in the late summer and fall in the Midwest. During the fall take advantage of locally grown crops and enjoy the best nature has to offer.

While most fruits should be tree-ripened for best flavor, pears are the exception. They should be picked when full-sized but unripe. They can then be left in a basket, bowl or in a paper bag at room temperature to ripen. They will be sweet and wonderful.

Both apples and ripe pears can be stored long term in the fridge or in a cool cellar. They are still best however, when used within a few weeks of harvest.

In most recipes apples and pears can be used interchangeably. Both can be baked, poached, fried and added to salads. If you are cooking with one and run a little short, like apples for a cobbler you can make up the difference with a few pears. Measure and use the same amounts.

Both fruits will discolor quickly after being cut. Whether you are cooking them or using them fresh you must treat them immediately after cutting. To a quart of cool water you can add any one of the following: ¼ c. lemon juice, 1 T. salt, 1,000 mg vitamin C, crushed and dissolved or 1 t. citric acid. Other juices such as pineapple, apple, or orange can be used at full or half strength, although they don't work as well.

There are so many apple to choose from we sometimes aren't sure what apples can be used for cooking, which are for eating and which are for both. At reputable apple marts you will see signs posted that will give you some guidance but there are always new apples out there.

Among common varieties Red Delicious and Gravenstein are best eaten fresh. Most other apples are good for cooking and eating, but some hold their shape better and work well for baked apples. These would include Rome Beauty, Golden Delicious, Northern Spy, Newton Pippin, York Imperial, and Cortland. Both Rome and York Imperial are considered to be best as cooking apples.

For a fun twist on an old favorite try dipping pears instead of apples in caramel. Just add sticks and dip as you would for apples. For an elegant touch you can also dip the pears a second time in melted chocolate, leaving some of the caramel exposed. Do this after the caramel has set up. You can also dip the bottom of the pears in toasted, chopped nuts or sprinkles, if you like.

Helpful Hints

Many recipes for pie and other apple desserts will give a range of amounts for sugar. This is because not all apples are created the same. For sweet apples you may want to add less sugar and more for tart apples. You may have to experiment to find the right amount for your taste. I like to make notes on my recipes so I remember what I did the next time.

For a fresh taste add ½ c. of diced apples or pears to muffin batter. Add a little cinnamon as well.

Both apples and pears go well with cheeses. The best apples to serve in salads and on cheese trays are Golden Delicious and Cortland because they discolor more slowly. Still pre-treat to retard discoloration. You can also dust apple and pear slices with cinnamon or cinnamon sugar to keep them looking fresh on a cheese plate.

Autumn Chicken Salad

4 boneless, skinless chicken breast halves
6 c. torn mixed salad greens
3 T. chopped green onions
1 rib celery, diced
½ c. carrots cut in thin strips
12 green beans, ends trimmed and cooked 3 minutes, then chilled in ice water
1-2 c. diced apples or pears
3-4 T. walnuts or toasted, hulled pumpkin seeds

Vinaigrette
1/3 c. apple cider or juice
3 T. olive oil
3 T. cider vinegar
1 t. dried thyme
1 t. Dijon mustard
1 t. sesame oil
salt and pepper to taste

Whisk dressing ingredients together. Place chicken breasts in a shallow dish and drizzle a little of the dressing over them. Chill the rest. Let chicken marinade for 30 minutes then grill or broil until cooked, brushing with some of the dressing still in the dish. Discard any unused marinade. Cut chicken into strips. To assemble salads divide greens among 4 salad plates. Place 3 beans on each plate, to one side and in a fan shape. Arrange chicken strips in a fan shape on beans. Sprinkle with onions and celery. Arrange carrots in a fan on other side of dish from beans. Place apples or pears near carrots, sprinkling a piece or two over the chicken. Sprinkle with seeds and drizzle with reserved dressing. Serves 4.

Apple and Cheese Salad

1 c. walnuts or pecans, toasted
4-6 c. salad greens, washed and spun dry
1 c. shredded cheddar cheese or ½ c. crumbled feta or bleu cheese
2 Granny Smith or other tart apples
1 T. chopped fresh mint or parsley
1 T. snipped chives or green onions, optional

Dressing
3 T. white wine vinegar
2 T. lemon juice
2 t. sugar
¼ c. olive oil
3 T. dried minced onion
2 T. water
salt and pepper to taste

In container with tight fitting lid shake dressing ingredients together and chill until ready to use. To toast nuts place on a baking sheet in a 350 degree oven for 15 minutes. Cool. When ready to serve the salads divide the greens among 4 plates or arrange greens on a platter. Core the apples and cut in slices. Toss apples with the dressing. Place apples on greens, then top with remaining ingredients. Serves 4.

Ham and Apple Salad

1 red apple, cored
2/3 c. mayonnaise
2 T. cider vinegar
½ t. Dijon mustard
2 c. diced celery
4-6 c. cooked rice
2 c. diced ham or turkey ham
3 apples, cored and diced
1 green onion, diced
salt and pepper to taste

Combine first 4 ingredients in blender until smooth and set aside. Combine remaining salad ingredients in medium bowl and toss with dressing. Serve over salad greens, if desired, Serves 4.

Spirited Applesauce

½ c. butter or margarine
2 c. chunky-style applesauce
¼ c. sugar
½ c. rum dark preferred
1 t. cinnamon
½ t. ground cardamom
¼ t. ground nutmeg
pinch of cloves

Combine all ingredients in a saucepan and simmer over low heat, stirring frequently until thickened. Makes about 2 cups. Use as a glaze on pork, lamb or poultry. Serve on the side as you would cranberry sauce. Can be served warm or cold. Also good with breakfast sausages or as a dipping sauce.

Pear Sauce

½ c. sugar
½ c. balsamic vinegar
1 lb. pears, cored, peeled and diced
2 T. dried minced onion
1 t. minced garlic
dash hot sauce
pinch cinnamon
salt and pepper to taste

Combine all ingredients in a saucepan and cook over medium heat until thickened, about 20 minutes. Stir often to avoid burning. Serve with pork or lamb roasts. Also great with turkey. Makes about 2 cups.

Pork with Pear Sauce

1 lb. pork loin, sliced or 4 pork chops
oil
1 large onion, sliced
salt and pepper to taste
pear sauce, see previous recipe

In skillet cook pork in oil, turning to brown evenly until juices run clear when meat is pierced. Remove meat and add onions, sautéing until onions are browned. Return pork to pan, adjust seasonings and add 1 c. of the pear sauce. Cook 10 minutes, or until heated through and bubbly. Serves 4.

Open-Faced Turkey and Apple Sandwiches

4 slices roast turkey
salt and pepper to taste
2 oz. cream cheese
2 T. mayonnaise
4 slices rye bread
4 slices Swiss cheese
1 crisp apple, sliced thin

Season turkey slices and set aside. Combine cream cheese and mayonnaise and spread on bread slices. Top with cheese, then turkey and finish with apple slices. Serves 4.

Cider Rice Pilaf

4 T. butter or margarine
1 c. brown rice, uncooked
½ c. chopped celery
½ c. chopped onion
¼ c. chopped parsley
1 t. thyme
1 t. grated fresh ginger
salt and pepper to taste
2 2/3 c. apple cider

Cook rice in butter until golden. Add vegetables and cook until onion is tender. Add remaining ingredients and bring to a boil. Reduce heat to low and cook, covered, for 50-60 minutes, or until all liquid is absorbed and rice is tender. Makes 6 side dishes. Goes well with pork or roast chicken.

Smoked Turkey and Pear Salad

1¼ lb. smoked turkey, diced
½ c. chopped celery
½ c. chopped green onions
1/3 c. mayonnaise
2 T. chopped fresh parsley
3 ripe pears, cored and diced
salt and pepper to taste

Dressing
½ c. oil
¼ c. cider vinegar
1 T. sugar
dash salt and pepper
½ lb. salad greens, washed and torn into bite-sized pieces
croutons

In medium bowl combine turkey with next 5 ingredients. Season to taste and chill. In jar with tight-fitting lid combine dressing ingredients. Place greens in a large bowl and toss with the dressing. Divide among 4 serving plates and top with the turkey mixture and croutons. Serves 4.

"Pearadise" Pork Tenderloin

1¼ lb. pork tenderloin, trimmed and cut in 1-inch thick slices
4 T. butter or margarine
4 firm but ripe Anjou pears, cored and cut into ½-inch thick wedges
1 t. sugar
½ c. minced onion
½ t. rosemary
½ c. pear nectar
2 T. sherry
salt and pepper

Between layers plastic wrap pound pork to ¼-inch thickness. Set aside. In skillet cook pears in 2 T. of the butter with sugar until deep golden, about 8 minutes. Remove from skillet and add remaining butter to skillet. Salt and pepper the pork before cooking it in batches, about 3 minutes per side. Remove pork from pan and add onions, cooking until browned. Add rosemary, pear nectar and sherry, cooking until sauce reduces by half. Return pears to pan to heat through. Place pork on serving platter and top with pears in sauce. Serves 4.

Beef in Cider Sauce

1 lb. round steak, cut into bite sized strips
1 T. oil
½ c. apple cider
¼ c. chopped onion
4 t. cornstarch
2 T. brown sugar
½ t. salt
¼ t. cinnamon
½ c. apple cider
2 T. vinegar
1 medium apple, cored and chopped
2 c. hot cooked rice or hot noodles

In large saucepan brown meat in hot oil. Drain off fat and add the first ½ c. of cider and the onion. Bring to boil, reduce heat and simmer, covered about 40 minutes. In small bowl combine the cornstarch with the sugar, seasonings, remaining cider and vinegar and stir until smooth. Stir in apple and add to beef mixture, cooking until thickened and bubbly. Cook and stir 3 minutes more. Serve over rice or noodles. Serves 4.

Apple Crumb Cake

Cake Batter
2 c. flour
2 t. baking powder
½ t. salt
½ stick (¼ c.) butter, softened
¾ c. sugar
1 egg
½ c. milk
2 c. chopped peeled, cored apples

Topping
½ c. sugar
¼ c. flour
½ t. cinnamon
½ stick (¼ c.) butter, chilled and cut into bits

Combine dry ingredients and set aside. In mixing bowl with electric mixer, beat butter and sugar until light and fluffy. Beat in egg and milk. Add flour mixture gradually until just mixed in. Fold in apples. Grease and flour an 8 or 9-inch pan and add prepared batter. Combine topping ingredients until they resemble coarse crumbs. Sprinkle over batter in pan and bake in a preheated 375 degree oven and bake for 35-45 minutes. Use toothpick to test.

Note: I used a 9-inch round pan and it worked fine.

Classic Apple Cake

1 c. oil
4 eggs
1 t. vanilla
1/3 c. orange or lemon juice
3 c. flour
2 c. sugar
3 T. baking powder
¼ t. salt
4 medium apples, peeled, cored, and sliced

Cinnamon Mixture
½ c. sugar
2 t. cinnamon

Combine first four ingredients and set aside. Mix together the next four ingredients. Make a well and stir in egg mixture to make a stiff batter. Mix ½ c. sugar and 2 t. cinnamon and set aside. Grease a 9x13-inch pan or a Bundt pan. Preheat oven to 350 degrees. Place ½ of batter in prepared pan. Arrange apple slices on batter and sprinkle on ½ of the cinnamon mixture. Pour on remaining batter and sprinkle with remaining sugar mixture. Bake 1-1½ hours.

Apple Oatcakes

¾ c. oatmeal
2 c. hot water
¾ c. butter
1½ c. brown sugar
3 eggs
2 c. flour
1 c. wheat-germ
1½ t. cinnamon
1½ t. baking soda
1½ t. baking powder
¼ t. vanilla
¼ t. nutmeg
2-3 cored and chopped yellow or green apples, peeled if desired

Over low heat cook oatmeal, water and butter for 15-20 minutes, stirring often. Allow to cool down. In medium bowl beat together brown sugar and eggs. Stir in flour, wheat germ, seasonings, baking powder and baking soda. Stir in oatmeal mixture. Just before cooking the oatcakes, add chopped apples. Cook in skillet as you would any pancake. Mixture will be very thick. That is normal. Also, you can do all but add the apples a day ahead and chill overnight. Then in the morning stir in apples and cook. Makes about 6 cups of batter. Batter can be frozen as can cooked oatcakes. Serve with warm maple syrup along with real whipped cream and chopped nuts as toppings.

Easy Fruit Cobbler

4 c. peeled, cored and sliced apples or pears
½ c. sugar
1 T. plus 2/3 c. baking mix, like Bisquick or Jiffy Mix
½ t. cinnamon
2 T. packed brown sugar
¼ c. butter or margarine
2 T. milk

In 1-quart shallow casserole, combine fruit, sugar, and 1 T. of the biscuit mix and cinnamon. In medium bowl combine remaining biscuit mix with sugar. Cut in butter or margarine to resemble coarse crumbs. Stir in milk to make a soft dough. Drop by spoonfuls over fruit mixture. Bake in a preheated 400 degree oven for 30 minutes, or until toothpick inserted into dough comes out clean. Let stand 5 minutes. Serves 4-6.

Easy Apple Granola Bake

4 apples, peeled and sliced
¼ c. raisins
¼ c. water
¾ c. rolled oats
1/3 c. flour
¼ c. wheat germ
¼ c. margarine
2 T. honey
1 t. cinnamon

Coat a 9-inch round pan with non-stick spray. Place apples, raisins and water in bottom of pan. Combine remaining ingredients and sprinkle over apples. Bake in a preheated 350 degree oven for 35 minutes. Makes 4 servings.

Autumn Sweet and Sour Cabbage

2 T. oil
1 large onion, sliced thin
8 c. shredded cabbage
2 c. chopped apples and pears, peeled if desired
½ c. cider vinegar
2 T. balsamic vinegar
¼ sugar, or more to suit your taste
salt and pepper to taste

Sauté onion in oil until golden brown. Add cabbage and fruit and cook over medium high heat, stirring often until cabbage is wilted. Add remaining ingredients and cook until most of the liquid is evaporated. Adjust seasonings. Serves 4-6.

Note: You can serve this dish just as it is or you can add 8 oz. of cooked noodles when you add the vinegar for cabbage and noodles. Some people also like to make this dish with crumbled bacon or diced ham.

No-Bake Apple Cranberry Relish

4 medium tart apples, cored, peeled if desired
2 c. fresh cranberries
2 small navel oranges, peeled
1-1½ c. sugar

In processor or food grinder chop fruit into ¼-inch pieces. Stir in sugar and chill until ready to use. Makes 5 cups.

Waldorf Pita Sandwiches

4 c. cooked cubed chicken
2 apples, cored and diced
2 ribs celery, diced
½ c. raisins
½ c. chopped toasted walnuts or pecans
salt and pepper
mayonnaise
6 pita breads, halved
lettuce leaves

Combine chicken with next four ingredients. Season to taste. Add mayonnaise according to your taste. Place a lettuce leaf in each pita half then spoon filling into pitas. Makes 6 sandwiches.

Oat Bran Apple Muffins

¾ c. oat bran
½ c. whole wheat flour
½ c. whole bran cereal
¼ c. brown sugar
1 T. baking powder
½ t. cinnamon
¼ t. salt
1 egg, beaten
¾ c. skim milk
3 T. oil
1 small apple, cored, peeled and chopped
½ c. raisins
2 T. sugar
1 T. flour
1 t. margarine, melted
¼ t. cinnamon

In medium bowl mix together first 7 ingredients. In small bowl combine egg, milk and oil and add to flour mixture, stirring until just moistened. Fold in apple and raisins. Batter will be lumpy. Divide batter among 12 greased or paper-lined muffin cups. Combine remaining ingredients and sprinkle over batter. Bake in a preheated 400 degree oven for 12-15 minutes, or until lightly browned. Makes 1 dozen.

Pear Oatmeal Muffins

1 (16 oz. can) pear halves
1½ c. flour
1 T. grated orange peel
2 t. baking powder
1 t. cinnamon
½ t. salt
½ t. baking soda
1 c. rolled oats
1 egg, beaten
1/3 c. honey
¼ c. oil
cinnamon sugar, optional

Drain pears and reserve ¼ c. of the syrup. Chop the pears fine. Combine flour with the powder, salt, soda, cinnamon, oats and peel. Set aside. Combine egg with the reserved syrup, honey and oil. Add egg mixture to flour mixture and stir until flour is just moistened. Fold in pears. Divide batter among 12 greased muffin cups and sprinkle with cinnamon sugar, if desired. Bake in a preheated 400 degree oven for 20-25 minutes. Makes 12.

Chapter 18:
Bread Baking

Choosing Yeast

There are several types of yeast out there and they can often be used interchangeably if you know what changes to make. Keep all yeast refrigerated or frozen for best shelf life.

Cake Yeast was the first widespread commercial yeast. A small cake is the same as a single packet of dry yeast. A large cake of yeast is the same as a three strip package of yeast. That is why dry yeast comes packaged in threes. Cake yeast is sensitive to high temperatures and must always be dissolved in warm water before adding to a recipe.

Active Dry Yeast comes in three packs, two packs, 4 oz. jars and even pound bags. A packet is a level tablespoonful and you may wish to buy in bulk to save money and then just measure out your own. Active dry yeast can be mixed with
Warmer water than cake yeast and can be mixed directly with dry ingredients instead of being proofed.

Quick Rising Yeast is a strain of yeast that is tolerant of hotter temperatures that other types. Hot water causes this yeast to react more quickly and dough to rise faster than ever. However, the main liquid in the recipe has to be water and the water has to be hot for this yeast to be any faster than other yeast.

Butter Coffeecake Braids

4 c. flour
2 T. sugar
1 t. salt
½ c. butter or margarine
1 packet yeast
¼ c. warm water
2 t. sugar
1 c. evaporated milk
2 eggs, beaten

Combine flour with sugar and salt. Cut in butter or margarine and set aside. Dissolve yeast in warm water and 2 t. sugar and set aside. Combine milk with eggs. Stir in yeast mixture and add to flour mixture stirring well. On lightly floured surface knead dough until dough is smooth, about 5 minutes. Dough will be very sticky. Cover and let rise until doubled, about 1½ hours. Divide dough in half and then each half into thirds. Roll dough into ropes and braid three ropes together. Repeat with remaining 3 ropes. Place braids in 9x5-inch greased bread pans and cover with a towel. Place in a warm, draft-free place and allow to rise until doubled, about 1½ hours. Bake in a preheated 350 degree oven for 25 minutes. Glaze loaves while warm with a mix of powdered sugar, a little milk, butter, and vanilla. Toasted almonds or walnuts can be added, if desired. Makes 2 loaves.

Note: You can also refrigerate the dough after kneading it if you would prefer. Just place dough in an oiled bowl, cover with plastic wrap and chill overnight. Roll and shape dough into braids when cold from the fridge. Allow to rise, covered, until doubled in bulk, about 2-3 hours. Bake as directed.

You can also place loaves on a greased baking sheet for a longer, flatter bread rather than in loaf pan.

This is a versatile dough that can be used for doughnuts, Danish and other pastries. It is also a favorite at family reunions and great for sandwiches. Mom and Dad would use this dough to make jelly doughnuts, a Polish tradition. Roll out dough to ½-¾-inch thick and cut out with a biscuit cutter. Re-roll scraps. Cover and allow doughnuts to rise until doubled in bulk, about 1-2 hours. Fry a few at a time in oil or shortening heated to 375 degrees. Cook until golden brown on both sides and drain on paper towels. This process will only take a couple of minutes. Either use a pastry bag to fill with jelly or custard or roll in powdered sugar or cinnamon sugar. You can also coat with a thin glaze.

Whole Wheat Bread

2 packages active dry yeast
3 c. warm water
¾ c. brown sugar
4 c. all-purpose flour
4 t. salt
1 c. hot water
1 stick butter, melted
8 c. whole wheat flour (2½ lbs.)

Dissolve yeast in ½ c. of the warm water and ¼ c. of the brown sugar. Add remaining warm water and brown sugar and the salt. Add all-purpose flour and beat until smooth. Cover and let rise until doubled, about 1 hour. Stir down the resulting sponge and add the remaining ingredients, mixing until smooth. Knead dough for 10 minutes. Place dough in bowl and grease lightly. Cover and let rise until double, about 1 hour. Punch dough down and let rest 10 minutes. Cut into thirds and shape each piece into a loaf. Place in 9x5-inch greased bread pans. Cover and let rise until doubled. Bake at 375 degrees for 30-35 minutes. Remove from pans to cool. Yields 3 loaves.

Challah

2 c. hot water
1 T. each sugar, salt and oil
1 package active dry yeast
¼ c. warm water
About 8 c. flour
2 beaten eggs
poppy or sesame seeds, optional

In large bowl combine hot water, salt, sugar and oil. Dissolve yeast in warm water in small bowl and add to oil/water mix. Stir in 1 c. of the flour and eggs, reserving 2 T. of the eggs for later. Gradually stir in enough of the flour to make soft dough. When dough pulls away from sides of bowl remove to floured surface. Knead dough, adding flour as necessary about 8-10 minutes. Dough should be smooth and elastic. Place dough in a lightly greased bowl, turning to grease top, cover with a towel and allow to rise in a warm, draft free place until doubled, about 1 hour.

Punch dough down and divide into 8 equal pieces. Roll three of the pieces into 12-inch ropes. Place in a greased 9x5-inch loaf pan. Take one of the remaining pieces of dough and divide into thirds. Roll the pieces into 3-nine-inch ropes and place on top of the braid already in the pan. Repeat with remaining dough and cover. Allow to rise until doubled in bulk, about 1 hour. Preheat oven to 400 degrees. Brush loaves with reserved eggs and sprinkle with sesame or poppy seeds, if desired. Bake 40-45 minutes. When done loaves will be nicely browned and sound hollow when tapped. Makes 2 loaves.

Note: Bread dough can also be placed on greased baking sheets instead of in loaf pans. The result will be longer and flatter, but very pretty.

Judi's Herb Braids

5½-6½ c. flour
2 packages quick rising yeast
¼ c. dried toasted shallots or onions
2 T. each dried marjoram and parsley
1 T. each dried oregano and minced garlic
1 T. honey
2 t. dried thyme
2 t. salt
¼ c. olive oil
2¼ c. hot water

In a mixing bowl combine 2 c. of flour with the rest of the ingredients and mix until smooth. Beat with electric mixer 4 minutes then add 1 c. additional flour and beat 1 minute longer. Stir in flour ½ c. at a time until soft dough forms. Turn onto surface and knead, adding flour gradually until dough is smooth and elastic. Place dough in lightly greased bowl and turn to cover. Cover with a towel and let rise until doubled, about 30 minutes. Turn dough onto surface and cut in half. Cut each half into thirds. Roll each piece of dough into an 18-inch rope. Loosely braid three ropes together and repeat with the remaining dough. Place on greased baking sheet and cover until doubled in size, about 20 minutes.
Bake in a preheated 375 degree oven for 25-30 minutes, or until bread sounds hollow when tapped lightly. Makes 2.

Variations
Whole Wheat: Add 2 c. of whole-wheat flour to replace 2 c. of white flour.

Try adding ¼ c. of wheat germ, oat bran or 2 T. of seeds (sesame, pumpkin, sunflower, poppy, etc.)

Regular yeast can be used, but rising times will be longer and water should be warm, not hot.

The Upper Crust

If you like crusty bread choose recipes that use only water as the liquid ingredient and are low in sugar, fat and eggs. Basic Italian and French breads are a mix of water salt yeast and flour. Some add a little cornmeal or sugar but they are unnecessary. Crusts can also be made crispier by misting the loaves with water during the first few minutes of baking or by placing a pan of boiling water in the bottom of the oven. Sometimes I even toss half a cup of water in the oven, on the bottom, just as I close the door and start baking the bread.

Crusts can also be brushed to affect appearance and texture.

Brush with egg whites or whole eggs for a glossy finish and to help seeds to stick. Sometimes you can thin them with a little water or milk.

Brushing with milk gives a chewier crust and a thin mixture of cornstarch and water is often used on rye breads to give them a chewier crust. This is called a deli wash.

Brushing with oil or butter right after baking will give your bread a soft glow and more tender crust.

Rich Squash Rolls

1 c. milk
4 T. butter or margarine
½ c. sugar
¼ c. brown sugar
1 t. salt
1 pkt. yeast
4-5 c. flour
1½ c. cooked butternut squash, strained, or 1 (16oz. can) squash or pumpkin
2 eggs, room temperature

Scald milk and butter. Place sugar and salt in large bowl and pour in milk mixture. Cool to lukewarm. Add yeast and 2 c. of flour. Beat at medium speed with mixer for 2 minutes. Add squash and eggs and mix until smooth. Add flour gradually to form a stiff dough. Knead on floured board for 7-8 minutes. Place in a greased bowl, turning dough to coat evenly. Cover with a towel and allow to rise until doubled. Punch dough down and shape into rolls. Dough can be placed in a greased cake pan where they will touch each other as they rise making softer rolls. You can also place them in muffin tins, or shape into rolls and place on greased baking sheet for crispier rolls. Cover and let rise until doubled. Bake at 375 degrees for about 25 minutes. Butter tops while warm. Makes 2½-3 dozen.

Variation: You can also add ½ t. ground nutmeg, 1-2 T. chopped chives or 1 T. parsley flakes for a little different flavor.

Pumpernickel Bread

2 packages active dry yeast
½ c. warm water
2 c. lukewarm strong coffee
¼ c. each molasses and unsweetened cocoa
2 T. caraway seeds
2 t. salt
5-6 c. flour
2 c. rye flour
cornmeal
1 egg white, slightly beaten

In large bowl dissolve yeast in warm water. Stir in coffee, molasses, cocoa, seeds, salt and 3 c. of flour. Beat with wooden spoon about 2 minutes. Stir in rye flour and enough of the remaining regular flour to make soft dough. Turn onto floured surface and knead until dough is smooth, about 10 minutes. Place in greased bowl, turning to grease top, cover and let rest until doubled, about 1 hour. Grease large baking sheet and sprinkle with cornmeal. Set aside.

Punch down dough, divide in 2, and form into balls. Place on baking sheet and cover. Let rise until double, brush with egg whites, slash tops and bake at 375 for 35-40 minutes. Makes 2 loaves.

Rueben Loaf

3¼ c. flour
1 T. sugar
1 t. salt
1 package quick-rising yeast
1 c. hot water
1 T. oil
¼ c. Thousand Island dressing
6-8 oz. thin sliced corned beef
4 oz. sliced Swiss cheese
1 c. sauerkraut, rinsed and squeezed dry
1 egg white, beaten
caraway seeds

Set aside 1 c. of the flour. Combine remaining flour with the other dry ingredients in a medium bowl. Stir in water and oil and gradually stir in enough flour to make a soft dough. Turn onto lightly floured surface and knead until dough is smooth and elastic, about 5 minutes. Roll dough into a rectangle about 16 x 8. Spread dressing down center middle of dough. Top with meat slices, cheese and sauerkraut. Cut one-inch wide strips of dough from filling to edge on both sides. It will sort of look like fringe. Alternating sides, fold strips up and over the filling at an angle. Carefully lift loaf onto greased baking sheet and place at an angle. Cover with a towel and place sheet on top of a roasting pan half-filled with simmering water for 15 minutes. Brush with egg white and top with seeds. Bake in a preheated 400 degree for 20-25 minutes or until golden brown. Cool slightly before slicing. Serve warm and refrigerate leftovers.

Note: Have fun with other fillings including spinach with cheese, chicken, pizza etc. I brush the dough with oil before spreading pizza sauce when making a pizza bread to keep the bread from getting soggy.

Philadelphia Sticky Buns

Dough
1/3 c. milk
¼ c. sugar
½ t. salt
¼ c. butter or margarine
¼ c. warm water
1 package active dry yeast
1 egg
2½ c. flour

Topping
¼ c. butter or margarine, softened
¼ c. brown sugar
½ c. pecan or walnut halves

Filling
¼ c. soft butter or margarine
½ c. brown sugar
½ c. raisins
½ t. cinnamon

In small pan heat milk until bubbles just form around edges. Remove from heat; stir in sugar, salt and butter or margarine. Allow to cool to lukewarm. Dissolve yeast in warm water in medium bowl and stir in milk mixture, egg and 2 c. of the flour. Mix by hand until dough leaves sides of the bowl. Turn onto lightly floured surface and knead until dough is smooth and elastic, adding more flour if needed. Lightly oil dough in bowl and cover with a towel allowing to rise in a warm place until doubled, about 1-1½ hours. Meanwhile, make topping. Cream together butter and brown sugar and spread on bottom and sides of 9x9-inch baking pan. Sprinkle with nuts and set aside.

Punch down dough and roll into a 16x12-inch rectangle. Spread with the softened butter, sprinkle on the brown sugar, cinnamon and raisins. Roll up from long side. Cut crosswise into 12 pieces. Hint: Using a knife tends to flatten the rolls. Instead use a piece of thread, string or even dental floss. Slide piece of string under dough where you wish to slice. Holding string ends above roll cross the ends over each other and pull outward. String will cut through easily. Repeat with remaining rolls. Place in prepared pan and cover with cloth, allowing to rise until doubled, 1-1½ hours.

Bake 25-30 minutes in a preheated 375 degree oven. Invert onto board and let stand 1 minute. Remove pan. Serve warm. Makes 12.

Seeds

Seeds add flavor, texture and contrast to breads and rolls. Some favorite toppers are caraway seeds, sesame, flax, fennel, poppy seeds, and dill seeds. Other decorative touches can be adding oatmeal, coarse salt, cracked wheat, or even sunflower and pumpkin seeds. Seeds can be folded into the dough or sprinkled on top. Mix several seeds together for a festive look

Oatmeal Bread

5-5½ c. flour
1 package active dry yeast
1½ t. salt
1 1/3 c. water
¼ c. milk
¼ c. molasses
¼ c. margarine
1 egg
1 c. old fashioned oatmeal

In large bowl mix 1 c. of the flour with yeast and salt. In small pan heat together next 4 ingredients until warm. Pour into bowl with flour mixture and beat 2 minutes. Stir in 1 c. additional flour and egg and beat 2 minutes longer. Stir in oatmeal and 1 c. more flour and stir, adding enough flour to form soft dough. Turn onto lightly floured surface and knead, adding flour as needed until dough is smooth and elastic. Place dough on a greased bowl, turning to grease top and cover, allowing to rise in warm place until doubled in bulk, about 1 hour.

Grease a large baking sheet and set aside. Punch dough down and divide in half. Shape each half into a ball and place on prepared sheet. Cover with towel and allow to rise until doubled, about 1 hour. Bake in a preheated 375 degree oven for 30 minutes or until done. Loaves are done when they sound hollow when tapped lightly. Makes 2 loaves.

This versatile dough can also be shaped into loaves and places in 8x4-inch greased loaf pans. Baking time will remain the same. Dough can also be divided into 24 equal pieces and shaped into dinner rolls. Bake rolls at 375 degrees for 15 minutes.

Rich Hot Rolls

¾ c. milk
½ c. each shortening and sugar
1 t. salt
2 packages active dry yeast
½ c. warm water
4-5 c. flour
2 eggs

Heat together milk and shortening until warm. Stir in sugar and salt. Dissolve yeast in warm water and add to milk mixture with 2 c. of flour. Beat 3 minutes. Beat in eggs. Stir in flour until soft dough forms. Knead on floured surface until dough is smooth and elastic. Place in oiled bowl and cover. Let rise until doubled. Punch dough down and divide in 24-30 pieces. Roll each piece into a 6-inch rope and tie in a knot. Place rolls 2-inches apart on greased baking sheets and cover until doubled, about 1 hour. Bake in a preheated 375 degree oven for 12-15 minutes. Brush with melted butter, if you like. Serve warm. Makes 24-30.

Whole Wheat Swiss Bread

3 c. flour
2½ -3 c. whole wheat flour
2 packages active dry yeast
2 T. sugar
2 t. salt
1 c. each milk and water
4 oz. diced Swiss cheese
3 T. butter or margarine
oil

Combine 2 c. of the flour with the yeast, sugar and salt in a mixing bowl. Heat together water and milk with cheese and butter until warm, cheese does not have to melt. Add to flour mixture and beat 3 minutes. Stir in remaining white flour and beat 2 minutes. Stir in enough whole wheat flour to make a soft dough. Knead on floured surface until smooth and elastic. Cover with bowl and let rest 20 minutes. Divide dough in half and shape into loaves by rolling out and then rolling into a loaf and sealing seams. Place in greased 8x4-inch loaf pans and brush with oil. Cover with plastic wrap and place in fridge. Chill 2–24 hours. Remove from fridge and remove plastic wrap allowing to stand while oven preheats. Bake at 375 degrees for 35-40 minutes. Remove from pans and brush with butter. Cool. Makes 2 loaves.

Whole Wheat Sugar Bears

1½ c. sugar
1½ t. salt
2 packages active dry yeast
4 c. whole wheat flour
about 4 c. white flour
2 c. milk
1 c. butter or margarine
2 eggs
1 T. water

In large bowl combine sugar, salt, yeast, 2 c. of the whole wheat flour and 1 c. of the white flour. Heat together milk and butter until very warm (120-130 degrees) and blend into flour mixture. Beat with mixer on medium speed for 3 minutes. Reserve one egg white and beat remaining eggs into batter along with 1 additional cup of each of the flours. Beat 2 minutes. Stir in remaining whole wheat flour and then gradually stir in enough white flour to form a soft dough. Turn dough onto lightly floured surface and knead, adding flour, as necessary until dough is smooth, about 10 minutes. Place dough in large greased bowl and turn to grease top. Cover and let rise in a warm place until doubled in bulk, about 1 hour. Punch dough down and place on floured surface. Cover with bowl and let rest 15 minutes. Grease 2 large baking sheets and combine reserved egg white with water.

Divide dough into thirds. Cut one dough piece in half. Take dough piece and form into a ball for the body. Place on baking sheet and press down slightly. Cut remaining half of dough in half and take one piece of the dough and form into a ball for the head. Brush one side with egg white and place against one side of the body, tucking under slightly. Roll remaining piece of dough into a 6-inch rope and cut off a 2-inch piece for the snout.

Point one end slightly and brush bottom with egg white and place on bear between head and body.

Pinch a small piece for nose and place on snout. Cut remaining dough into 5 equal pieces for feet and ears. Form 4 pieces into balls and brush with the egg wash. Tuck under body. Cut remaining piece into 2 pieces and flatten slightly for ears. Brush with egg white and tuck under head. With kitchen shears cut feet for toes and snip in "eyes" and a belly button. Repeat with remaining dough to make 2 more bears.

You'll need to get 2 bears on one sheet. Cover and let rise until doubled, about 1 hour. Preheat oven to 375 degrees and brush bears with remaining egg wash. Bake bread using 2 oven racks for 15 minutes then switch positions in the oven and bake 10 minutes longer. Cool on wire racks. Makes 3 bears.

Croissants

1 package active dry yeast
1 c. very warm water
¾ c. evaporated milk
1 t. salt
1/3 c. sugar
1 egg
5 c. flour
4 T. melted butter, cooled
1 c. firm butter
additional melted butter for brushing
1 egg beaten with 1 T. water

Dissolve yeast in water. Stir in milk, salt, sugar, egg and one c. of flour. Beat into a smooth batter and stir in melted butter. Set aside. With pastry blender cut firm butter into remaining flour until particles are the size of small peas. Stir in milk mixture gently until all flour in moistened. Cover and refrigerate at least 4 hours.

Turn dough onto lightly floured surface and knead a few strokes. Divide into fourths and roll each into a circle. Divide circle into 8 pieces and brush with melted butter. Starting at wide end roll up loosely and place on greased baking sheet with point tucked under. Allow 2-3-inch between rolls and curve slightly into an arc, if desired. Cover with a towel and allow to rise in a warm place for at least 2 hours or until nearly doubled. Brush with egg wash just before baking. Bake in a 325 degree oven for 35 minutes or until golden. Brush again with butter. Makes 32.

Note: You can add up to 2 c. of whole wheat flour in place of 2 c. of the white flour for whole wheat croissants. You can also brush the dough with fruit preserves instead of butter before rolling up or you can sprinkle with chopped chocolate and roll up.

Hot Cross Buns

2/3 c. sugar
1 t. salt
2 packages active dry yeast
about 5 c. bread flour
1½ c. milk
½ c. butter or margarine
2 eggs
1 c. raisins

Icing
¾ c. powdered sugar
1 T. milk

In bowl combine sugar, salt, yeast and about 1½ c. flour. Heat together milk and butter until very warm. Beat milk mixture into to flour mixture and beat 2 minutes with electric mixer. Beat in 1 egg and 1 c. flour and beat 2 more minutes until batter thickens. Stir in raisins and enough additional flour to make a soft dough. Turn dough onto a floured surface and knead until smooth, about 10 minutes. Place dough in greased bowl, turning to grease top, cover with a towel and allow to rise in a draft free place until doubled in bulk, about 1 hour.

Place dough on floured surface and divide into 15 equal pieces. Cover with towel and let rest 15 minutes. Meanwhile grease a 9x13-inch pan. Form dough into smooth balls and place in prepared pan. Cover and let rise until doubles, about an hour. Preheat oven to 350 degrees. Beat remaining egg. Cut a cross in each bun and brush with the egg. Bake for 25 minutes or until buns are golden. Remove buns to wire rack to cool 15 minutes. Make frosting, place in decorating bag and pipe onto buns. Makes 15.

Chapter 19:
Holiday Baking

Some tips
To make holiday baking easier

Make a list (shopping) and check it twice. Nothing is more frustrating than getting ready to bake and finding that you are missing one ingredient or something is too old to use. Go over your recipes in the kitchen so you can go over inventory as you make your list.

Read through the directions before starting to make sure your ingredients are ready. You may need to let an ingredient like butter or eggs come to room temperature, or you might need to toast nuts. Better to get it all ready before you get started than to find out you aren't ready.

Make sure you have enough of the basics. There are about 10 cups of sugar in a five-pound bag and about 20 cups of flour in a five-pound bag.

Make sure ingredients are fresh. High fat foods like nuts and butter should be kept refrigerated or frozen for best flavor. These foods can become rancid if stored too long at room temperature. I like to buy nuts in season, which is fall and winter and freeze them for all year. The price is usually better and they will keep fine in the freezer.

Check your powder. Baking powder can lose its fizz if it is too old. To test what you have at home, place 1 t. of baking powder in a cup and add 2 T. of boiling water. It should bubble up. If nothing happens get a fresh tin.

Make one day and bake another. If you are making cookies try making and chilling the dough all at one time and then just chill or freeze it until you are ready to bake it. Cookie dough can be frozen for up to a couple of months with no problem. This way you can concentrate on just one thing, clean up that mess and the next day just do the baking. Cookie dough will keep in the fridge for a week if it contains no eggs and 4 days if it does. I even will decorate the cookies another day if I can, just to keep down the chaos in my too small kitchen.

Two can be as easy as one. If you are making quick breads for gifts it is usually no problem to double the batch and get that much more baking out of the way. I like to but pretty foil pans so I can bake and give the bread in the same pan. At stores like Joshen Paper, Michaels, and cake decorating stores you can find an assortment of containers with lids for even easier packaging.

Keep it simple. I like to make really fancy desserts, too, but sometimes there just isn't the time. You can dress up a simple cake with drizzles of melted chocolate, fancy sprinkles, chocolate curls and edible glitter. A fun way to dress up a cake is to place a doily on the top of the cake and then dust the cake with cocoa (for a white frosted cake) or powdered sugar (for a dark frosted cake) or even cinnamon or cinnamon sugar. Gently lift off the doily and you will have a lacy design on your cake. Use window stencils for other designs.

Holiday Pound Cake

1¼ c. sugar
1 (8 oz. package) cream cheese, softened
1½ c. butter or margarine, softened
2¼ c. cake flour
2 t. baking powder
4 eggs
1½ t. almond extract
½ c. light brown sugar
1 t. almond extract
1 (3½ oz. can) flaked coconut
4 oz. sliced blanched almonds

Preheat oven to 350 degrees. Grease and flour a 13x9-inch pan. In large bowl combine sugar, cream cheese and 1 c. of the butter or margarine. Beat together until light and fluffy. Add flour, powder eggs and the almond extract. Mix on low until well-blended and then beat on high for 2 minutes. Pour batter into prepared pan and bake 25-30 minutes. Test for doneness by inserting a toothpick. Cool cake on a rack for 10 minutes. Meanwhile, preheat broiler. In small saucepan combine remaining butter or margarine with remaining ingredients and heat until butter has melted. Spread over cooked cake and place under broiler 7-9-inches from heat source for 1 minute. Topping should brown a little. Cool before serving. Serves 12-15.

Hearth Loaf

1/3 c. butter, softened
2/3 c. sugar
2 t. grated lemon or orange peel
½ t. cinnamon
2 eggs
3 T. milk
1 t. lemon juice
1 t. each baking powder and salt
½ t. baking soda
2 c. flour
1½ c. peeled shredded apples
1 c. raisins
½ c. chopped nuts

Cream together butter, sugar, peel and cinnamon. Beat in eggs until light and fluffy. Stir in milk and lemon juice. Stir in dry ingredients then fold in apples, raisins and nuts. Bake in a greased 9-inch loaf pan in a preheated 350 degree oven for 1 hour. Use a toothpick to test for doneness. Cool 15-20 minutes before removing from pan. Yield: 1 loaf.

As with other quick bread you can make this recipe and bake it in smaller pans for gift-size loaves. Baking temperature is the same. Time will vary so check after 30 minutes and test for doneness as usual.

Cheese Puffs

1 lb. sharp cheddar cheese, grated
½ c. butter or margarine
½ t. salt
¼ t. cayenne pepper or 2 drops hot pepper sauce
1¾ c. flour

In mixer or food processor combine cheese and butter or margarine until smooth. Add remaining ingredients and blend until pretty smooth. Roll out onto lightly floured surface to ¼-inch thickness. Cut into thin strips or use mini cookie cutters to make shapes. Place on ungreased baking sheet nearly touching as they do not spread and bake in a preheated 350 degree oven for 15-20 minutes. Bottoms should be lightly browned. Makes about 100. They freeze well.

Holiday Cranberry Bread

4 c. flour
2 c. sugar
1 T. baking powder
2 t. salt
1 t. baking soda
½ c. shortening
2 eggs
1¾ c. orange juice
2 T. grated orange peel
2 c. fresh or frozen cranberries. chopped or 1½ c. dried cranberries
1 c. walnuts, chopped

Preheat oven to 350 degrees. Grease and flour 2 9x5-inch loaf pans. In large mixing bowl mix dry ingredients. Cut in shortening to resemble coarse crumbs. In medium bowl beat together eggs, juice, and orange peel. Stir into flour mixture and stir just until moistened. Fold in cranberries and nuts. Spoon batter into prepared pans and bake 55 minutes, or until toothpick inserted in center comes out clean. Cool in pans 10 minutes, then remove from pans and cool on wire racks. Makes 2.

Herbed Sweet Potato Biscuits

2¼ c. flour
1 T. baking powder
½ t. grated lemon peel
¼ t. each baking soda, dried basil and dried thyme
1 egg, beaten
1½ c. shredded sweet potato, about 1 large
½ c. fine chopped green onions
½ c. sour cream
2 T. butter or margarine, melted

Stir together dry ingredients in large bowl and set aside. Combine remaining ingredients and add to flour mixture mixing until just blended. Turn onto lightly floured surface and knead a few times until dough just stays together. Press into an 8-inch square and cut into four squares. Cross cut each square into four triangles. Place on greased baking sheet and bake in a preheated 425 degree oven for 20 minutes. Makes 16.

Dog Biscuits

3½ c. flour
1 c. each rye flour and cornmeal
2 c. cracked wheat or wheat germ
½ c. powdered milk
1 packet active dry yeast
1 T. salt
2 c. chicken or beef broth
1 beaten egg mixed with 1 T. water

Combine dry ingredients then add broth stirring until well blended. Roll out on lightly floured surface and cut into canine-friendly shapes. I use bones, cats, squirrels, hearts and rabbits. Place on ungreased baking sheet and brush with the egg wash. Bake in a preheated 300 degree oven until hard, about 40-45 minutes depending on thickness. Store in an airtight container until ready to serve to your favorite pooch. Woof!

Honey Date Nut Bread

¾ c. boiling water
1 c. pitted whole dates, chopped
1 egg
1 c. honey
1 T. butter or margarine, melted
1 t. vanilla
2 c. flour
1 t. baking soda
½ t. salt
1 c. chopped nuts

In small bowl pour water over dates and let stand until cool. Do not drain. You can do this early in the day or day ahead and refrigerate until ready to use. In small bowl beat eggs until lemon-colored, about 2 minutes. Beat in honey, butter and vanilla. Stir in dates and water. Combine dry ingredients and add to batter until smooth. Stir in nuts. Pour batter into 2 7x3-inch greased loaf pans or 1 9x5-inch greased loaf pan. Bake in preheated 350 degree oven 50 minutes for small pans and 65 minutes for large. Test for doneness with a toothpick. Cool in pan 10 minutes then turn out of pan and cool on wire rack. Makes 2 small or 1 large loaf.

Hawaiian Wedding Cake

2 c. flour
2 eggs
1 (20 oz. can) crushed pineapple in its own juice, undrained
1 c. coconut
1 c. sugar
1 c. chopped walnuts
2 t. baking soda

Preheat oven to 350 degrees. Grease a 9x13-inch pan. Combine all ingredients in a bowl and mix well. Pour into prepared pan and bake 35 minutes or until golden brown on top. Cool and dust with cinnamon sugar or frost. Serves 12.

Frosting
8 oz. cream cheese, softened
¾ c. powdered sugar
1 stick butter or margarine, room temperature

Beat all together until fluffy. Frost cake and refrigerate until ready to eat.

Warm Cranberry Cake

2 c. biscuit mix
½ c. sugar
1/3 c. milk
2 T. oil
1 egg
2 c. fresh or frozen cranberries, chopped

Preheat oven to 350 degrees. Grease and flour a 9x9-inch pan. Combine all ingredients except cranberries and beat 30 seconds. Stir in berries and place in prepared pan. Bake about 35 minutes, using toothpick to test for doneness. Serve warm.

White Chocolate Cheesecake with Cranberry Swirl

1½ c. cranberries
¾ c. orange juice
¼ c. sugar
3 T. raisins
2 T. cranberry or orange liqueur
1 T. grated orange peel
6 oz. white chocolate, chopped fine
1½ lb. cream cheese, room temperature
¾ c. sugar
4 eggs

Combine first 6 ingredients in saucepan and cook until berries are tender, about 8 minutes. Stir as needed. Process until smooth, strain and allow mixture to cool. Can be done 1 day ahead.

Preheat oven to 350 degrees. Melt white chocolate over double boiler, set aside and allow to cool a little. Beat cheese with sugar until fluffy. Beat in eggs one at a time. Mix in white chocolate and pour ½ of mixture into 9-inch spring form pan. Drop half of cranberry mixture in by spoonfuls and swirl into batter. Repeat with remaining ingredients. Bake about 40 minutes until edges are puffed and golden. Center will not be set. Cool completely before refrigerating. Serves 10.

Note: You can use any graham crust recipe for this cheesecake if you like. Follow any directions involving pre- baking of the crust. With a crust add about 10-15 minutes baking time to the cheesecake.

Baker's Hint: When cleaning up after using flour always wash surfaces with cold water first to dissolve the flour. Hot water will cause the flour to get gummy. After flour residue is gone wash in hot soapy water and rinse.

Coconut Cake Squares

1 white cake, prepared and frozen solid
1 c. cocoa
1¼ c. sugar
2 c. water
1 t. vanilla
½ c. desiccated coconut (available at cake supply stores and some health food stores)

Cut frozen cake into small squares, or cake can be baked in regular or mini cupcake tins. Keep cake frozen until ready to use. Meanwhile, combine remaining ingredients, except coconut in a medium saucepan. Bring to a boil then simmer 5 minutes. Remove from heat and cool completely.

Using toothpicks or fondue forks, dip cake in sauce let drain a few seconds, then roll in the coconut. Can be used right away or frozen again for later use.

Christmas Tree Coffee Cake

Dough
4-4½ c. bread flour
½ c. sugar
1½ t. salt
2 packages active dry yeast
¾ c. milk
½ c. water
½ c. butter or margarine
1 egg

Filling
1 lb. cream cheese, softened
½ c. sugar
¼ t. nutmeg
dash salt
¼ t. vanilla
1 (20 oz. can) pineapple in its own juice drained and squeezed dry

Topping
11 red candied cherries, halved
2 c. powdered sugar
3 T. milk
red and green sugars

For dough in large mixing bowl combine 2 c. of the flour with the sugar, salt and yeast. Heat together the milk, water and butter or margarine until very warm. Add to flour mixture and beat 2 minutes. Add egg and 1 more cup of flour and beat 2 more minutes. Stir in enough of the remaining dough to make a stiff batter, about 1 c. Cover bowl tightly with foil or plastic wrap and refrigerate for at least 2 hours or up to 3 days before using. For filling combine all ingredients for the filling except the pineapple and beat until smooth. Stir in pineapple and set aside until ready to use. Remove dough from fridge cut in half. Roll out one piece on lightly floured surface into a 10x11-inch rectangle.

Spread with half the filling, leaving an-inch at the end of 11-inch side. Roll up from eleven-inch side. Use thread or dental floss to cut through dough in 1-inch pieces by placing thread under roll and crossing ends. Pull outward and thread should cut through dough. If you aren't having any luck you can always use a knife, but they tend to flatten the rolls. On a greased baking sheet arrange the slices (you should have 11) into a tree shape. Start with one on the top and then a row of 2 below then 3 and then 4. The last roll will serve as the trunk. Cover dough with plastic wrap and set in a warm place to rise. Repeat with the remaining dough and filling. When dough is risen, about 1-2 hours bake in a 375 degree oven for 15 minutes then cover edges with foil to prevent over browning and return to oven for 10 minutes more. Cool on wire rack. Place half a cherry in the middle of each roll. Make a glaze with powdered sugar and milk and drizzle over. Sprinkle with the sugars. Makes 2 trees, 11 rolls each. Can be frozen up to a month ahead. Defrost in a 350 degree oven for 10 minutes and apply toppings.

Chef Pastry Mix/Biscuit Mix

8 c. sifted, all-purpose flour
1 c. powdered milk
1 c. powdered buttermilk
¼ c. baking powder
1 T. salt
2 c. shortening

Sift dry ingredients together 3 times. Cut in shortening to resemble cornmeal. Keep in an airtight container. Store in a cool dry place and use within six months.

Polish Poppy Seed Bread

Dough
¾ c. milk
¼ c. sugar
¼ c. honey
¾ t. salt
½ c. butter or margarine
½ c. warm water
2 pkt. yeast
2 eggs, room temperature
5-6 c. flour

Filling
1 (12 oz. can) poppy seed filling
2 t. toasted poppy seed

Glaze
1 egg yolk
1 T. milk

Scald milk and add next 4 ingredients. Dissolve yeast in warm water. Allow to stand 5 minutes. When milk mixture is cooled to lukewarm add to water mixture and stir to blend. Beat in eggs and 2½ c. of the flour. Beat 3 minutes and then start stirring in flour until dough starts to form into a ball. Place on floured surface and knead until dough is smooth and elastic, about 8 minutes. Place dough in greased bowl, turning to grease top and cover. Allow to rise until doubled in bulk, about 1 hour. Meanwhile combine filling ingredients and set aside and grease large cookie sheet. Punch dough down and cut in half. Roll one half into a 12x9-inch rectangle. Cut rectangle into 3 12x3-inch strips. Divide half of the filling down center of the strips and pinch edges to seal. Braids strips together and place on baking sheet. Repeat with remaining dough and cover, allowing to rise until doubled, about 1 hour. Preheat oven to 350 degrees. Brush dough with egg wash and bake 25 minutes or until golden. Makes 2.

Cranberry Bounce

1 lb. fresh or frozen cranberries, coarsely chopped
2 c. sugar
4 c. vodka

Place berries in jar with tight fitting lid and add sugar, stirring to dissolve. Seal and let stand several hours or overnight. Add vodka and let stand 2-4 weeks. Strain and pour through coffee filters or cheesecloth to remove any sediment. Bottle and label for home use or gifts. Makes about 5 cups.

Maple Cookies

1 c. butter
1 c. sugar
½ c. maple syrup
1 egg yolk
3 c. flour
½ t. salt

Glaze
2 c. powdered sugar
½ c. maple syrup

Cream together sugar and butter. Stir in syrup. Sift in flour and salt. Chill dough. Roll out chilled dough and cut out in leaf shapes. Bake at 350 degrees for 12 minutes. Cookies should be lightly browned around the edges. You can decorate by marking raw leaves with veins or by spreading cooled cookies with glaze. Glaze will harden.

Yule Log

Cake
1/3 c. cake flour
1/3 c. cocoa
2 T. cornstarch
½ t. baking soda
¼ t. salt
4 eggs, separated
¾ c. sugar, separated
powdered sugar

Filling Frosting
6 oz. white chocolate
¼ c. whipping cream or milk
1 c. cold butter, cut in bits
1 c. powdered sugar

Chocolate Frosting
6 T. butter or margarine, softened
¾ c. cocoa
2 2/3 c. powdered sugar
1/3 c. milk
1 t. vanilla

Line a 15x10-inch jellyroll pan with wax paper or parchment. Grease and flour lined pan. In medium bowl mix dry ingredients well. In separate bowl beat together egg yolks and ¼ c. of the sugar until lemon-colored. Set aside. Beat egg whites until foamy and start to add remaining ½ c. of sugar gradually while beating. Beat egg whites until stiff peaks form. Fold 1/3 of the egg whites into yolk mixture. Alternately fold in flour mixture and remaining egg white mixture. Spread batter in pan and smooth out. Bake in a preheated 350 degree oven for about 15 minutes. Use toothpick to test for doneness. While cake is baking dust a linen towel with powdered sugar on flat surface.

When cake is done turn cake onto sugared cloth and gently peel off wax paper or parchment. Trim off cake edges, if needed. Starting at long end roll up cake and lay on table to cool with seam side down. When cake in cooled unroll and remove cloth. Frost with white chocolate frosting to within ½-inch of the edges and re-roll. Place seam side down on work surface and cut a diagonal slice off each end, about 2-3-inches wide. Using a little of the chocolate buttercream attach each of the slices (with the flat side against the cake) to form cut-off branches. Use remaining frosting to frost cake and then use a fork to make lines to resemble bark. You can decorate with real leaves, powdered sugar (for snow) or meringue mushrooms. Serves 8-12.

Filling Frosting
Combine white chocolate and cream or milk in microwave safe bowl and heat in microwave until just warm enough to melt. Stir until smooth and let stand until room temperature. Beat in cold butter with mixer until smooth and fluffy. Beat in powdered sugar until smooth.

Chocolate Frosting
Beat butter or margarine until smooth. Combine cocoa and powdered sugar and beat into butter alternately with the milk and vanilla. Beat until smooth. You made need a little more milk to make the frosting spreading consistency.

Meringue Mushrooms

3 egg whites at room temp
pinch of salt
¾ c. superfine granulated sugar
cocoa for dusting mushroom caps

With electric mixer beat 2 of the egg whites and salt until soft peaks hold. Add 1/3 c. of the sugar and beat until very stiff peak form. Using a pastry bag pipe small mounds of meringue onto parchment-covered baking sheets to form mushroom stems. To form caps pipe rounded mound onto parchment and use a wet finger to smooth the top. Bake in 180 degree oven (using racks in bottom and top third of oven for 2-8 hours switching tray positions every hour. Leave in until meringue is hard. Cool and scrape a little bit of meringue out of the bottom of each cap so stem ends will fit in. Beat remaining egg white with remaining sugar as you did the first time. Use this mixture to bond the tops and stems of your mushrooms. Place in 180 degree oven again and bake for about 45 minutes, or until joints are firm. Store in an airtight container until ready to use. These are best used within a few days of preparation. Just before using on your Yule log dust the tops of the "mushrooms" with a little cocoa. Place here and there on the Yule log.

Garlic Batter Bread

1 c. milk, scalded
3 T. olive oil
2 T. sugar
2 t. salt
2 packages active dry yeast
1 c. lukewarm water
2 t. dry minced garlic
4 c. flour
½ c. grated Parmesan cheese

Combine first 4 ingredients and allow to cool to lukewarm. Dissolve yeast in water and add to milk mixture. Add remaining ingredients and beat until blended. Cover and let rise until doubled, about 45 minutes. Stir down and place in well-oiled 1½ quart casserole. Bake at 375 degrees for about 1 hour. Serve with herb butter.

Nisu

½ c. warm water
2 packages active dry yeast
2 c. milk
½ c. sugar
2-3 t. cardamom
1 t. salt
6 T. shortening
6-7 c. flour, preferably bread flour
2 eggs

Dissolve yeast in water and set aside. Place milk in large bowl and add the sugar, cardamom, salt and shortening. Heat in microwave until liquid is very warm. Shortening will not be completely melted. Stir mixture until sugar is dissolved. Place 2 c. of flour in a mixing bowl and add the milk mixture, eggs and yeast mixture. Beat on medium speed for 3 minutes. Add 1 c. more of the flour and beat 2 minutes more. Stir in enough of the remaining flour to make a soft dough. Turn onto a floured surface and knead until dough is firm and smooth, about 10 minutes. Place in an oiled bowl and turn dough to coat. Cover with a towel and allow to rest until doubled in bulk, about 1 hour. Punch dough down and divide into 3 pieces. Roll each piece into a loaf and place in a greased 8x4-inch bread pan. Cover and allow to rise until doubled in bulk, about 45 minutes. Bake in a 375 degree oven for 30 minutes or until golden and loaf sounds hollow when tapped lightly. Makes 3 loaves.

Holiday Wreath Bread

4-4½ c. flour
1/3 c. plus 2 T. sugar
1 t. salt
1 t. ground cardamom
2 packages active dry yeast
½ c. butter or margarine
½ c. water
½ c. milk
½ c. raisins
2 eggs, slightly beaten
2 T. chopped nuts

In mixing bowl combine 1 c. of flour with 1/3 c. sugar, salt, cardamom and yeast. In microwave safe dish combine butter or margarine, water, milk and raisins and heat until very warm (120 degrees) and add to flour mixture. Beat 2 minutes. Set aside 2 T. of the beaten eggs and add the rest of the eggs to the batter along with another cup of flour. Beat 2 more minutes. Add enough flour to make a soft dough and turn onto floured surface. Knead, adding flour as necessary until dough is smooth and elastic. Place in greased bowl and turn to coat. Cover and let rise until doubled in bulk, about 1 hour. Punch dough down and divide into thirds. Roll out each piece into a 30-inch long rope. Braid dough. Grease an 8-oz. heat-proof custard cup and invert on greased baking sheet. Wrap braid around cup, pinching ends together. Cover and let rise until doubled in bulk, about 45 minutes. Before baking brush braid lightly with reserved egg and sprinkle with remaining sugar and nuts. Bake in a preheated 375 degree oven for 25-30 minutes. Loaf should be golden and sound hollow when tapped lightly. Cool on rack. Makes 1 loaf. Can be decorated with a ribbon for a nice hostess gift.

Ribbon Cake

1 yellow cake mix
1 jar lemon curd
1 jar raspberry spreadable fruit (like Polaner's)
1 jar apricot spreadable fruit
whipped cream frosting

Bake cake according to package directions in 2 9-inch round cake pans. Cool overnight. When cakes are cool split each layer in half horizontally. Place 1 cake layer on a platter and spread with lemon curd. Add second layer and spread with the raspberry fruit spread. Add next cake layer and spread on the apricot fruit spread. Top with remaining cake layer and frost or cover and chill until ready to frost. Cake must be kept chilled until ready to serve. Serves 16.

Note: You can use your favorite buttercream frosting if you would rather even canned frosting.

Whipped Cream Frosting

2 c. whipping cream
¼ c. sugar

Beat together until stiff peaks form.

Chapter 20:
Coffee House Treats

Tiramisu Cheesecake

Espresso Syrup
4 t. dried instant coffee or espresso
1/3 c. water
¼ c. sugar
2 T. coffee liqueur

Cheesecake
12 to 16 lady fingers
1 lbs. cream cheese
½ lbs. mascarpone cheese
2/3 c. sugar
1 t. pure vanilla
1 T. orange liqueur (optional)
4 eggs
2 egg yolks
1/3 c. whipping cream

Topping
16 to 20 lady fingers - quartered
½ c. unsalted butter
½ c. sugar
2 t. espresso or instant coffee dissolved in 1 to 2 tbsp. hot water
non-stick cooking spray
confectioner's sugar for dusting or 1/3 c. semi-sweet chocolate - grated

Lightly spray a 9-inch spring form pan or 9-inch deep tart pan with non-stick cooking spray. Preheat oven to 350 degrees.

Syrup
In a small saucepan, stir water with coffee and sugar. Heat just to dissolve sugar. Remove from heat and cool to room temperature. **Stir in liqueur.**

Cake

Arrange ladyfingers in pan, cutting or trimming to fill out pan bottom with cookies. Brush syrup over cookies and allow to soak in. Re-apply to use up syrup. In an electric mixer on slow speed, cream the cream cheese with sugar. Add vanilla, (orange liqueur), eggs, egg yolks and heavy cream. Pour over prepared cake crust. In a small saucepan, over low heat, melt the butter with the sugar. Using a whisk, briskly blend in the dissolved coffee. Pour into a medium sized bowl. Toss quartered ladyfingers into this mixture. Arrange on top of cake. Bake until just set - about 30 minutes. Chill for 4 hours or overnight. Dust with confectioner's sugar or grated chocolate. Makes 10-12 servings

Rich Brownies

This recipe has been around for decades and is said to have originated with the famous actress.

2 oz. unsweetened chocolate
½ c. unsalted butter
1 c. sugar
2 eggs, lightly beaten
½ t. vanilla
¼ c. flour
¼ t. salt
1 c. chopped walnuts

Preheat oven to 325 degrees. Butter and flour and 8-inch square pan. Melt chocolate and butter together over low heat or in microwave. Remove from heat and stir in sugar then stir in eggs and vanilla. Stir in flour, salt and nuts and pour into prepared pan. Bake until toothpick inserted in center of brownies comes out clean, about 40 minutes.

Black and White Cookies

1¾ c. sugar
1 c. unsalted butter, room temp.
4 large eggs
1 c. milk
½ t. vanilla extract
¼ t. lemon extract or
2½ c. cake flour
2½ c. all-purpose flour
1 t. baking powder
½ t. salt

Frosting
4 c. confectioner's sugar
1/3 to ½ c. boiling water
1 oz. bitter or semi-sweet chocolate

Preheat the oven to 375 degrees. Line two baking sheets with parchment paper. In a large mixing bowl, combine sugar and butter until fluffy. Stir in eggs, milk, vanilla, extracts, until smooth. Fold in flours, baking powder, and salt. Stir until mixed. Using a soup spoon (or a small ice cream scoop) drop spoonfuls of dough onto baking sheet, leaving 2-inches of room between them. Bake until edges are browned, 20-30 minutes.

Frosting
Place confectioner's sugar in a bowl. Gradually stir in boiling water until you have a thick spreadable mixture. Remove half of frosting to a bowl and stir in melted chocolate. With a brush, decorate each cookie half with white frosting, half with chocolate. Let set until thoroughly dry.

About 2 dozen cookies.

Chocolate Apple Bread

2 T. sugar
¼ t. ground cinnamon
¼ c. finely chopped walnuts
2 c. all-purpose flour
½ t. salt
½ t. baking powder
½ t. baking soda
½ t. ground cinnamon
¼ t. ground nutmeg
½ c. margarine, softened
1 c. white sugar
2 eggs
1 t. vanilla extract
2 T. buttermilk
1 c. chopped apples
½ c. walnuts
¼ c. semi-sweet chocolate chips

Topping
In a small bowl mix the sugar, cinnamon and finely chopped walnuts. Set aside.

In medium bowl combine flour, salt, baking powder, baking soda, cinnamon, and nutmeg. Set aside. In a separate large bowl cream butter and sugar. Add eggs and vanilla extract, and mix well. Gradually beat in flour mixture alternately with buttermilk. Stir in apples, walnuts, and semi-sweet chocolate chips. Pour into a greased 9x5-inch loaf pan. Sprinkle with topping. Bake in a preheated 350 degree oven for 50 to 60 minutes. Cool for 15 minutes. Remove from pan. Cool on a wire rack.

Caramel Scones

3 c. flour
½ c. unsalted butter
1/3 c. sugar
½ t. salt
1 T. baking powder
modest pinch of nutmeg or cloves
¾ to 1 c. milk or cream
1 egg
1½ t. pure vanilla
½ t. butterscotch extract (optional)
1 c. butterscotch chips
½ c. grated walnuts (optional)

Topping
1/3 c. butterscotch chips - finely chopped in food processor
1 egg white, whisked
confectioner's sugar (optional)

Preheat oven to 425 degrees. Line top sheet of doubled up baking sheets with parchment paper. In a food processor, place the flour and butter and pulse to break up butter. Add sugar, baking powder, salt and nutmeg or cloves and pulse to combine. Turn out dough into a large bowl. Make a well in the center and stir in cream, vanilla, butterscotch extract and egg. Stir to make a soft dough. Fold in butterscotch chips. Use ice cream scoop to make scones placing scoops of dough onto baking sheet. Brush tops with egg white and add ground butterscotch chips. Bake until browned, 16-18 minutes. Dust with confectioner's sugar when cool. Makes about 18-22 depending on size.

Russian Tea Biscuits

5 c. flour
½ c. sugar
1 t. baking powder
1 t. baking soda
¼ t. salt
1½ c. butter, softened
2 eggs, separated
2/3 c. orange juice
1 1/3 c. preserves (strawberry, seedless raspberry or plum preferred)
1 c. chopped walnuts
1 c. raisins, dark or golden
1 t. cinnamon
3 T. sugar

Combine dry ingredients in a mixing bowl and cut in butter until mixture is the size of peas. Stir in egg yolks and orange juice. Knead until dough is well blended. Divide dough into 4 equal pieces. Roll out a piece of dough ¼-inch thick into an 8x10-inch rectangle. Spread with 1/3 c. of the preserves and sprinkle with ¼ c. each of the raisins and nuts. Roll up jelly roll fashion and set, seam side down, on ungreased baking sheet. Repeat with remaining dough. Beat egg whites until foamy and brush on dough. Combine cinnamon and sugar and sprinkle on dough. Bake in a 350 degree oven for 25-35 minutes, or until golden. Slice while warm into 6 pieces for each roll. Makes 24.

Classic Babka

Dough
1½ c. water
2 T. yeast
pinch sugar
2 eggs
2 egg yolks
1 t. vanilla
2 drops almond extract
1 t. lemon juice
¾ c. sugar
1 t. salt
1/3 c. milk powder
1 c. unsalted butter, softened in small pieces
6 c. (approx.) flour

Egg Wash
1 beaten egg
sugar for sprinkling

Babka Fillings
Chocolate Filling
1½ c. semi-sweet chocolate chips
½ t. cinnamon
¼ c. cocoa
½ c. sugar
3 T. unsalted butter or margarine

Cinnamon Filling
¼ c. unsalted butter
1 c. brown sugar
2 T. corn syrup
2-4 t. cinnamon
¾ c. chopped walnuts, optional

In a large mixing bowl, whisk together water, yeast and pinch of sugar. Let stand about five minutes to allow yeast to swell and dissolve. Stir in eggs; egg yolks, vanilla, almond extract, lemon juice, sugar, salt and milk powder. Fold in softened butter and flour. Mix dough, then knead as it becomes a mass (with a dough hook or by hand) for about 8 to 10 minutes - until smooth and elastic. Place dough in a well-greased bowl and place entire bowl in a plastic bag and seal. Allow to rise until puffy, about 45-90 minutes. (Can also be refrigerated overnight to resume next day, allowing dough to warm up a bit before proceeding).

Divide dough in two equal parts. Cover with a tea towel and let rest ten minutes. Line a large baking sheet with parchment paper or generously grease two 9-inch spring-form or layer cake pans. If making one large babka, generously butter a 10-inch tube pan.

On a lightly floured board, roll dough into a 16 by 16-inch square. Arrange or spread on filling of choice (below) all over dough surface. Roll up dough into a large jellyroll. Cut in half. Place both halves in prepared pan, beside each other - it doesn't matter if they are a little squished. Brush with egg wash and sprinkle with some sugar. Place loaf pan in a plastic bag and let rise until babka is flush or over top of pan.

Repeat with other half of dough, using a different filling, if desired. To use all of dough in one large babka, procedure is the same but you will be using all of dough at once. Roll dough out into a 20-inch square (instead of 16 by 16) and proceed as above. A large babka is especially dramatic but two smaller ones give you two flavor and assembly options.

Preheat oven to 350 degrees. Bake 35-45 minutes (50-70 minutes for one large babka) until medium brown. Cool pan fifteen minutes before removing to a rack or serving plate.

Chocolate Filling
Grind chocolate chips, cinnamon, cocoa, sugar, and butter in a food processor to make a loose paste. You can also use a chopped up, imported Swiss chocolate bar, semi-sweet or milk chocolate.

Cinnamon Filling
In a food processor, process the butter, sugar, corn syrup, cinnamon and walnuts to make a loose paste. You can substitute maple syrup for corn syrup.

Poppy Seed Tea Cake

Streusel
6 T. sugar
6 T. flour
¼ c. butter, melted
1 t. cinnamon
¾ t. cardamom

Cake
2 1/3 c. cake flour
1½ t. baking powder
1 t. baking soda
¾ t. cardamom
½ t. salt
1½ sticks butter, room temp.
1 c. plus 2 T. sugar
2 eggs
1 c. sour cream
¼ c. orange juice
2 t. grated orange peel
1 t. vanilla
1/3 c. poppy seeds

For streusel topping combine all ingredients in a small bowl with a fork until mixture forms into clumps. Set aside. For cake grease and flour a 12-cup angel food cake pan with a removable bottom. Sift together first 5 ingredients and set aside. Beat butter and sugar together until fluffy. Beat in eggs one at a time. Beat in sour cream, orange juice and flavorings. Beat in dry ingredients until blended. Stir in poppy seeds. Pour batter into prepared pan and bake in a 350 degree oven for 25 minutes. Remove cake and sprinkle with streusel topping. Return to oven for about 20 minutes longer. Use toothpick to test for doneness. Cool cake in pan on rack. Use knife to loosen pan from edges and center tube. Remove pan side and cut cake to remove from base. Place on platter. Serves 10-12.

Pumpkin Maple Scones

3 c. flour
2 c. white sugar
½ c. brown sugar
½ c. unsalted butter - in chunks
½ c. pumpkin (canned or homemade)
¾ t. salt
½ t. pumpkin pie spice (or ¼ t. each: cloves and allspice)
½ t. cinnamon
4 t. baking powder
1/3 c. whipping cream or milk (cream is better)
½ t. vanilla
½ t. maple extract (or syrup to taste)
½ c. pecans, chopped

Preheat oven to 450 degrees. Double up two baking sheets (one inside the other) and cover top sheet with parchment paper. Mix dry ingredients together in a food processor. Cut in butter, then stir in pumpkin puree, cream, vanilla and maple extract. Stir in nuts. Make a soft dough. Knead gently on a floured board until smooth. Cut into thick disks - about 1-inch high by 2½-inches wide. Brush tops with cream and top with some brown sugar. Bake for 12 to 15 minutes. Cool well.

Oatmeal Orange Scones

2½ c. flour
2 c. oatmeal
1 c. sugar
1 t. salt
1 T. baking powder
½ t. baking soda
½ c. very cold, unsalted butter - cut into chunks
1 egg
½ c. orange juice
2 t. grated orange peel
1 c. raisins, plumped and well dried

Glaze
milk
sugar
orange zest

Line a large baking sheet with parchment paper (double two sheets if you have them - one inside the other). Preheat oven to 425 degrees. In a large bowl, place flour, oatmeal, sugar, salt, baking powder, baking soda and mix together. Cut or rub in butter to make a mealy mixture. Stir in egg and orange juice. Add orange peel and raisins. Mix to make a soft dough. Turn out onto a lightly floured board and knead for a few minutes. Roll or pat out into a thickness of ½-inch. Using a serrated cookie cutter cut into disks or rounds. Brush with milk and sprinkle with sugar and orange zest. Bake until nicely browned - about 14 minutes. Makes about 24.

Lemon Poppy Seed Muffins

1/3 c. milk
¼ c. vegetable oil
2/3 c. nonfat lemon yogurt
1 egg
1¾ c. all-purpose flour
¼ c. white sugar
2 T. poppy seeds
1 T. lemon zest
¼ t. lemon extract
2½ t. baking powder
½ t. baking soda
½ t. salt
½ c. confectioners' sugar
2½ t. lemon juice

Preheat oven to 400 degrees. Grease the bottoms only of 12 muffin cups. Beat the milk, oil, lemon yogurt and egg together. Stir in the flour, white sugar, poppy seeds, lemon zest, lemon extract, baking powder, baking soda and salt. Mix until just combined. Divide batter evenly between muffin cups. Bake for 16 to 18 minutes or until golden brown. Drizzle with glaze immediately and let cool on racks. Makes 12.

Glaze
Stir the confectioners' sugar with the lemon juice and mix until smooth and of drizzling consistency. Add drops of milk if thinning is necessary.

White Chocolate and Ginger Biscotti

1 c. white sugar
1/3 c. brown sugar
1/3 c. melted unsalted butter
1 t. molasses
½ t. vanilla
¼ c. ground or coarsely chopped white chocolate
2¼ c. (approximately) flour
2 eggs
½ t. salt
2 t. baking powder
1½ t. cinnamon
1¼ t. ginger
½ t. cloves
¼ t. allspice

Coating
4-6 oz. white chocolate - chopped bars or white chocolate wafers - melted and cooled

Blend sugars, butter, eggs, molasses and vanilla. Stir in dry ingredients. Stir to make a stiff dough. Knead on a lightly floured board. Roll to a thickness of ½-inch. Cut into stars or other preferred shape. Line a baking sheet with parchment paper. Bake at 350 degrees until firm - about 25 minutes. Cool well. Dip into melted chocolate. Makes 18-24.

Easy Bear Claws

1 package frozen puff pastry (2 sheets) thawed
1 (10-12 oz. can or jar) almond filling
1 c. chocolate chips
1 T. shortening

Open one pastry sheet onto lightly floured surface and spread with half of the filling. Roll up loosely, jelly roll fashion, leaving seam side down on surface. Cut roll in half and each half into thirds. You will have 6 pieces total. On one closed edge of each pastry use scissors (preferred) or a sharp knife to cut 3 "toes". Do not make cuts on open filling sides. Pull apart slightly. Place 2-inches apart on ungreased baking sheet. Repeat with remaining dough and filling. Bake in a preheated 425 degree oven until golden, about 20-25 minutes. Cool on wire rack. Melt together chocolate and shortening in microwave-safe bowl in microwave. Stir to smooth and dip top of each claw into chocolate. Set on rack or wax paper to set up chocolate. You can also put in the fridge for a few minutes to harden chocolate quicker. Makes 12.

Variations
For filling you can use cinnamon sugar instead of almond filling or even use another filling flavor like poppy seed.

For topping you can use a powdered sugar glaze or even just powdered sugar.

Tiramisu

5 egg yolks
¼ c. sugar
½ c. Marsala wine (not cooking wine)
1 c. whipping cream
2 T. sugar
1 lb. mascarpone cheese
2 c. strong coffee, room temp.
2 T. sugar
½ c. brandy
1 T. vanilla
48 ladyfingers
3 T. cocoa

Make zabaglione (egg custard). In double boiler, over simmering water, beat together egg yolks and sugar until lemon colored. Stir in Marsala and continue cooking, stirring constantly until mixture thickens and will mound on a spoon. This will take about 10 minutes. Remove from heat and cool down. You can place in bowl in fridge 30 minutes or so. Beat together whipping cream and sugar until stiff peaks form. Beat in mascarpone and chilled zabaglione. Chill 1 hour. Stir together coffee with remaining sugar, brandy and vanilla and set aside. Assemble tiramisu by placing 16 of the ladyfingers in the bottom of a 9x13-inch pan. Drizzle about 1/3 of the coffee mixture over the ladyfingers, about 1 T. each. Top with 1/3 of the cream mixture and sprinkle with 1 T. of the cocoa. Repeat this process 2 more times until all ingredients are used. Chill until ready to serve. Serves 12.

Citrus Topped Cake

1 package lemon cake mix
12 oz. orange marmalade
2/3 c. flaked coconut
¼ c. butter or margarine, softened

Preheat oven to 350 degrees. Grease generously and flour 10-inch Bundt pan. Combine marmalade, coconut and butter or margarine and pour into prepared pan. Prepare cake mix according to package directions and pour in pan. Bake 50-55 minutes or until toothpick tests clean. Cool cake 10 minutes and invert onto serving plate. Serves 12.

Blueberry Crumb Cake

Cake Batter
2 c. flour
2 t. baking powder
½ t. salt
½ stick (¼ c.) butter, softened
¾ c. sugar
1 egg
½ c. milk
1 pint blueberries

Topping
½ c. sugar
¼ c. flour
½ t. cinnamon
½ stick (¼ c.) butter, chilled and cut into bits

Combine dry ingredients and set aside. In mixing bowl with electric mixer, beat butter and sugar until light and fluffy. Beat in egg and milk. Add flour mixture gradually until just mixed in. Fold in blueberries. Grease and flour an 8 or 9-inch pan and add prepared batter. Combine topping ingredients until they resemble coarse crumbs. Sprinkle over batter in pan and bake in a preheated 375 degree oven and bake for 35-45 minutes. Use toothpick to test.

Note: I used a 9-inch round pan and it worked fine.

Marble Pound Cake

fine dry breadcrumbs
1 lb. butter
1 T. vanilla
3 1/3 c. sugar
10 eggs
4 c. flour
½ t. almond extract
¼ t. baking soda
2 T. instant coffee, dry
¾ c. chocolate syrup

Place rack in oven about 1/3 of the way up from bottom. Grease a 10-inch tube pan and line bottom of pan with parchment paper. Grease paper and dust lightly with the breadcrumbs. Set aside. Preheat oven to 350 degrees. Cream together butter and vanilla then pour in sugar slowly. Beat 2-3 minutes, scraping sides, if needed. Beat in eggs, 2 at a time until thoroughly combined. On lowest speed slowly add flour and mix only until flour is just worked in. Remove half of batter (5 c.) to another bowl and add almond extract to it. Place in prepared pan and smooth batter out. In mixing bowl add soda, coffee and syrup to remaining batter. Beat until smooth and pour over white batter. Level by rotating pan back and forth quickly. Place foil loosely over top of pan and place in oven. Bake 30 minutes before removing foil. Reach in and get foil quickly to avoid leaving oven door open too long. Bake an additional 70-80 minutes. Use toothpick to test for doneness. Cool cake 10 minutes before removing from pan to finish cooling. Makes 1 cake.

Chocolate Lovers' Biscotti

¾ c. brown sugar
½ c. butter, room temperature
2 eggs
¾ c. chocolate syrup
2½ c. flour
2 t. baking powder
½ t. salt
1 c. chocolate chips (mini, regular or flavored)
1 c. chopped nuts
3 oz. white chocolate

Grease 2 9x5-inch loaf pans and set aside. Beat sugar and butter together than beat in eggs and syrup. Beat in dry ingredients. Dough will be soft. Stir in chips and nuts. Divide batter in prepared pans and use spatula to spread evenly. Bake in a 350 degree oven for about 35 minutes. Tester inserted in center should come out clean. Turn loaves onto rack and cool 15 minutes. Reduce oven temperature to 300 degrees. Using a serrated knife cut loaves into ¾-inch slices. Place cut side down on baking sheet and bake about 9 minutes. Turn slices over and bake an additional 10 minutes. Cool completely. Melt white chocolate and drizzle over biscotti. Allow to set up. Makes about 2 dozen.

Fruit Filled Ladder Loaf

3 oz. cream cheese
¼ c. butter or margarine
2 c. biscuit mix (Bisquick or Jiffy) or homemade
½ c. chopped nuts
¼ c. milk
½ of a (12-oz. can) cherry or apricot cake and pastry filling
powdered sugar glaze

In mixing bowl cut cheese and butter or margarine into baking mix until crumbly. Add nuts and milk and mix well. Knead on lightly floured surface until dough just holds together. Roll dough into a 12x8-inch rectangle on a piece of wax paper and turn dough onto greased baking sheet. Remove wax paper. Spread filling down middle third of dough and cut slits in dough at 1-inch intervals down length of dough (like fringe.)

Pull strips of dough over filling alternately from each side and pinch together. Bake in a 425 degree oven for about 15 minutes. Drizzle with powdered sugar glaze while still warm or dust with powdered sugar when cool. Makes 1 loaf.

Almond Biscotti

2 c. flour
1 t. baking powder
¼ t. salt
1 c. sugar
4 eggs
2 T. Amaretto liqueur
1 T. lemon juice
2 t. grated lemon peel
2 c. coarsely chopped almonds, about 9 oz.

Combine dry ingredients and set aside. Beat sugar and 3 eggs together until light and lemon colored, about 3 minutes. Mix in liqueur, juice and peel. Beat in dry ingredients and stir in almonds. Mixture will be very sticky. Spray large baking sheet with non-stick coating. By spoonfuls transfer dough to baking sheet forming 2 14-inch long strips. Using floured hands shape each strip into 2½-inch wide log. Whisk remaining egg and brush over top of logs. Bake in a 350 degree oven for about 30 minutes. Logs should be light golden and firm to touch. Transfer to cutting board and using a serrated knife, cut into ¾-inch thick slices. Return slices to baking sheet cut side down and bake 6 minutes. Turn slices over and bake 5-6 minutes more. Transfer to wire rack and cool completely. Can be stored in airtight container for a week. Makes about 40.

Hazelnut Biscotti

3 c. flour
2 t. baking powder
½ t. salt
3 eggs
1 c sugar
¼ c. butter or margarine, melted
¼ c. olive oil
1½ t. vanilla
1 t. grated orange peel
1 c. hazelnuts, toasted, peeled and chopped

Combine dry ingredients and set aside. Mix together eggs, sugar, butter or margarine, oil, vanilla and peel. Beat until smooth and stir in flour mixture and nuts. Grease a large baking sheet and place dough on sheet, forming into a 16x4-inch log. Bake at 325 degrees until tester inserted in center comes out clean, about 30 minutes. Cool 15 minutes and leave oven on. Use serrated knife to cut into ½-inch thick slices. Place cut side down on baking sheet and return to oven for 10-12 minutes. Turn over and bake 10-12 minutes longer. Cool. Makes about 24.

Easter Egg Biscotti

1 c. shortening
1½ c. sugar
4 eggs
5 t. baking powder
1 t. salt
2 t. vanilla
1 c. milk
6 c. flour
hard cooked eggs, plain or dyed
powdered sugar glaze

Sugar Glaze
2 c. powdered sugar
2-3 T. milk or orange juice
1 t. vanilla
food coloring, if desired

Preheat oven to 350 degrees. Cream together shortening and sugar. Beat in eggs. Add next 4 ingredients and blend until smooth. Stir in flour 2 c. at a time. Dough should be pliable. If dough is too sticky add a little more flour. Take a piece of dough about the size of a large egg and place on a greased baking sheet. Indent middle slightly and then place an egg in the center, pressing down slightly. It should look like a nest. Continue with remaining dough allowing about 2-3-inches in between as they grow. You can fit 6-8 on a large baking sheet. Bake 20–25 minutes or until browned on the bottom. Cool on wire rack before drizzling with frosting. Makes 24-30.

Sugar Glaze
Mix together until smooth and of drizzling consistency.

Chapter 21:
Cookies, Cookies and More Cookies

Cookie Baking Know How

Types of Cookies

Bar: Spread or pressed into pans, baked and cut into squares

Drop: Soft dough dropped or spooned onto baking sheet, very quick and easy

Rolled: Dough is normally chilled then rolled out on wax paper or floured surface, cut into shapes

Refrigerator: Dough is rolled into logs, usually chilled and then sliced and baked

Pressed: Pressed through a machine into shapes or strips, usually very rich

Molded: Sturdy dough shaped by hand and often decorated later

Ingredients

Butter is usually best and never use diet margarine unless the recipe was specifically designed to use it.

Use only pure granulated sugar when recipes call for "sugar". Some less expensive brands are a sucrose and dextrose blend and may cause crisp cookies to be soft. This type of sugar also cannot be used in jelly recipes.

All-purpose flour is best although you can use some whole wheat pastry flour. You'll need to experiment a little, substituting about ¼ of the regular flour for the whole wheat pastry flour. Some recipes may react better than others to the higher fiber flour. Avoid regular whole wheat flour and don't use flour labeled as bread flour.

Eggs means large eggs unless otherwise stated and should be used at room temperature if possible.

Baking

Check cookies at minimum time listed in recipe. If cookies are browning on the bottom too quickly but not fully baked try doubling the cookie sheets. It will give you a little more insulation on the bottom and costs far less than buying air-bake cookies sheets.

Don't open the oven any more than needed and close promptly. Every peek causes the temperature to drop 25 degrees and will add to the bottom heat the cookies endure as the oven re-heats itself.

Don't place cookies too close to the edge of pans with sides. They radiate heat and can burn cookie edges. Leave about 1½-2-inches or turn the pan over and bake on the bottom. There will be no sides and you can bake closer to the edge of the pan.

Shiny pans are better for cookies and dark pans are better for breads.

Grease pans with solid shortening or butter (when baking temperatures are less than 375 degrees) or use non-stick spray. Unless called for don't use oil it will sometime stick.

Note: Don't grease pans unless the recipe calls for you to do so. Cookies baked on greased sheets will spread out more so allow more space between dough.

Storing and Freezing

To store crisp cookies place in a container with a loose-fitting lid or cover lightly with foil. Sealing crisp cookies up can sometimes make them get soggy. In humid weather, however you might want to keep them in sealed containers in the freezer and just remove a few to defrost as needed.

Soft cookies should always be stored in containers with tight fitting lids to prevent hardening. In humid weather place them between layers of wax paper to prevent sticking.

If you want to mail cookies avoid crisp and frosted types. Soft cookies travel best.

Both raw cookie dough and baked cookies can be frozen. If you have the freezer space it can be a great help to get some of your holiday baking out of the way ahead of time.

Dough can be frozen 6-9 months. Wrap in plastic wrap and place in freezer bags. Always label and date the package. Defrost in refrigerator and bake as directed.

Cookies can be frozen up to a year, but will begin to lose some of their flavor after 6 months. Use sturdy container and place layers of plastic wrap between cookies to prevent drying out. You should defrost cookies in their container, with the lid on to keep the cookies from getting soggy. When thawing there will be condensation on the package. If you take the cookies out of their container while frozen condensation will form on the cookies. Not so much of a problem with crisp cookies, but soft cookies are very moist and tend to get wet if defrosted unwrapped. If you only want to remove some of the cookies you can just place them in a bag and leave seal it up. Leave them to thaw on the counter and any condensation will form on the bag.

Extra Notes

Remember: Your cookies are only as good as the ingredients you use. Dried fruits should be moist and fresh. Nuts should be stored in a freezer or refrigerator until ready to use. Make sure they have not gotten stale or rancid. Taste one to be sure. If nuts don't taste fresh, pitch them and buy fresh. Nuts should stay fresh in the fridge for 3-6 months and frozen for up to a year (some will stay fresh a bit longer, so taste to be safe).

Before starting always make sure you have all the ingredients out and ready to use,

To save time around the holidays I like to do all my mixing in one evening (or afternoon) and then refrigerate or freeze the dough for baking on another day. I can make a dozen batches or dough at one time then put away all the mixing bowls and ingredients. If I am doing cookies that require decorating after baking I will often do that on yet another day to keep any one job as simple as possible. Remember, with the exception of bar cookies, most cookies bake for very short times and over bake before you know it. When baking them I like to have as few distractions as possible and always use a timer.

Snow People

Dough
3½ c. flour
1 t. baking powder
1 c. butter or margarine, softened
1 (8 oz. package) cream cheese, softened
2 c. sugar
1 egg
1 t. vanilla
¼ t. almond extract

Decorations
mini chocolate chips or mini M&Ms
kisses or mini peanut butter cups, halved

Frosting
2 c. powdered sugar
few drops green food coloring
milk
extra powdered sugar for sprinkling

Mix dry ingredients and set aside. Cream together butter and cream cheese until smooth. Beat in sugar until light and fluffy. Beat in egg and flavorings then stir in dry ingredients. Chill dough overnight. For each snow person rolls out 3 balls of dough1-inch, ¾-inch and ½-inch in diameter. Place balls in descending order on ungreased baking sheet. Press together lightly. Leave 2-inches between cookies. Use 2 mini chocolate chips for eyes in smallest ball and use either chips or M&Ms for buttons (2 on largest ball and 1 in medium). Bake in a preheated 325 degree oven for about 18 minutes or until edges are firm and bottoms are lightly browned. Cool on baking sheet 1 minute then remove to rack to finish cooling. Combine powdered sugar with green food coloring and just enough milk to make a frosting that can be piped. Use a little dab of frosting to attach either a chocolate kiss (unwrapped) or half of a peanut butter cup as a hat. Pipe a small amount of frosting to form a scarf. Dust cookies with a little extra powdered sugar. Makes 48.

Roscoe Village Gingerbread Cookies

2 c. flour
2 t. baking soda
1 t. cinnamon
¾ t. ginger (fresh grated preferred)
½ t. cloves
¼ t. salt
1 c. sugar, plus extra for rolling
¾ c. shortening
¼ c. molasses
1 egg

Mix together dry ingredients and set aside. Beat together sugar with shortening, molasses and egg until light. Stir in dry ingredients and roll dough into 1-inch balls. Roll balls in additional sugar. Place 2-inches apart on ungreased baking sheet. Bake in a preheated 350 degree oven for 10-12 minutes. Edges should look dry. Cool on sheet for a few minutes and then move to rack. Makes about 36.

Puppy Kibble

12 oz. chocolate chips
1 c. peanut butter
2 sticks margarine or butter
1 (13 oz. box) Crispix cereal
2 c. powdered sugar

In saucepan melt together chocolate chips, peanut butter margarine over low heat. Stir until smooth. Place cereal in large bowl and pour over chocolate mixture. Using large spoon gently toss mixture until cereal is well coated. Place mixture on baking sheets or large trays to cool. Put cooled mixture in clean bowl and sprinkle with powdered sugar stirring until coated. Mixture resembles dog kibble. Store in a cool, dry place.

Thumbprint Cookies

½ c. shortening (part butter or margarine)
¼ c. brown sugar
1 egg, separated
½ t. vanilla
1 c. flour
¼ t. salt
¾ c. finely chopped nuts
jelly, preserves

Mix shortening, sugar, egg yolk and vanilla and blend until smooth. Stir in flour and salt. Roll teaspoonfuls of dough into balls. Dip in the reserved egg white and then roll in the nuts. Place on ungreased baking sheet and make in indent with your finger or a spoon in the middle of each cookie. Bake in a preheated 350 degree oven 10-12 minutes and cool on rack. Fill indent with jelly or preserves. Makes 3 dozen cookies.

Jan Hagel

1 c. butter or margarine
1 c. sugar
1 egg, separated
2 c. flour
½ t. cinnamon
1 T. water
½ c. finely chopped nuts

Lightly grease jellyroll pan. Mix butter, sugar and egg yolk then stir in flour and cinnamon. Pat into pan. Beat egg white with water until frothy and spread over dough. Sprinkle on nuts and bake in a 350 degree oven for 20-25 minutes or until lightly browned. Cut immediately into tiny strips, makes about 50.

Buckeyes

1½ lb. powdered sugar
1½ c. peanut butter
2 sticks softened margarine
candy making chocolate (available at many grocery stores) or use dip recipe found in chocolate fans

Mix together sugar, peanut butter and margarine. Chill. Roll into balls, flatten slightly. Dip in melted chocolate to cover about ¾ of the surface. Using a toothpick or fondue fork makes this job a lot easier. Allow to harden on wax paper. Store in a cool place. Can be frozen.

Sugar Cookies

1 c. butter or margarine
1 c. sugar
1 egg
1 t. vanilla
3 c. flour
2 t. baking powder
3 T. milk
extra sugar for sprinkling, if desired
royal icing, **next recipe**

Beat butter and sugar until fluffy. Beat in egg and vanilla. Combine dry ingredients and add to butter mixture. Beat in milk. Heat oven to 375 degrees. Roll dough on lightly floured surface to about 1/3-inch thickness. Cut out with lightly floured cutters and sprinkle with sugar or colored sugar if you like and if you are not going to frost them. Bake on an ungreased baking sheet for 10-12 minutes. Cool on baking sheet 3 minutes before placing on wire rack to cool completely. Frost when cooled. Makes about 4 dozen.

Decorating your cookies
You can use tube of pre-made frosting or you can tint canned frosting, however the best way is to use royal icing. Because royal icing contains egg whites it gets hard. Cookies have a smooth appearance and can be stacked.

You can also use colored sugar and sprinkles and mini chocolate chips for eyes.

Royal Icing

1 lb. powdered sugar
½ t. cream of tartar
5¼ t. egg white powder
6 T. water
½ t. vanilla, optional
assorted food colorings

In large mixing bowl combine dry ingredients and mix well. Add water and vanilla and beat until light and fluffy, about 10 minutes. Divide into small bowls and tint each batch as needed. Keep bowl covered with a damp towel while waiting to use so frosting will not dry out.

ALWAYS USE PASTUERIZED EGG WHITES OR POWDERED EGGS WHITES TO PREVENT SAMONELLA.

Holiday Chocolate Fans

1 lb. phyllo dough, thawed
1 c. butter or margarine, melted
12 oz. chocolate chips
2 T. shortening
1 c. finely chopped nuts or coconut, pistachios are extra nice

Remove phyllo from box, still rolled up and cut crosswise into 5-6 equal pieces. Keep unused dough covered in a damp towel to prevent drying out. Take one piece of dough and open it up, cutting it in half crosswise. Take 1 sheet and brush with butter. Place another sheet on top and brush again with butter. Place third piece of dough on top and butter again. Starting at short end begin to fold the dough in ¾-inch folds, accordion style. Pinch together at one end and fan out the dough at the other. It should look like a little fan. Place on ungreased baking sheet and repeat with remaining dough. Bake at 375 degrees for 5 minutes. Cool. Melt chocolate and shortening together in microwave or on top of double boiler. Stir to smooth. Dip tip of wide end of fans in melted chocolate and then in the nuts or coconut. Place on a rack to cool and harden. Makes about 65 fans. Can be frozen.

Cream Wafers

1 c. butter or margarine
1/3 c. heavy whipping cream
2 c. flour
extra fine or granulated sugar

Frosting
¼ c. butter or margarine, softened
¾ c. powdered sugar
1 T. milk
1 t. vanilla
food coloring, if desired

Mix butter or margarine, cream and flour well. Wrap and chill at least an hour. Roll chilled dough 1/8-inch thick on lightly floured board. Cut out into 1½-inch rounds or even little hearts or stars. Transfer cookies to a sheet of wax paper heavily coated with extra fine or granulated sugar and coat both sides. Place on an ungreased baking sheet and prick each cookie 4 times with a fork. Bake at 375 degrees 7-9 minutes until lightly browned and puffy. Cool on rack. Mix frosting ingredients. Put 2 cookies together with frosting to make "sandwiches".

Russian Teacakes

1 c. butter or margarine
½ c. powdered sugar, plus extra for coating
1 t. vanilla
2¼ c. flour
¼ t. salt
¾ c. finely chopped nuts, nearly ground

Mix butter, ½ c. sugar and vanilla well. Stir flour and salt together and then add to butter mixture. Mix well and stir in nuts. Wrap dough and chill. Heat oven to 375 degrees. Roll dough into 1-inch balls and place 1-inch apart on ungreased baking sheet. Bake 10-12 minutes. Cookies should be lightly browned on the bottom. While still warm, roll cookies in powdered sugar. Dust again with sugar once cooled. Makes about 4 dozen.

Snickerdoodles

1 c. shortening
1½ c. sugar
2 eggs
2¾ c. flour
2 t. cream of tartar
1 t. baking soda
¼ t. salt
2 T. sugar
2 t. cinnamon

Mix shortening, sugar and eggs. Combine next 4 ingredients and add to egg mixture. Combine sugar and cinnamon in shallow bowls. Roll dough in 1-inch balls and roll in cinnamon sugar. Place 2-inches apart on ungreased baking sheet and bake in a preheated 375 degree oven for 9-11 minutes. Makes 6 dozen.

Pecan Tassels

Dough
3 sticks butter or margarine
8 oz. cream cheese, softened
3 c. flour

Filling
3 eggs
1 c. light or dark corn syrup
1 c. sugar
2 T. butter or margarine, melted
1 t. vanilla
1¼ c. pecans or walnuts, coarsely chopped

Mix all dough together and chill well before using.

Combine all filling ingredients, except nuts. Set aside until ready to use.

To make cookies: press a small amount of dough into a mini muffin pan and press to coat the pan evenly and thinly. There is no easy way to say this. Practice makes perfect when it comes to these cookies. After a few thousand, well, hundred you'll get pretty quick at making the dough shells. Sprinkle a little of the nuts in the bottom of the shell and pour in prepared filling about 7/8 full. Sprinkle with a few more nuts and bake in a preheated 350 degree oven for 20-25 minutes. Makes about 4 dozen.

Hint: make a few first to make sure that you don't over fill them or that you make the shells too thick or thin. Better to make 3 or 4 than 2 dozen before you find your filling bubbling over in the oven.

Foldovers

tassel dough, see recipe
assorted fruit pie fillings
powdered sugar

Roll out chilled dough into squares or circles. Spoon a little fruit filling into the center and pinch 2 ends or corners together. Bake in 350 degree oven for about 12 minutes, or until golden on edges. Cool and dust with sugar.

Versatile Butter Cookies

1 c. butter or margarine
1 c. sugar
1 egg
1 t. vanilla
2¼ c. flour
1 t. baking powder
¼ t. salt

Beat sugar and butter together until fluffy and then beat in egg and vanilla. Combine dry ingredients and stir into butter mixture. Chill dough at least a couple of hours. Roll dough into ¾-1-inch balls and roll in sugar, sprinkles or nuts. Place 2-inches apart on ungreased baking sheet and bake in a preheated 375 degree oven for 8-10 minutes. Cookies will flatten somewhat. Makes about 6 dozen cookies.

Variations: You can bake plain cookies and then dip cooled cookies in melted chocolate and then in chopped nuts or sprinkles.

Form into balls and place on baking sheet then press a nutmeat into the center of each. When cool you can drizzle with a small amount of melted chocolate or glaze.

Chocolate Peanut Clusters

12 oz. chocolate chips
1 can sweetened condensed milk
2 c. crispy rice cereal
1 c. peanuts

In microwave safe dish, melt chocolate and stir in milk. Add cereal and nuts and drop by teaspoonfuls on wax paper lined baking sheet. Chill until firm then store in a closed container at room temperature. Makes about 40 candies.

Cookie-Candies

1 c. butter or margarine
¾ c. powdered sugar
1 T. vanilla
2 c. flour
½ c. rolled oats
½ c. chocolate chips
¼ c. milk
finely chopped nuts
assorted sprinkles
shredded coconut

Cream together butter, sugar and vanilla. Stir in flour and oats. Shape teaspoonfuls of the dough into different shapes like rounds, ovals, cones cubes etc. Try to make them look like little candies. They will hold their shape very well while baking. Bake in a 325 degree oven for 20-25 minutes on an ungreased baking sheet. Cool. In microwave safe dish combine chocolate and milk and melt. Dip tops of cookies in chocolate mixture and then in one of the toppings you have. Chocolate topping will harden up after a while. Makes about 4 dozen.

Martha Merrick's Shortbread

1 c. sugar, plus extra for sprinkling
2 c. butter or margarine
4 c. flour

Cream together sugar and butter. Stir in flour and press into 9x13-inch baking dish. Sprinkle with extra sugar and cut into squares. Bake in a 300 degree oven for an hour or until light brown around edges. Re-cut while warm. Makes 4 dozen.

Chinese Almond Cookies

¾ c. sugar
¾ c. softened butter or margarine
1 egg
2 T. water
1 t. baking powder
1 t. almond extract
¼ t. salt
2½ c. flour
whole almonds, about 1/3 c.

Combine all ingredients except flour and nuts and beat until smooth. Stir in flour. Shape dough into 1-inch balls and place 2-inch apart on lightly greased baking sheet. Dip bottom of buttered glass in sugar and use it to flatten cookies a little. Press an almond into the center of each. Bake in a 350 degree oven for 8-12 minutes. Cookies should be firm to the touch, but not brown. Makes 3-4 dozen.

Hazelnut Ovals

¾ c. butter, softened
½ c. brown sugar
1¾ c. flour
¾ c. hazelnuts, skinned and lightly toasted, chopped
30 additional whole hazelnuts, toasted and split in half

Beat together butter and sugar. Beat in flour and stir in nuts. On lightly floured surface roll dough into a 15-inch log and wrap in wax paper. Chill 30 minutes. Slice dough in ¼-inch thick slices and place on lightly greased baking sheet. Press nut half in center of each cookie. Bake in preheated 350 degree oven for 15-18 minutes. Makes 60.

Santa Claus Cookies

1 c. granulated sugar
½ c. shortening
2 T. milk
1 t. grated lemon or orange peel
1 egg
2 c. flour
1 t. baking powder
½ t. baking soda
½ t. salt
miniature marshmallows
red sugar
raisins or chocolate chips
red cinnamon candies or red mini M&Ms
shredded coconut

Creamy Frosting
1½ c. powdered sugar
½ t. vanilla
2-3 T. water

Cream together first 5 ingredients. Stir in flour, baking powder, baking soda and salt. Shape dough into 1¼-inch balls and place 2-inches apart on ungreased baking sheet. Flatten cookies with bottom of glass bottomed lightly buttered and dipped in sugar. Bake in preheated 400 degree oven for 8-10 minutes or until edges are light brown. Cool. Spread each cookie with a little frosting and place a marshmallow on cookie for tassel of Santa's hat. Sprinkle red sugar on top third of cookie for hat and add 2 raisins or chips for eyes in middle third of cookie. Add cinnamon candy or M&M for nose. Coconut is sprinkled on bottom third for beard. Do one cookie at a time so frosting will not dry out too quickly. Makes about 1½ dozen.

Creamy Frosting
Beat all together until of spreading consistency.

Oatmeal Chocolate Chip Cookies

1 c. shortening
1 c. brown sugar
½ c. sugar
1 t. vanilla
2 eggs
1½ c. flour
1 t. salt
1 t. baking soda
2 c. oatmeal
12 oz. chocolate chips

Cream together shortening and sugars. Add vanilla and eggs and blend well. Stir in dry ingredients then add chips. Drop by heaping teaspoons on greased baking sheet and bake in a 350 degree oven for 8-10 minutes.

Chocolate Sparkles

1 c. butter or margarine, softened
1¼ c. sugar
2 eggs
2 oz. unsweetened chocolate, melted
½ t. vanilla
2 2/3 c. flour
2 t. cream of tartar
1 t. baking soda
½ t. salt
¼ c. sugar

Cream together butter and sugar. Beat in eggs, chocolate and vanilla. Stir in next four ingredients. Chill dough. Shape dough into 1-inch balls and roll in ¼ c. sugar. Place about 2-inches apart on ungreased baking sheet. Bake in a preheated 400 degree oven for 8-10 minutes. Makes 5-6 dozen.

Lemon Squares

1 c. flour
½ c. butter or margarine
¼ c. powdered sugar
2 eggs
1 c. sugar
2 T. lemon juice
½ t. baking powder
¼ t. salt

Mix together flour, butter or margarine and powdered sugar and press into the bottom of an 8x8-inch pan. Bake in a 350 degree oven for 20 minutes. Beat together remaining ingredients and pour over baked crust. Return to oven for 20-25 minutes or until golden and puffed. Cool. Cut. Makes 16 squares.

Viennese Shortbread

1 c. butter or margarine
½ powdered sugar
½ t. vanilla
2 c. flour
¼ t. baking powder

Mocha Filling
2/3 c. powdered sugar
2 T. butter or margarine, softened
1 t. instant coffee dissolved in 1 t. boiling water

Heat oven to 375 degrees. Cream together butter, sugar and vanilla. Blend in flour and baking powder. Using medium star design of cookie press to make 3-inch strips on ungreased baking sheet. Bake about 7 minutes, or until very lightly browned. Cool and then put two cookies together with mocha filling.

Note: You can make these cookies in almost any cookie press design that is symmetrical. I have made flowers, trees and stars among others. Makes about 2 dozen double cookies.

Mocha Filling
Beat all ingredients together until smooth. Add a few drops of water if too dry.

Candy Cane Cookies

1 c. shortening (half butter or margarine)
1 c. powdered sugar
1 egg
1½ t. vanilla extract
1 t. vanilla
2½ c. flour
1 t. salt
½ t. red food coloring
½ c. granulated sugar
crushed candy canes or other peppermint candies, optional

Heat oven to 375 degrees. Mix together shortening, sugar, egg and flavorings well. Stir in flour and salt and divide dough in half. Tint half the dough with the food coloring and leave the other half plain. Using 1 t. of dough roll out 4-inch strip of dough in one color and repeat with the other. Lay side by side and twist together. Bend over top to form a cane. Roll out 1 cookies at a time as pre-rolled strips tend to dry out and crack when shaped. Place about an-inch apart on ungreased cookies sheet and bake about 9 minutes, or until lightly browned. While still warm sprinkle with sugar and some crushed candy, if you like. Makes about 4 dozen cookies.

Sandbakelser (Sand Tarts)

1/3 c. blanched almonds, ground
4 un-blanched almonds, ground
¾ c. butter or margarine
¾ c. sugar
1 egg white
1¾ c. flour

Mix all ingredients, except flour until smooth. Stir in flour and chill. Heat oven to 350 degrees. Press dough into tiny fluted molds. Dough should be in a thin layer. Place filled pans on baking sheet and bake for 12-15 minutes. Gently tap cookies out of molds. Makes 3½ dozen. Cookies are crispy and can be filled with jam, lemon curd or pie filling just before serving. Unfilled shells should be served upside down to show detail of design.

Butterscotch Lace Cookies

1 c. butter or margarine, melted
1½ c. brown sugar
2¼ c. rolled oats
½ t. salt
1 T. molasses, optional
3 T. flour
1 egg, lightly beaten
1 t. vanilla

Mix sugar and butter and pour over oats. Allow to stand at room temperature overnight. Heat oven to 375 degrees. Stir in remaining ingredients. Drop dough by teaspoonfuls on heavily greased cookie sheet 2-inches apart. Bake 5-7 minutes. Cookies spread. Allow to firm on cookies sheet a few minutes before removing. Makes 6 dozen. Cookies are thin a crisp and do not come out right in humid weather.

Death by Chocolate Cookies

1½ c. flour
½ c. cocoa
1 t. baking soda
1/8 t. salt
8 oz. semi-sweet chocolate, melted
4 oz. unsweetened chocolate, melted
1½ c. brown sugar
1½ sticks butter or margarine, softened
3 eggs
1 t. vanilla
2 c. chocolate chips

Preheat oven to 325 degrees. Sift together dry ingredients and set aside. Beat together sugar and butter, beat in eggs and vanilla and stir in melted chocolates. Stir in dry ingredients and chips. Drop rounded spoonfuls (2 T. per cookie) on lightly greased baking sheet. Bake 18-22 minutes. Good sizes cookies.

Craisin Nut Cookies

1 c. shortening
1 c. butter or margarine
1½ c. sugar
1½ c. brown sugar
3 eggs
1 T. grated orange peel
5 c. flour
1½ t. each baking soda and salt
2 c. chopped nuts
1 (6 oz.) package Craisins (sweetened dried cranberries)

Cream together first 6 ingredients and blend until smooth. Combine flour with soda and salt and add to sugar mixture. Stir in nuts and Craisins. Drop walnut sized balls on an ungreased cookie sheet about 2-inches apart. Bake in a preheated 350 degree oven for about 8-10 minutes or until golden brown. Makes about 7 dozen.

Lemon Meltaways

Dough
1¼ c. flour
¾ c. butter, softened
½ c. cornstarch
1/3 c. powdered sugar
1 T. lemon juice
1 t. grated lemon peel

Frosting
¾ c. powdered sugar
¼ c. butter, softened
1 t. lemon juice
1 t. grated lemon peel

In large bowl combine all dough ingredients and mix well. Divide dough in half and roll each half into an 8-inch roll. Wrap in plastic wrap and chill until firm, 1-2 hours. Slice chilled dough into ¼-inch slices and place 2-inches apart on a cookie sheet. Bake in a 350 degree oven for 8-12 minutes, or until cookies are set, but not brown. Cool completely on a rack. Combine frosting ingredients and beat until light and fluffy. Frost cooled cookies. Makes 4 dozen.

Chapter 22:
Chocolate Lover's Cookbook

Chocolate Know-How

Unsweetened chocolate is as the name implies, pure chocolate with no added sugar.

Bittersweet chocolate is sweetened a little, also called semi-sweet chocolate, but there are no guidelines for how much sugar is used. There is also more cocoa butter than in unsweetened chocolate. Chips tend to be sweeter than bars sold for baking. Sometimes also called dark chocolate. All may be used interchangeably in cooking.

Milk chocolate is also chocolate, but has more cocoa butter, sugar and milk or cream. Smooth and creamy it is also lighter in color and milder.

Cocoa is pure chocolate with most of the cocoa butter removed. It is used to make hot cocoa and in baking. Sometimes you will see it labeled Dutch process or European style. These cocoas have been treated to neutralize some of the acids and are less bitter. They are also darker and more reddish.

To substitute cocoa for unsweetened chocolate in a recipe combine 3 T. of cocoa and 1 T. of fat.

White chocolate isn't chocolate at all because it contains no chocolate. Some brands contain cocoa butter for better flavor. They are often called vanilla chips or white baking bars.

After chocolate is melting take care not to let water touch it. It will change textures and often be ruined for cooking. This is sometimes a problem when using a double boiler. If milk or cream is being added to chocolate during melting add before applying heat to insure proper texture.

Unsweetened chocolate can be turned into semi-sweet chocolate by adding 1 T. of sugar to each melted ounce. Three oz. of unsweetened chocolate and 3 T. of sugar will equal 4 oz. of semi-sweet chocolate.

Store chocolate at room temperatures, away from heat sources. Ideal temperatures are from 60-78 degrees. The white film that sometimes forms on chocolate is due to fat rising to the surface. Not pretty but harmless.

When cooking with chocolate always wear brown.

Chocolate Pecan Pie

1 unbaked pie crust
1 c. pecan halves
1 c. chocolate chips
1 c. corn syrup
½ c. sugar
½ stick butter
3 eggs, beaten
1 t. vanilla

Place nuts and chips in crust and set aside. Heat together syrup, sugar and butter and boil 2 minutes. Cool a little then stir in eggs and vanilla and pour over nuts. Bake in a preheated 375 degree oven for 45 minutes.

Flourless Chocolate Mousse Cake

½ c. each sugar and water
1 stick butter
12 oz. semi-sweet chocolate
6 eggs
¼ dark rum or other liqueur

Butter an eight-inch cake pan and line with parchment. In saucepan heat together water and sugar until they boil. Stir in butter and bring to boil. Remove from heat and stir in chocolate until melted. Beat in eggs until smooth and stir in rum. Pour batter into prepared pan and place pan in a roasting pan. Pour boiling water into roaster to come up sides of pan 1-inch. Bake in a preheated 325 degree oven for 45 minutes. Cool, invert onto plate.

Serve cake topped with whipped cream and decorate with raspberries, other fresh fruit or even toasted nuts. Dense and rich this cake serves 8-10.

Princess Brownies

1 package family size brownies
1 (8 oz. package) cream cheese, softened
1/3 c. sugar
1 egg
1 t. vanilla

Prepare batter according to package directions. Cream together cream cheese and sugar. Beat in egg and vanilla. In greased 9x13-inch pan spread brownie batter, reserving ½ c. Spread cream cheese mixture over brownie batter and spoon remaining batter on top. Cut through several times with a knife to get a marble effect. Bake at 350 degrees for 35-40 minutes. Cool and cut into squares.

Extra Extra Fudgy Brownies

4 oz. semi-sweet chocolate
1 stick butter or margarine
1 c. plus 2 T. sugar
3 eggs
7 T. flour
½ c. plus 2 T. chopped nuts

Heat oven to 325 degrees and grease an 8x8-inch pan. Melt chocolate and butter in microwave. Remove and let cool 5 minutes. Stir in sugar and beat 25 seconds with a mixer. Add eggs one at a time, mixing just until yolk is broken and egg is dispersed. Add flour on low speed and blend about 20 seconds. Stir in ½ c. of the nuts and spread batter in pan. Sprinkle with remaining nuts and bake about 25 minutes. Tester would emerge with a moist crumb. Cool 1 hour before cutting. Makes 9-12.

Frozen Mocha Cheesecake

1¼ c. chocolate cookie crumbs
¼ c. sugar
¼ c. butter or margarine, softened
8 oz. cream cheese
1 (14 oz. can) sweetened condensed milk
2/3 c. chocolate syrup
2 T. instant coffee crystals
1 t. hot water
1 c. whipping cream, whipped

Combine crumbs, sugar and butter and press into 9-inch spring form pan. Chill. Beat cheese until fluffy and beat in milk. Stir in syrup and dissolve coffee in water. Add to cheese mixture and fold in whipped cream. Pour into prepared crust and freeze until solid, at least 6 hours. Garnish with additional cookie crumbs if you like or with shaved chocolate. Keep leftovers frozen and use within a week for best flavor.

Fudge Cheesecake

Crust
1½ c. vanilla cookie crumbs
½ c. sugar
1/3 c. cocoa
½ c. melted butter or margarine

Filling
12 oz. chocolate chips
3 (8 oz. packages) cream cheese, softened
1 (14 oz. can) sweetened condensed milk
4 eggs
1 t. almond extract
1 t. vanilla
½ c. toasted slivered almonds

Crust
Combine all ingredients and press into the bottom of a 9-inch spring form pan. Bake in a 350 degree oven for 10 minutes. Set aside.

Filling
Melt chips over low heat and set aside. In bowl beat cheese until fluffy and beat in milk. Stir in chocolate, eggs and flavorings. Mix well and pour into crust. Bake in a 300 degree oven for 1 hour and 5 minutes or until set in center. Remove from oven and sprinkle with almonds. Cool and chill.

Hot Fudge Cinnamon Sauce

1 c. chocolate chips
2 T. butter or margarine
1 can sweetened condensed milk
dash salt
1 t. cinnamon
1 t. vanilla

In heavy saucepan, over medium heat, combine chocolate, butter, milk and salt. Heat, stirring constantly, until sauce has thickened, about 5 minutes. Remove from heat and stir in cinnamon and vanilla. Serve warm over ice cream. Makes about 2 cups.

Chocolate Chip Cake Mix Cookies

1 package cake mix (pudding in the mix recommended but not necessary)
½ c. margarine or butter, softened
1 egg
2 T. water
1 c. chocolate chips

Heat oven to 350 degrees. Combine all ingredients, except chips, in bowl and mix until well blended. Stir in chips. Shape dough into 1¼-inch balls and place 2-inches apart on ungreased baking sheet. Bake 9-12 minutes or until tops appear cracked. Cool 2 minutes before removing from baking sheets and cool on racks. Makes 32 cookies.

Note: I like to use a small ice cream scoop (about 1/3 c.) and I make about 16-18 large cookies. Bake 3-4 minutes longer. I can get 8 or 9 to a cookie sheet.

Chocolate Sorbet

12 oz. semi-sweet chocolate chips
3 c. water
1¾ c. sugar
1 T. instant coffee powder
1 t. cinnamon
dash of salt

Place chips in food processor. Meanwhile heat remaining ingredients to boiling. Slowly pour boiling liquid into running processor, blending until smooth. Scrape down sides of work bowl as needed. Chill. Process in ice cream machine. Transfer to container and freeze overnight. Or you can freeze in a shallow pan until solid. Soften a little than cut in chunks and puree in a food processor when ready to eat. Makes about 5 cups.

Hot Fudge Sauce

1 c. cocoa
¾ c. sugar
½ c. brown sugar
1/8 t. salt
1 c. heavy or whipping cream
½ c. butter or margarine cut into pieces
1 t. vanilla extract

In saucepan, stir together dry ingredients then stir in cream and butter. Heat to boiling and boil 1 minute. Remove from heat, cool 5 minutes and stir in vanilla. Makes 2½ cups.

Chocolate Chip Oatmeal Cherry Cookies

1 c. butter, softened
¾ c. sugar
¾ c. brown sugar
1 egg
1 t. vanilla
1½ c. flour
1 t. baking soda
1 c. oatmeal
1 c. chocolate chips
1 c. dried cherries
1 c. toffee chips

Cream together butter and sugars. Cream in egg and vanilla. Add flour and soda and cream until smooth. Stir in remaining ingredients, one at a time. Dough can be used right away, but should be chilled. Shape dough into logs about 1-inch across. Chill. Slice ½-¾-inch thick. Place on cookie sheet and bake in a preheated 350 degree oven for 8-10 minutes. Makes 2 dozen 3-inch cookies.

Chocolate Coconut Bowls

good quality semi-sweet chocolate
desiccated coconut
small balloons

Melt chocolate over simmering water. Meanwhile place coconut in bowl and blow up balloons to a diameter of about 4-inches. Remove chocolate from heat and dip bottom of balloons about 2-inches into chocolate. Allow excess to drip off and using your hands sprinkle coconut gently over wet chocolate surface. Place "bowls" on baking sheet and place in freezer for at least 30 minutes. Remove bowls from freezer one at a time. Pierce balloon and gently remove balloon and any remnants. Store in freezer until ready to use.

To serve you can scoop in any type of ice cream or sorbet, but you can also fill the bowls with any white or nearly white frozen confection. Soften first, then spoon in, level off and refreeze until ready to serve. Now the bowls look like little coconut halves. Garnish with mint sprigs, if desired.

No-Cook Fudge

4 c. sifted powdered sugar
8 oz. cream cheese, softened
4 oz. unsweetened chocolate, melted
½ c. chopped nuts
1 t. vanilla
dash of salt

Cream together sugar and cheese until smooth. Add remaining ingredients and mix well. Spread into a greased 8-inch square pan and chill several hours or overnight. Cut into squares and garnish with more nuts, if desired. Makes 1¾ lbs.

Easy Chocolate Glaze

6 T. butter
1 c. chocolate chips

Melt together over low heat, stirring often until smooth. Can be poured over cakes for a shiny coating or used on brownies, cookies, etc. Makes about 2/3 cup. Hardens as it sets.

Chocolate Cabbage Cake

This is probably the oddest cake you'll ever make, but it is easier than you might think and a real show stopper.

1 box chocolate cake mix
1 double recipe chocolate frosting
1½ lbs. melting chocolate, sold in some grocery stores and in candy-making stores.
6 or seven large cabbage leaves, washed and dried

Find 2 bowls that are about 1 quart each and are oven-proof. I use a stainless steel bowl and a Pyrex bowl. Grease and flour and set aside. Prepare cake mix according to package direction and divide batter in the 2 bowls. Bake until cake tests done, usually a little longer than the time given for 8-inch round pans. Cool 15 minutes and remove from pans. Prepare frosting and set aside. In double boiler or in microwave-safe dish melt chocolate, stirring often. Using a pastry brush paint the inside of 5 cabbage leaves with the chocolate, spreading evenly and leaving a ½-inch border on the edge of the leaves. Prop leaves to maintain their curve. These will be used on the cake. Paint the outside of the other leaves, laying them relatively flat to dry. These will be used on the platter. When chocolate has set-up gently peel the leaves away. In hot weather I put them in the fridge to harden quickly. The chocolate leaves sometimes break, but three or four good-sized leaves will be enough, or you can re-melt and reapply chocolate to more leaves.

OK here goes.

Hold one cake half in your hand round side up. Frost round side of cake and gently place frosted side down on platter. Frost top of cake and place second cake on top, flat side down. Frost rest of cake. Using extra frosting as glue start to attach the leaves to your round cake to resemble a head of cabbage. Press 3 leaves around cake, pressing lightly into place. Use broken pieces to fill in gaps around top of cake. Remaining leaves can be placed on the plate. Because of the imprint the cabbage leaves will leave on the chocolate the cake really looks like head of cabbage. Serves 12-15.

Aunt Josie's Ho Ho Cake

1 Duncan Hines dark chocolate cake mix

White Icing
5 T. flour
1¼ c. milk
1 c. sugar
½ c. shortening
½ c. margarine
1 t. vanilla

Chocolate Icing
3 packets choco-bake
1 stick margarine, melted
1 t. vanilla
3 c. powdered sugar
2½ T. hot water

Prepare cake according to package directions, baking in a jelly roll pan. Cool before frosting. Make white frosting by cooking flour, sugar and milk together in saucepan, stirring constantly, until thickened. Cool completely, then chill. Beat remaining ingredients together until smooth and fluffy. Beat in cooled custard until fluffy smooth. Frost cake. Chill.

For chocolate frosting mix all ingredients together and frost over white layer. Store cake in a cool place.

Chocolate Covered Goodies

Dipping a wide array of foods in chocolate can make an easy dessert or a terrific hostess gift. You can use semi-sweet chocolate for any of the following choices. For dipped fruits you can also use milk or dark chocolate.

Liquid lecithin is sold in health food stores and some drug stores as a dietary supplement. When added to melted chocolate it thins it out and makes it shinier. If you are using melting discs that are not real chocolate you do not need the lecithin, but you might want to add 1 or 2 T. of shortening to the discs to make them softer once set. You can also use the white "chocolate" sold as almond bark, chips, disc form and in bars in the baking aisle.

For every 6 oz. of semi-sweet chocolate add up to 1 T. of lecithin after the chocolate has melted, adding one teaspoon at a time. Use more for dipped fruit and less for items like leaves where a firmer end product is desirable.

Strawberries, other fruits
You can dip fresh berries or other fruits like candied pineapple, dried apricots, dried mango, dried papaya. Don't confuse this process with fondue. Since fondue is eaten right away fruits like bananas, fresh pineapple or cut up apples work in fondue but not for dipping. Using clean, cold berries will help the chocolate to set up faster. I sometimes chill dried and candied fruit, too to speed up the process.

Marshmallows (full size)
Spear onto a fondue fork and allow excess to drip off before setting on wax paper.

Nuts and easy candy
Clusters are the easiest way to coat nuts and raisins. Melt chocolate and add nuts or raisins to it stirring to coat well. Place mixture by spoonfuls on tray covered with wax paper. You can add mixed nuts or fruit and nuts and even mini marshmallows or coconut for super easy candy.

Potato chips
Place wax-paper lined baking sheets next to the chocolate and have unbroken chips within reach. Using small metal tongs hold onto a chip and dip in chocolate until coated. Pull out of chocolate and tap tongs on side of pan a couple of times to remove excess chocolate and to even up the coating. Place on prepared sheet and continue with rest of the chips. Keep chocolate over low heat during this time to keep thin.

Oreo's
Always a treat. Just hold cookie in a pair of small tongs and dip about 2/3 of the way down in the chocolate. Tap on pan side to remove excess chocolate and place on prepared sheet as you would for chips and fruit.

Pretzels
The process here is much like the chips, but I like to use a fondue fork to hold the pretzel and I let them set up on cooling racks. You can also sprinkle freshly dipped pretzels with nonpareils, if you like.

Chow Mein Noodles
Dump chow mein noodles into melted chocolate and stir to coat well. Drop by rounded spoonfuls onto waxed paper for tasty crunchy clusters.

Crisped Rice
You can use store-bought cereal for this candy, or you can buy special extra crispy rice at candy making stores. Add to melted chocolate and drop by rounded spoonfuls onto wax paper.

Granola
Treat like crisped rice. Just stir, spoon out and let set up for a different treat.

Graham Crackers
Break the crackers into halves or quarters and treat as you would the potato chips.

Frozen Bananas
One of the great treats of summer. Just peel ripe bananas and stick them on Popsicle sticks. For really big bananas you can cut them in half. Dip bananas in chocolate to cover and then roll in chopped nuts. You can set them directly in the freezer to set up and then wrap and keep frozen until ready to eat.

Leaves
Chocolate leaves can add elegance to any dessert, especially when paired with edible flowers. You can use lemon or lime leaves, available at florist shops or rose leaves and even fresh bay leaves. Sturdy leaves that are lined, but have a smooth texture work, but only use leaves that are non-toxic. Brush the back sides of the leaves with chocolate, being careful not to drip to the other side. When chocolate is set peel away the leaf and you will have a beautiful chocolate leaf.

Spoons
These make lovely little gifts and are easy to make. Get heavy duty plastic spoons in silver or gold. Dip just the bowl of the spoon in chocolate and allow excess to drip off. Lay curved side up on wax paper and set in fridge to set up. When set you can

wrap each spoon in a piece of cellophane tied with a ribbon on the stem.

Use your imagination to come up with other things to dip. Let's face it, most anything tastes better with chocolate.

Pretzel Kisses

midget pretzels
Hershey's kisses
M&M's

Line a baking sheet with foil and place pretzels on the foil, using only pretzels that have all three loops. Unwrap kisses and set one on top of each pretzel, balancing them in the middles. Place the tray in a 350 degree oven for 3-4 minutes, or until kisses just start to look wet and get glossy. Remove from oven and immediately place an M&M in the center of each softened kiss pressing down slightly. Cool before eating. These are especially nice with holiday color M&M's, or in pastels for baby showers.

Fudgy Buttons

2 T. butter or margarine
1½ t. cocoa
½ c. powdered sugar
½ t. milk
2 T. creamy peanut butter

In small saucepan or in microwave-safe dish melt butter. Add cocoa and stir well. Stir in sugar then add milk and stir until smooth. Mix in peanut butter. Drop by teaspoonfuls onto wax paper flatten tops to form 1-inch patties. Makes about 1½ dozen.

Chocolate Dipping Sauce

1 c. heavy cream
¼ c. milk
1½ t. instant coffee powder
¾ c. sugar
10 oz. semi-sweet chocolate
2 T. butter

Combine cream, milk and coffee powder in saucepan and heat until very warm. Add sugar and stir until sugar is melted. Add chocolate and butter and stir until melted, but do not allow to boil. Serve with fruit and cake squares for dipping, thin with cream, if needed. Makes 2 2/3 cups.

Cocoa Mint Hearts

9 c. powdered sugar
1 c. cocoa
½ c. butter, softened
½ c. water
2 t. peppermint extract

In large bowl combine ingredients until well blended. You can add more water, if needed, 1 t. at a time. Divide mixture into 2 pieces and shape in balls. Place each between sheets of wax paper and roll out to ¼-inch thickness. Cut out with tiny cutters and place on foil-lined tray. Chill several hours, then wrap up in colored foil or place in tiny candy bags. Makes 80.

Whoopie Pies

Cookies
2 c. flour
2 t. each baking soda and baking powder
½ t. salt
1 stick unsalted butter, at room temp.
1 c. packed brown sugar
1 t. vanilla
2 eggs
1/3 c. cocoa
¾ c. milk

Cream Filling
3 T. flour
1 c. milk
1 stick unsalted butter, at room temp.
2 t. vanilla
2¼ c. powdered sugar

Heat oven to 375 degrees. Line baking sheets with foil and coat with non-stick spray. Combine dry ingredients and set aside. Beat butter and sugar together until creamy. Beat in vanilla and eggs then beat in cocoa. Alternately beat in flour mixture and milk. Drop 2 T. of dough on prepared sheets for each cookie, spacing 3-inches apart. Shape into 2¼-inch rounds, trying to keep them even as they will be sandwich cookies later. Bake 12-14 minutes, cookies should spring back when touched lightly. Let sit on baking sheet 5 minutes then transfer to rack to cool.

Prepare filling: Combine flour and milk in saucepan until smooth. Heat over medium, stirring until thickened and bubbly. Cook 1 minute. Remove from heat and whisk in 2 T. of the butter. Place wax paper directly on surface of the mixture and let sit until cool to the touch about 45 minutes. Beat in remaining butter, vanilla and powdered sugar until smooth and fluffy.

Sandwich cookies together in pairs with about 2 T. of the filling. Store between wax paper in airtight container. Makes 15.

Chocolate Pound Cake

1 c. cocoa
2 c. flour
½ t. baking powder
1 t. salt
2 T. instant coffee powder
3 sticks butter
3 c. sugar
2 t. vanilla
5 eggs
1 c. buttermilk
¼ c. water

Preheat oven to 325 degrees. Grease and flour a 10-inch tube pan. Sift together dry ingredients and set aside. Cream butter with mixer until smooth. Add sugar slowly while beating. Beat at high speed for 5 minutes. Stir in vanilla and beat in eggs one at a time beating briefly after each addition. Beat in flour mixture alternately with the liquid. Beat until batter is smooth and pour into prepared pan. Bake in top third of oven for 1 hour and 20 minutes or until tester comes out clean. Let cake rest in pan 20 minutes before inverting onto plate.

Chocolate Angel Food Cake

2/3 c. cake flour
1/3 c. cocoa
1½ c. sugar, divided
12 large egg whites
1½ t. vanilla extract
1½ t. cream of tartar
½ t. salt

Preheat oven to 375 degrees. Sift flour, cocoa and ¾ c. sugar together 3 times and set aside. Beat egg whites in large bowl on low speed until foamy, about 5 minutes. Add vanilla, cream of tartar and salt and gradually increase speed to medium while beating in remaining ¾ c. sugar, one tablespoon at a time. This will take 5 minutes. Continue beating until stiff peaks form, about 2 minutes longer. Sift one third of flour mixture over egg mixture and fold in. Repeat 2 more times and pour prepares batter into ungreased 10-inch tube pan. Run a knife through to remove any large air pockets. Bake 35-40 minutes until cake springs bake when touched lightly. Invert pan onto funnel or bottle to cool. Remove from pan when cool. Serves 12.

Chocolate Shortbread

1 c. butter, room temperature
¾ c. sugar
2 c. flour
1/3 c. cocoa
¼ t. salt
8 oz. semi-sweet chocolate

Beat together butter and sugar until well blended. Mix together dry ingredients and slowly beat into butter mixture, stirring it in at the end. Line a cookie sheet with foil or parchment and press dough out on prepared sheet into a 12x6-inch rectangle that's about ½-inch thick. Bake in a 325 degree oven for 30 minutes. Cool on sheet 5 minutes. Trim edges to make straight and cut into 3x1-inch rectangles. Cool on rack. Melt chocolate and dip cookies in it. Place on wax paper until firm. Makes 24-28 bars.

Chocolate-Orange Scones

1½ c. baking mix, like Jiffy or Bisquick or homemade
1 T. grated orange peel
¾ c. heavy cream
½ c. milk chocolate chips or 3 oz. milk chocolate, chopped

Combine baking mix and orange peel in medium bowl. Stir in cream to make a soft dough that forms into a ball in the bowl. On floured surface gently knead in chocolate and press or roll dough to ¾-inch thickness. Cut into 2¼-inch rounds, re-rolling scraps. You should get 8. Place on and ungreased cookie sheet and bake in a preheated 425 degree oven for 8-10 minutes.

Double Chocolate Variation: Knead 3 T. of cocoa into dough with the chocolate chips.

Chocolate Shortcakes

2 c. flour
½ c. sugar
1/3 c. cocoa
1 t. baking powder
½ t. baking soda
1 c. chocolate chips
1 2/3-1¾ c. chilled whipping cream
melted butter
additional sugar

Preheat oven to 325 degrees. Combine dry ingredients in large bowl and stir in chips. Add just enough cream to form a dough firm enough to roll out. On well-floured surface and with well-floured hands press dough out to ¾-inch thickness. Run knife under dough to prevent sticking. Cut dough out with 2-2½-inch biscuit cutter or with fun shapes like stars or hearts. Re-press scraps and cut out more shortcakes. Depending on the size of the cutter you should get about 24 small shortcakes. Brush tops with butter and then sprinkle with sugar. Place sugar side down on baking sheets and butter and sugar the tops. Bake until shortcakes feel firm to the touch and tester comes out with a few moist crumbs. Serve with ice cream, fresh berries and whipping cream.

English Toffee Crunch

1½ c. sugar
2 sticks butter (not margarine)
3 T. water
1 T. light corn syrup
¾ lb. milk chocolate, either discs from a candy making supply store or Hershey bars
½ c. very finely chopped walnuts

Over low heat, stirring constantly, cook sugar, butter, water and corn syrup until mixture reaches hard crack stage (300-320 degrees). Pour onto ungreased jellyroll pan tilting quickly in all directions to get toffee as thin as possible. It hardens up unbelievably quickly so work fast. I like to warm the cookie sheet a little in the oven so it buys me a few extra seconds to thin out the toffee. Harden in fridge about five minutes or let stand at room temperature until cooled down. Melt chocolate in double boiler and spread half of it over toffee, spreading to edges. Sprinkle with half the nuts and return to fridge it harden chocolate. Turn toffee onto another sheet and coat the bottom with the remaining chocolate and nuts. Chill until chocolate hardens then break up into bite sized pieces.

Note: you can use even more chocolate if you like a thicker coating. Store in a cool, dry place in an airtight container. Makes 1½ lbs.

Chocolate Peanut Butter Pie

½ c. melted semi-sweet chocolate chips (about ¾ c. before melting)
1/3 c. peanut butter
2/3 c. cold sweetened condensed milk
1 1/3 c. cold heavy whipping cream
1 purchased chocolate graham cracker crust

Place chocolate in one bowl and peanut butter in another. Place half of the milk and half of the cream in each bowl. Beat with mixer until the thickness of mayonnaise. Alternately spoon mixtures into crust and run a knife through to swirl. Chill until set. Serves 8.

Chocolate Pecan Bars

1¼ c. flour
1 c. powdered sugar
½ c. cocoa
1 c. cold butter or margarine
1 (14 oz. can) sweetened condensed milk
1 egg
2 t. vanilla
1½ c. chopped pecans

Preheat oven to 350. In larger bowl combine dry ingredients and cut in butter or margarine to resemble coarse crumbs. Press firmly into bottom of 13x9-inch baking dish. Bake 15 minutes. Meanwhile, beat together milk, egg and vanilla. Stir in nuts and spread over chocolate layer. Bake 25 minutes, or until lightly browned. Cool, cut in bars and store, covered in fridge. Makes 2-3 dozen.

Chocolate Turtles

16 soft and chewy caramels
¼ c. chopped pecans
½ c. milk chocolate chips, melted
12 raisins
12 pecan halves, quartered (halved lengthwise and crosswise)

Knead caramels and chopped pecans together and divide into 12 balls. Press flat and stick a raisin in each for the head. Stick caramel disc on a fork and drizzle with chocolate, coating raisin, too. Place on wax paper and tuck 4 pieces of pecan in chocolate for feet. Allow to set up and remove from paper. Makes 12.

Mocha Brownies

5 oz. semi-sweet chocolate
1/3 c. butter or margarine
2/3 c. flour
½ t. salt
½ t. baking powder
4 eggs
1¼ c. sugar
2 t. vanilla
1¼ c. graham cracker crumbs, preferably chocolate
1 c. coarsely chopped nuts

Coffee Glaze
2 T. milk
1 T. butter or margarine
1 t. instant coffee powder
1½ c. powdered sugar

Melt together chocolate and butter. Sift together next 3 ingredients and set aside. Beat together eggs, sugar and vanilla and stir in all remaining ingredients and pour batter into a greased 9x9-inch pan. Bake in a 350 degree oven for 40-45 minutes. Glaze while hot. Cut into squares after cool.

Coffee Glaze
Heat together 2 T. milk, 1 T. butter or margarine and 1 t. instant coffee powder. Stir into 1½ c. powdered sugar and stir until smooth.

Chapter 23:
Cupcakes -
Little Cakes, Big Flavor

Chocolate Pecan Cupcakes

4 oz. semi-sweet chocolate
1 c. butter
1 c. all-purpose flour
1¾ c. sugar
4 eggs
1 t. vanilla extract
2 c. chopped pecans

Preheat oven to 325 degrees. Line 24 muffin cups with paper liners. In the top of a double boiler, combine chocolate and butter. Heat, stirring occasionally, until mixture is melted and smooth. Remove from heat and allow to cool to lukewarm. Sift flour and sugar together into a large bowl. With mixer on low speed, beat in eggs one at a time. Stir in chocolate mixture, vanilla and pecans. Fill muffin cups 2/3 full. Bake in the oven for 25 minutes. Do not over bake. Tops should be shiny but give slightly when touched. Makes 24.

Black and White Cupcakes

1 (18.25 oz. package) devil's food cake mix
1 (8 oz. package) cream cheese
1 c. sugar
1 c. mini semisweet chocolate chips

Preheat oven according to directions on package. Line muffin pans with paper liners. Prepare the cake mix according to package directions. In separate bowl, combine softened cream cheese and sugar. Fold in chocolate chips. Fill the cupcake papers 1/3 full with the chocolate cake mix. Top with the cream cheese mixture. Bake according to box instructions or until the cream cheese mixture just starts to turn a light golden color. Makes 30.

Note: I like to top these cupcakes with vanilla frosting on ½ and chocolate frosting on the other half.

Chip and Cream Filled Cupcakes

1 (18.25 oz. package) devil's food cake mix
4 oz. cream cheese
¼ c. sugar
1 egg
1 pinch salt
1 c. semisweet chocolate chips

Preheat oven to 350 degrees. Lightly grease muffin pans. Prepare cake mix according to package directions. Combine cream cheese and sugar, cream until light and fluffy. Add egg and salt, beating well. Spoon batter into greased muffin pans, filling 2/3 full. Drop a few chocolate morsels in the center and spoon 1 t. of the cream cheese mixture on top of the chocolate morsels. Bake at 350 degrees for 25 minutes. Let cupcakes cool before serving. Makes 24-30.

Peanut Butter Cupcakes

1½ c. brown sugar
½ c. shortening
1 c. peanut butter
2 eggs
1½ c. milk
1 t. vanilla extract
2½ c. all-purpose flour
1 t. baking soda
2 t. cream of tartar
1 pinch salt

Preheat the oven to 350 degrees. Line cupcake pans with paper liners, or grease and flour. In bowl, mix the brown sugar, shortening and peanut butter until light and fluffy. Beat in the eggs one at a time, then stir in the vanilla. Combine dry ingredients; stir into the batter alternately with the milk. Spoon into the prepared pans. Bake for 15 to 20 minutes in the oven, until the top of the cupcakes spring back when lightly pressed. Cool in the pan for at least 10 minutes before removing to a wire rack to cool completely. Makes 24.

Spicy Chocolate Zucchini Cupcakes

2 c. all-purpose flour
1 t. baking soda
½ t. salt
1 t. cinnamon
½ t. nutmeg
pinch of cloves
¼ c. unsweetened cocoa
½ c. butter, softened
½ c. olive oil
1 ½ c. sugar
2 eggs
½ c. buttermilk
1½ t. vanilla
2½ c. grated zucchini
1 c. chocolate chips

Preheat oven to 325 degrees. Grease and flour 18 muffin cups or use paper liners. Mix together the dry ingredients. Set aside. In a large bowl, cream together the butter, olive oil and sugar until light and fluffy. Beat in the eggs one at a time, then stir in the buttermilk and vanilla. Beat in the flour mixture, just until incorporated. Stir in the grated zucchini and chocolate chips. Pour batter into prepared pans. Bake in the preheated oven for 25 to 30 minutes, or until the top of the cupcakes springs back when lightly pressed. Cool in pans over a wire rack for at least 10 minutes before removing from baking cups. Makes 18.

"Twinkle" Cupcakes

If you grew up loving those cream-filled chocolate cupcakes - try these.

3 c. all-purpose flour
2 c. sugar
1/3 c. unsweetened cocoa
2 t. baking soda
1 t. salt
2 eggs
1 c. buttermilk
1 c. water
1 c. vegetable oil
2 t. vanilla

Cream Filling
¼ c. butter
¼ c. shortening
2 c. confectioners' sugar
1 pinch salt
3 T. milk
1 t. vanilla extract

Preheat oven to 375 degrees. Line muffin cups with paper liners. In a large bowl, mix together the flour, sugar, cocoa, baking soda and salt. Make a well in the center and pour in the eggs, buttermilk, water, oil and vanilla. Mix well. Fill each muffin cup half-full of batter. Bake in the preheated oven for 15 to 20 minutes, or until a toothpick inserted into the center of the cake comes out clean. Allow to cool. Make filling: In a large bowl, beat butter and shortening together until smooth. Blend in confectioners' sugar and pinch of salt. Gradually beat in milk and vanilla. Beat until light and fluffy. Fill a pastry bag with a small tip. Push tip through bottom of paper liner to fill each cupcake. Makes 36.

S'Mores Cupcakes

1 (18.25 oz. package) white or yellow cake mix
½ c. water
3 egg whites
24 milk chocolate candy kisses
about 1 c. Graham cracker crumbs
1 (7 oz. jar) marshmallow cream

Preheat oven to 350 degrees. Line 24 muffin cups with paper liners. Place about 1 t. of crumbs in the bottom of each liner. In a large bowl, combine the cake mix, water and egg whites. Beat for 2 minutes at high speed of an electric mixer. Divide batter evenly among paper lined cups, filling about 2/3 full. Place a chocolate kiss in each cupcake, pressing in lightly. Spoon 1 t. graham cracker crumbs onto each cupcake. Bake at 350 degrees for 18 to 25 minutes. Remove from the oven and top each cupcake with 1 t. marshmallow crème. To do this place marshmallow cream in a Pastry bag or plastic bag. Snip off a corner and squeeze some of the marshmallow on each cupcake. Return to oven for about 1 minute to melt slightly. Makes 24.

Ice Cream Cone Cupcakes

1 cake mix
1 box flat bottomed ice cream cones
1 can of frosting or two c. homemade frosting
candy sprinkles

Preheat oven to 350 degrees. Prepare cake batter according to package directions. Place about 24 cones in muffin tins to hold them up and fill 2/3 full with batter. Bake for about 20 minutes, or until cupcakes puff to top of cones. Test with a toothpick. Cool and frost to look like ice cream. Decorate with sprinkles. Makes about 24.

Apple Banana Cupcakes

2 c. all-purpose flour
1 t. baking soda
1 t. salt
1 t. cinnamon
¼ t. nutmeg
2/3 c. shortening
1 c. sugar
2 eggs
1 t. vanilla extract
¼ c. buttermilk
1 c. ripe bananas, mashed
2 apples, peeled, cored and shredded

Preheat oven to 375 degrees. Grease and flour 24 muffin cups, or use paper liners. Sift together the flour, baking soda, salt, cinnamon, and nutmeg. Set aside. In a large bowl, cream together the shortening and sugar until light and fluffy. Beat in the eggs one at a time, then stir in the vanilla and buttermilk. Beat in the flour mixture, mixing just until incorporated. Fold in the mashed bananas and shredded apples. Fill each muffin cup half full. Bake in the preheated oven for 20 to 25 minutes, or until a toothpick inserted into the center comes out clean. Allow to cool. Makes 24.

Note: I like these just sprinkled with a cinnamon combined with powdered sugar.

Black Forest Cupcakes

1 (18.5 oz. package) chocolate cake mix
2 containers whipped topping, thawed
1 (21 oz. can) cherry pie filling

Preheat oven according to box directions for cupcakes. Line 36 cupcake pans with cupcake liners. Mix cake according to package directions. Fill cupcake liners slightly less than half full. You want the cupcake to bake up close to level with the top of the liner. Bake according to package directions. Cool completely. After cupcakes are cooled completely, frost with a level layer of whipped topping. Spoon remaining topping into pastry bag fitted with a star decorating tip. Pipe around the edges of the cupcakes. Spoon a small amount of cherry pie filling in the center of each. Refrigerate and enjoy! Makes 36.

No-Bake Strawberry Cupcakes

¾ c. graham cracker crumbs
¼ c. chopped nuts
¼ c. butter, melted (½ a stick)
1 c. fresh strawberries, sliced thin
4 oz. cream cheese
1 (10½ oz. can) sweetened condensed milk
1 c. whipping cream, whipped just before starting

Line 12 muffin pans with paper or foil cup liners. In a medium bowl, combine graham cracker crumbs, chopped nuts and melted butter, mixing well to blend. Spoon mixture evenly into prepared pans. Press mixture with a spoon to firm bottom. Beat cream cheese until fluffy. Add condensed milk and ½ c. of the berries and mix until well blended. Fold in whipped cream. Spoon evenly into baking cups. Freeze for at least 5 hours. When ready to serve, remove liners. Place cakes onto individual serving plates. Garnish with remaining slices of strawberry. Serve promptly. Makes 12.

Spicy Carrot Cupcakes

2 c. flour
2 t. baking soda
2 t. cinnamon
½ t. allspice
½ t. nutmeg
1 c. sugar
1 t. salt
4 eggs, beaten
1½ c. oil
3 c. grated carrots
1 c. chopped nuts
cream cheese frosting, **recipe follows**

Line 24 muffin tins with paper liners or grease. Set aside. Preheat oven to 350 degrees. Mix dry ingredients together and set aside. In another bowl blend wet ingredients and stir until smooth. Stir in carrots. Spoon batter into prepared pans, filling about 2/3 full. Bake for about 18 minutes or until toothpick inserted in center comes out clean. Cool on wire rack. Frost once cooled and top with chopped nuts. Store in fridge. Makes 24.

Frosting
8 oz. cream cheese
1 lb. powdered sugar
½ stick margarine
2 t. vanilla

Beat together until smooth.

Gingerbread Cupcakes

5 T. unsalted butter, softened
½ c. sugar
½ c. molasses
1 egg
1 egg yolk
1¼ c. all-purpose flour
1 T. cocoa powder
1 t. ginger, fresh grated preferred
1 t. cinnamon
½ t. allspice
½ t. nutmeg
¼ t. salt
1 t. baking soda
½ c. hot milk

Preheat the oven to 350 degrees. Grease or line with paper liners 12 muffin tins. Cream butter with the sugar. Add the molasses and the egg and egg yolk. Sift together the flour, cocoa powder, spices and salt. Dissolve the baking soda in the hot milk. Add the flour mixture to the creamed mixture and stir until just combined. Stir in the hot milk mixture. Pour the batter evenly into the prepared tins. Bake for 20 minutes or until slightly springy to the touch. Allow to cool a few minutes in the pan and remove to a rack to cool. Frost once cooled, cream cheese frosting preferred. Makes 12.

Molten Chocolate Cupcakes

1 c. unsalted butter or unsalted margarine
8 oz. semi-sweet chocolate chips, or bars, cut into bite-size chunks
5 large eggs
½ c. sugar
pinch of salt
4 t. flour

Garnish
1 (6 oz. container) raspberries, barely moistened and rolled in about
½ c. sugar right before serving

Adjust oven rack to middle position; heat oven to 450 degrees. Line 12 muffin tins with paper liners. Spray muffin papers with vegetable cooking spray. Melt butter and chocolate in a medium heat-proof bowl over a saucepan of simmering water; remove from heat. Beat eggs, sugar and salt with a hand mixer in a medium bowl until sugar dissolves. Beat egg mixture into chocolate until smooth. Beat in flour until just combined. Divide batter among muffin cups. Bake until batter puffs but center is not set, 8 to 10 minutes. Carefully lift cakes from tin and set on a work surface. Pull papers away from cakes and transfer cakes to dessert plates. Top each with sugared raspberries and serve immediately. Makes 12.

Note: You can throw these in the oven as you sit down for dinner and have them ready just in time.

Mint Surprise Cupcakes

2¼ c. all-purpose flour
2½ t. baking powder
1 t. salt
2/3 c. margarine, softened
1 c. brown sugar
¾ c. white sugar
2 eggs
1 t. vanilla extract
1¼ c. buttermilk
24 small chocolate covered mints, **like Junior Mints**

Preheat oven to 350 degrees. Grease 24 muffin cups, or use paper liners. Mix together the flour, baking powder and salt. Set aside. In a large bowl, cream together the margarine, brown sugar and white sugar until light and fluffy. Beat in the eggs one at a time, then stir in the vanilla. Beat in the flour mixture alternately with the milk, mixing just until incorporated. Fill each muffin cup 1/3 full, and place a mint in the center of each. Top with remaining batter until cups are 2/3 full. Bake in preheated oven for 18 to 20 minutes, or until golden brown, and tops spring back when lightly tapped. Makes 24.

Chessman Cupcakes

1 (18.25 oz. package) white cake mix
2 (9-inch) unbaked pie crusts
1 (10 oz. jar) jam, **any you like**

Preheat oven to 350 degrees. You will need 24 un-greased muffin tins for this recipe. (You may want to spray tops of muffin pans with nonstick cooking spray so cake does not stick). Prepare cake mix according to package directions; set aside. Roll out pastry dough to 1/8-inch thickness. Using a floured, round cookie cutter that is slightly bigger than the muffin cups, cut 24 circles of dough. Place one dough circle in each muffin cup, pressing dough gently into bottom and sides. Dough should come about halfway up the sides of each muffin cup. Place a rounded tablespoon of jam into each pastry-lined cup. Pour prepared cake batter into each cup over jam and pastry, filling just to the top of each cup. Bake in preheated oven for 25 to 30 minutes or until a toothpick inserted into the cake comes out clean. Let cool briefly in pans, then loosen with knife and remove cakes to wire rack to cool completely.

Classic White Cupcakes

1 c. sugar
½ c. butter
2 eggs
2 t. vanilla extract
1½ c. all-purpose flour
1¾ t. baking powder
½ c. milk

Preheat oven to 350 degrees. Line a muffin pan with 12paper liners. In a medium bowl, cream together the sugar and butter. Beat in the eggs, one at a time, then stir in the vanilla. Combine flour and baking powder, add to the creamed mixture and mix well. Finally stir in the milk until batter is smooth. Pour or spoon batter into the prepared pan. Bake 20 to 25 minutes. Cupcakes are done when they springs back to the touch. Makes 12.

Sour Cream Lemon Cupcakes

1 c. butter or margarine, softened
2 c. sugar
3 eggs
2 t. grated lemon peel
1 t. vanilla extract
3½ c. all-purpose flour
1 t. baking soda
½ t. each baking powder and salt
2 c. sour cream

Frosting
9 T. butter or margarine, softened
6¾ c. confectioners' sugar
6 T. lemon juice
1 T. vanilla extract
¾ t. grated lemon peel
3 T. milk

In a mixing bowl, cream butter and sugar. Beat in eggs, one at a time. Add lemon peel and vanilla; mix well. Combine dry ingredients; add to creamed mixture alternately with sour cream (batter will be thick). Fill 30 greased or paper-lined muffin cups with ¼ c. of batter. Bake at 350 degrees for 25-30 minutes or until a toothpick inserted near the center comes out clean. Cool for 10 minutes; remove to wire racks to cool completely. For frosting, cream butter and sugar in a small mixing bowl. Add lemon juice, vanilla, lemon peel and milk; beat until smooth. Frost cupcakes. Makes 30.

Coconut Orange Cupcakes

1 c. sugar
2/3 c. vegetable oil
2 eggs
1 c. orange juice
3 c. all-purpose flour
1 T. baking powder
1 t. baking soda
¾ t. salt
1 (11 oz. can) mandarin oranges, drained
1 c. vanilla or white chips

Topping
1 c. flaked coconut
1/3 c. sugar
2 T. butter, melted

In a mixing bowl, combine the sugar, oil, eggs and orange juice; mix well. Combine dry ingredients; stir into orange juice mixture just until moistened. Fold in oranges and chips. Fill 24 greased or paper-lined muffin cups two-thirds full. Combine topping ingredients; sprinkle over cupcakes. Bake at 375 degrees for 15-20 minutes or until golden brown. Makes 24.

Banana Cupcakes

½ c. shortening
1½ c. sugar
2 eggs
1 t. vanilla extract
1 c. mashed ripe bananas
¼ c. buttermilk
2 c. all-purpose flour
1 t. baking powder
¾ t. baking soda
½ t. salt

Frosting
½ c. butter or margarine, softened
2½ c. confectioners' sugar
3 T. milk

In a large mixing bowl, cream shortening and sugar. Add the eggs, vanilla, bananas and buttermilk. Combine the flour, baking powder, baking soda and salt; add to banana mixture. Fill 18 paper-lined muffin cups two-thirds full. Bake at 350 degrees for 15-20 minutes or until a toothpick comes out clean. Remove to wire racks to cool completely. In a small mixing bowl, cream the butter, sugar and enough milk to achieve desired spreading consistency. Frost cupcakes. Makes 18.

Spicy Pumpkin Cupcakes

1 c. all-purpose flour
¾ c. whole wheat flour, whole wheat pastry flour preferred
1 t. each baking powder and baking soda
½ t. each salt and ground cinnamon
¼ t. ground nutmeg
2 eggs, lightly beaten
1 c. canned pumpkin
½ c. vegetable oil
½ c. honey
1/3 c. water
½ c. each chopped walnuts and miniature chocolate chips

In a large bowl, combine the first seven ingredients. Combine the eggs, pumpkin, oil, honey and water; mix well. Stir into dry ingredients just until combined; fold in walnuts and chocolate chips. Fill greased or foil-lined muffin cups three-fourths full. Bake at 350 degrees for 20-25 minutes or until a toothpick comes out clean. Cool for 10 minutes before removing from pans to wire racks to cool completely. Makes 15.

Rich Chocolate Sour Cream Cupcakes

1 devil's food cake mix
2 T. unsweetened cocoa
1 c. sour cream
½ c. oil, I like olive oil
½ c. water
3 eggs
2 t. vanilla

Preheat oven to 350 degrees. Line 18-20 muffin pans with paper liners and set aside. Combine cake mix with remaining ingredients and beat on low 1 minute. Scrape down sides of bowl and beat on high for 2 minutes more. Fill muffin pans with batter about ¾ full. Bake 28-30 minutes using a toothpick to test for doneness. Cool before frosting. Makes 18-20.

Mocha Cupcakes

¼ c. butter, softened
2/3 c. sugar
1 egg
½ t. vanilla extract
14 T. all-purpose flour
¼ c. baking cocoa
½ t. each baking soda and salt
¼ t. each baking powder and cinnamon
¼ c. strong brewed coffee, room temperature
3 T. buttermilk
1 c. prepared chocolate frosting
¾ t. instant coffee granules
1 t. hot water

In a small mixing bowl, cream the butter and sugar. Beat in egg and vanilla. Combine the flour, cocoa, baking soda, salt, baking powder and cinnamon; add to creamed mixture alternately with coffee and buttermilk. Coat muffin cups with nonstick cooking spray or use paper liners; fill half full with batter. Bake at 350 degrees for 18-20 minutes or until a toothpick comes out clean. Cool for 5 minutes before removing from pan to a wire rack to cool completely. Place the frosting in a bowl. Dissolve coffee granules in hot water; stir into frosting until smooth. Frost cupcakes. Makes 8.

Strawberry Cupcakes

2/3 c. whole fresh or frozen strawberries, thawed
1½ c. all-purpose flour, sifted
1 t. baking powder
¼ t. coarse salt
¼ c. whole milk, room temperature
1 t. pure vanilla extract
½ c. (1 stick) unsalted butter, room temperature
1 c. sugar
1 large egg, room temperature
2 large egg whites, room temperature

Preheat oven to 350 degrees. Line a 12-cup muffin tin with cupcake liners; set aside. Place strawberries in a small food processor; process until pureed. You should have about 1/3 c. of puree, add a few more strawberries if necessary or save any extra puree for frosting; set aside. In a medium bowl, whisk together flour, baking powder, and salt; set aside. In a small bowl, mix together milk, vanilla, and strawberry puree; set aside. In the bowl of an electric mixer fitted with the paddle attachment, cream butter on medium-high speed, until light and fluffy. Gradually add sugar and continue to beat until well combined and fluffy. Reduce the mixer speed to medium and slowly add egg and egg whites until just blended.

With the mixer on low, slowly add half the flour mixture; mix until just blended. Add the milk mixture; mix until just blended. Slowly add remaining flour mixture, scraping down sides of the bowl with a spatula, as necessary, until just blended.

Divide batter evenly among prepared muffin cups. Transfer muffin tin to oven and bake until tops are just dry to the touch, 22 to 25 minutes. Transfer muffin tin to a wire rack and let cupcakes cool completely in tin before icing. Makes 12.

Favorite Creamy Icing

½ c. shortening
½ c. margarine
1 c. powdered sugar
1 small can evaporated milk (5-6 oz.)
1 t. vanilla

Beat together shortening, margarine and sugar. Beat until smooth. Add milk and vanilla and beat until all traces of milk are gone.

Cream Cheese Frosting

8 oz. cream cheese
1 lb. powdered sugar
½ stick margarine
2 t. vanilla

Beat together until smooth.

Mocha Frosting

1 t. instant coffee granules
¼ c. milk
¼ c. unsweetened cocoa powder
6 T. butter
1½ t. vanilla extract
5 c. confectioners' sugar

Mix together; instant coffee or leftover coffee, milk, cocoa powder, butter or margarine, vanilla extract, and confectioners' sugar until of spreading consistency. Makes more than enough to frost 24 cupcakes.

Easy Chocolate Butter Cream

6 T. butter or margarine, softened
1/3-¾ c. cocoa, depending on how dark you want your frosting.
2 2/3 c. powdered sugar
1/3 c. milk
1 t. vanilla

Cream butter. Combine cocoa and sugar. Beat cocoa mixture in alternately with the milk until frosting is spreading consistency. Beat in vanilla. You may need an additional tablespoon of milk. Makes about 2 cups.

Creamy Chocolate Frosting

1 c. semi-sweet chocolate chips
4 T. butter
½ c. sour cream
1 t. vanilla extract
¼ t. salt
2¾ c. confectioners' sugar

Melt chocolate and the butter together. Let cool and blend in the sour cream, vanilla, and salt. Gradually add the confectioner's sugar until the frosting is of spreading consistency, beat well.

Chocolate Silk Frosting

2 2/3 c. confectioners' sugar
2/3 c. butter, softened
2 (1 oz. squares) each, unsweetened chocolate, melted
¾ t. vanilla extract
2 T. milk

In a medium bowl, blend confectioner's sugar, butter, melted chocolate and vanilla on low speed. Increase speed to high. Gradually add milk; beat until smooth and fluffy.

Crunchy Chocolate Peanut Butter Frosting

2 c. sugar
2 T. unsweetened cocoa powder
¾ c. evaporated milk
1 t. vanilla extract
2 c. crunchy peanut butter

Combine the sugar, cocoa, and milk in a medium saucepan. Bring to a boil, and cook for 3 minutes. Stir in the vanilla and peanut butter. Mix well. Spread over hot cake while frosting is also still hot. Let frosted cake cool before cutting.

Caramel Frosting

½ c. butter
1 c. packed brown sugar
¼ t. salt
6 T. milk
3 c. sifted confectioners' sugar

Melt butter in a saucepan, stir in the brown sugar and the salt. Bring to a boil and boil for 2 minutes, stirring constantly. Remove from heat and add the milk, stirring all the while. Return to heat and bring to a boil again. Remove from heat and allow to cool until lukewarm (approximately 20 to 25 minutes). Stir in the confectioners' sugar and beat until smooth and cool enough to spread. You might need to add a few drops of milk if frosting gets too stiff.

Cooked Custard Frosting

1 c. milk
2 T. all-purpose flour
1 c. butter, softened
1 c. white sugar
1 t. vanilla extract

Whisk milk into flour in small saucepan until smooth. Heat and stir until it boils and thickens. Cool thoroughly. Cream butter, sugar and vanilla in bowl until light and fluffy. Add thickened milk. Beat until mixture resembles whipped cream. Makes enough to frost 24 cupcakes, about 3½ cups.

Easy Chocolate-Peanut Butter Frosting

12 oz. semi-sweet chocolate chips
½ c. peanut butter

Melt both together in microwave and stir until smooth. Spread while warm on bar cookies, brownies or cookies. Firms up at it cools.

Easy Vanilla Frosting

¾ c. butter
6 c. confectioners' sugar
1/3 c. milk
1½ t. vanilla extract
¼ t. salt
2 T. milk

Beat butter in a large bowl until fluffy. Gradually add 3 c. of the sifted confectioners' sugar, beating well. Slowly beat in the vanilla, salt, and 1/3 c. of the milk. Gradually beat in the 3 remaining c. of confectioner's sugar. Beat in additional milk (1 to 2 T.) if needed, to make frosting of spreading consistency. If desired tint the frosting with 6 to 8 drops of food coloring.

Classic Butter Cream

1/3 c. butter
4½ c. sifted confectioners' sugar
¼ c. milk
1½ t. vanilla extract

In a bowl beat butter or margarine until fluffy. Gradually add 2 c. of the confectioners' sugar, beating well. Slowly beat in the ¼ milk and vanilla. Slowly beat in remaining sugar. Beat in additional milk, if needed, to make of spreading consistency. Tint with food color, if desired.

Chocolate Cream Cheese Frosting

1 (8 oz. package) cream cheese
¼ c. confectioners' sugar
¼ c. heavy whipping cream
1 c. semi-sweet chocolate chips

In double boiler melt chips and add heavy cream, mix until smooth take off of heat. In mixing bowl cream together sugar and cream cheese until smooth, slowly add chocolate mixture. Mixture will thicken up as the chocolate cools.

Super Fluffy Frosting

1 c. shortening
½ c. butter
1½ T. vanilla extract
2 lbs. confectioners' sugar
1/8 t. salt
4 T. water or milk

In a heavy duty mixer combine the shortening, butter or margarine, vanilla and water or milk. Add the sugar and salt, beat until well mixed. Add a tablespoon or two more of water or milk if needed. Turn mixer to the highest speed and beat for 15 minutes.

Pink Lemonade Frosting

2 c. heavy whipping cream
2 T. white sugar
3 fluid ounces frozen pink lemonade concentrate, thawed

In a large glass, metal or ceramic bowl beat whipping cream, sugar, and pink lemonade until fluffy and peaks form. Use immediately.

Strawberry Frosting

½ c. whole frozen strawberries, thawed
1 c. (2 sticks) unsalted butter, firm and slightly cold
pinch of coarse salt
3½ c. confectioners' sugar, sifted
½ t. pure vanilla extract

Place strawberries in the bowl of a small food processor; process until pureed. In the bowl of an electric mixer fitted with the paddle attachment, beat together butter and salt on medium speed until light and fluffy. Reduce mixer speed and slowly add confectioners' sugar; beat until well combined. Add vanilla and 3 T. strawberry puree (save any remaining strawberry puree for another use); mix until just blended. Frosting consistency should be dense and creamy, like ice cream. Makes enough for 1 dozen cupcakes.

Finishing Touches

Novelty cupcakes are all the rage. Animals are fun. For cats, dogs, pigs, cows etc use jelly beans, small chocolate covered mints, chocolate- covered raisins for noses. Eyes can be raisins, Craisins, M&M's, chocolate chips or any small candy. Spots can be mini-chips and whiskers can be string licorice or pretzel sticks. Ears can be frosting, rolled out Tootsie Rolls or caramels, pieces of cookies. Starburst candies (red or pink) can be rolled out and cut for tongues and fruit roll-up also make great tongues. You can just pile up frosting for snouts but I like to put pieces of marshmallow underneath and frost over. Use decorating tips for different types of fur and don't be afraid to tint frosting for blue dogs or pink kitties.

Make a bouquet of cupcakes-using a star tip start on the outside making a circle of petals. Then make the next circle of petals nearer the middle. Continue until the cupcake is covered in "petals". Finish with a small candy center or even a dusting of cinnamon or dried orange peel for pollen. You can mix colors, add leaves and play with different decorator tips.

Frosting is one way to top cupcakes but you can also use powder sugar glazes, powdered sugar, hot cocoa mix, cinnamon sugar or even powdered sugar with some cinnamon or cocoa powder in it. You can also use sweetened whipping cream and add a strawberry on top for a cassata cupcake.

If you are frosting the cupcakes you can tint a white frosting or use juice to tint the frosting when you are mixing it. Don't forget you can also use different extracts to make your frosting a different flavor. Nut extracts, mint and fruit flavorings are all good choices.

For a nice finish use a pastry bag and decorative tip the make your cupcakes look professional. You can also place two different frostings in the piping bag and get a two-toned frosting.

You can use the creamy filling in the Twinkle cupcakes for any cupcake you want to be cream-filled.

For a Boston Cream cupcakes just fill cooled vanilla cupcakes with a little prepared vanilla pudding. Cut a little hole in the bottom of the paper liner and use a piping bag to squeeze in the pudding. Soften chocolate frosting (canned or homemade) in the microwave a little and spread in the center of the cupcakes.

Have fun with decorating. You can top the frosted cupcake with sprinkles, fresh or dried fruit, nuts, chopped or whole, Maraschino cherries, small candies, powdered cocoa, cinnamon sugar, candy kisses, M&M's, grated citrus peel, fresh or candied flowers (make sure they have been grown without pesticides) or whatever else suits your taste.

Get seasonal. By using candy corn, jelly beans, seasonal M&M's etc. you can make cupcakes for any occasion or holiday.

Cupcakes on a tiered tray can be served as the cake for special occasions. They are easy for serving and for sending home with guests.

Cupcake only bakeries are springing up and can charge several dollars for a single cupcake!

If you are using canned frosting they can be whipped to make them fluffier and to increase the volume.

You can freeze cupcakes. If they are frosted place cupcakes on a plate or tray and place in the freezer until solid. Remove from the tray and wrap in a freezer-proof wrap. When ready to defrost remove or loosen covering and allow to thaw at room temperature. You can also place the cupcakes in a storage container with a tight fitting lid (Tupperware or Rubbermaid) and place in freezer. Thaw in the container. The reason for leaving them in the container to defrost is that condensation will take place on the container, not the cupcakes. If removed from their container to defrost they will become soggy. Cupcakes should be used with 3 months of freezing for best quality.

A serving of cupcakes is two.

For extra fun look for decorated papers. You can get holiday designs, bright colors, browns and foils. Check out cake and candy-making stores in your area for more choices

Speaking of cake decorating stores, they are also good sources for novelty sprinkles and toppings like candy flowers and other edible decorations.

Every Spring, I candy violets for later use in decoration. Just take clean dry violet blossoms (organic only) rinse and dry and set on paper toweling. In small bowl mix up powdered eggs whites according to package directions. In small bowl place extra fine or granulated sugar, gently dip violet blossom in egg mixture and then mix in the sugar. Place on paper toweling and repeat with remaining flowers. Leave flowers to dry for a couple of weeks or until brittle. Remove them to an airtight container and use them whenever you want an elegant finish for cupcakes and other baked goods.

Chapter 24:
Gifts from the Kitchen

Multi Bean Soup Mix

For 12 gifts you will need:

1 case of pint canning jars. (with lids and rings or 12 cellophane bags and ribbon)
24 c. of assorted dry beans
labels and directions
herb packets

Get as many types of beans as you can find at the grocery store. When estimating how many bags you will need to get, a 1 lb. bag of most beans fills a pint jar with a little extra, however lentils and split peas under fill the same jar. I get 13 lbs. for good measure and if I have some left over I save it for the next batch or for home use. I've also found that it usually takes a couple of stores to find a decent assortment of beans. Look for a variety of colors and sizes. Some of the things I try to include are: black beans, large and small limas, navy beans, yellow and green split peas, pinto beans, cranberry beans, black-eyed peas, brown and red lentils and kidney beans. Get a large bowl and add the beans. I usually have an empty jar and hand and measure as I go. Counting how many jars of beans I've placed in the bowl as I empty them into the jar and then empty the jar into the bowl. Measure a little generously, though. Small legumes tend to fill in spaces when several types are mixed and so 12 jars mysteriously become 11. It's more of a general guide than a precise measure. Mix the beans well and scoop them into the jars, adding the lids as you go. You could also use cellophane bags and ties instead of jars, if you like.

Herb Packets
12 lollipop bags
12 labels

and

¾ c. parsley flakes
½ c. dried diced onion
2 T. dried savory
1 T. dried oregano
1 T. dried marjoram
1 T. dried thyme
1 T. dried minced garlic
1 t. powdered bay leaf

You can adjust the herbs to taste or use what you have on hand. Other herbs or seasonings you could add would be basil, mint, chili powder, cumin or rosemary to name but a few. The blend recipe given is a mix of flavors I happen to like. Savory is sometimes called the "bean herb" because its flavor complements legumes. Thyme is also similar in flavor. Anyway, mix the herbs well and divide the mixture in the 12 bags. Use a couple of slightly rounded tablespoons per bag, depending on how powdered your herbs are. Fold over the labels and staple. Punch a hole in the corner of the label and affix to jar with stretchy loop or raffia or twine or even thin ribbon.

The Labels

I make labels that are the same size as 2 business cards. On the front add your own graphic and on the back the directions for the soup. The print on the back will have to be small.

Directions to include with soup mix:
Rinse beans and pick over. Place beans in large kettle of cold water and bring to the boil. Boil 3 minutes and remove from the heat. Let stand 1 hour then drain and rinse beans. Return beans to pot and add enough water to cover and simmer until beans are tender, about 2-3 hours. Meanwhile in large pot in 2 T. oil sauté 1 large onion (chopped) until tender. Add beans with water and 1 (28 oz. can) diced tomatoes. Add seasoning packet, water or broth if needed and salt and pepper to taste. Serves 6-8.

Horseradish Mustard

1 c. dry mustard
¾ c. white wine vinegar
1/3 c. dry white wine or dry sherry
¼ c. brown sugar
¼ c. granulated sugar
1 T. dried minced onion
2 t. caraway seeds
1½ t. salt
¼ t. coarse ground mustard
2 eggs, slightly beaten
1 T. prepared horseradish

Combine all ingredients, except eggs and horseradish in top of double boiler and let stand at room temperature for 2 hours. Whisk in eggs and cook over simmering water until mixture has thickened and eggs are cooked, about 10 minutes. Remove from heat and stir in horseradish. Pour into sterilized jar, cool and cover. Store in fridge for up to 3 months. Makes 2 cups.

Bavarian Mustard

¾ c. beer
2/3 c. dry mustard
2 T. sugar
2 T. cider vinegar
2 t. salt
1 t. celery seeds
½ t. fresh grated ginger or ¼ t. dry
1 egg, beaten

Combine all but the egg in the top of a double boiler and let stand 2 hours at room temperature. Stir in egg and cook over simmering water. Stirring constantly until mixture thickens and egg is cooked, about 10 minutes. Pour into sterilized jars and cool before covering. Store in fridge for up to 2 months. Makes 2 cups.

Spicy Mustard

1 c. dry mustard
2/3 c. dry white wine
½ c. vinegar, flavored with herbs or garlic
½ c. sugar
2 t. salt
1 t. basil
1 t. chili powder
1 t. dried minced garlic
1 t. oregano
½ t. cracked pepper
2 eggs, slightly beaten

Mix all ingredients, except eggs, in top of double boiler and let stand 2 hours at room temperature. Add eggs and cook over simmering water, stirring constantly until mixture thickens and eggs are cooked, about 10 minutes. Pour into sterilized jars and cool down before covering and refrigerating. Keeps in fridge for up to 2-3 months. Makes 2 cups.

French Herb Mustard

¼ c. dry mustard
¼ c. white wine vinegar
¼ c. white wine or dry sherry
¼ c. brown sugar
½ t. salt
½ t. tarragon
¼ t. dill seed
¼ t. celery seed
¼ t. ground cloves
3 egg yolks or 1 whole egg

Combine all ingredients, except eggs, in top of double boiler and let stand at room temperature 2 hours. Whisk in eggs and cook over simmering water, stirring constantly, until mustard thickens and eggs are cooked, about 5 minutes. Store in crock or jar in fridge for up to 1 month. Makes 1 cup, recipe can be doubled.

Sugared Nuts

4½ c. nuts
2 c. sugar
1 c. water
1 t. cinnamon
1 t. orange peel

Place all ingredients in heavy skillet and cook over medium heat stirring, often until all the water disappears. Whatever liquid in the pan will be clinging to the nuts and syrupy. Dump nuts onto 2 cookie sheets and break apart with wooden spoon to prevent clumping. As nuts cool, stir once or twice to remove any remaining clumps and to cool faster. Nuts will lose their glossy appearance and attain a sugary crust. If it looks like nut soup, you didn't cook them long enough, and must return all to the skillet and cook longer. As the nuts start to get drier during cooking, you can turn down the heat a little to prevent burning. Once you've made a few batches, though you will get good at judging when to stop cooking.

Store in an air tight container in a cool place for up to a month and they can be frozen for up to 6 months.

Note: If you like hot/sweet flavors you can add 1 t. hot sauce, or more to taste, to the nuts when you start cooking.

Candied Cashews

1 lb. cashews, preferably raw
2 egg whites
½ c. sugar
½ c. brown sugar
½ t. cinnamon
1 stick butter or margarine

Place cashews on jelly roll pan and warm in a 325 degree oven for about 10 minutes. Meanwhile, beat egg whites until stiff. Combine sugars and cinnamon and fold into the egg whites. Remove nuts from oven and fold into egg white mixture. Melt butter or margarine and pour in the jelly roll pan used to warm nuts. Spread nut mixture evenly in prepared pan and bake 30 minutes, stirring once every 10 minutes.

Seasoned Almonds

¼ c. butter or margarine
2 t. salt
1 t. garlic powder
1 t. onion powder
1 t. Worcestershire sauce
1 t. chili powder
dash cayenne
4-5 c. almonds

Melt butter or margarine and toss with the seasonings. Toss in nuts until evenly coated. Place in jelly roll pan and bake in a 300 degree oven for 20 -25 minutes, stirring once or twice. Cool and store in airtight container for up to a month or can be frozen for up to 6 months.

Sweet and Savory Nuts

¼ c. butter or margarine
1 t. salt
1 t. parsley
1 t. savory, powdered
¼ c. sugar
4 c. nuts, any type

Melt butter or margarine and combine with seasonings and sugar. Toss with nuts in bowl and spread on baking sheet. Bake in a 350 degree oven for 15 minutes, stirring once. Store cooled nuts in an airtight container for 1 month or can be frozen for up to 6 months.

Citrus Sugar

1 c. sugar
1 T. orange, lemon, lime or tangerine peel
½ t. cinnamon
½ t. nutmeg
1/8 t. allspice

Mix all ingredients and place in pie pan. Place in a preheated 200 degree oven for 15 minutes, stirring every 5 minutes. Cool sugar before storing in airtight jar or you can powder the sugar in a blender for 10 seconds or so before storing. Use in tea, on sugar cookies, on toast and bagels or with fresh fruit and yogurt.

Note: You can also make a citrus mint variation by combining sugar with citrus peel and 1 T. dried mint leaves, omitting other flavorings. This sugar is great in lemonades and iced teas.

Sesame Salt

1 c. sesame seeds
¼ c. salt
1 t. paprika
1 t. onion powder
¼ t. pepper
¼ t. garlic powder

In skillet over medium heat toast sesame seeds, stirring or tossing to cook evenly until seeds are light brown. Stir in salt and cook 5 minutes more. Cool mixture completely and add remaining ingredients. Process in blender or spice grinder until mixture in powdered. Makes ¾ c. Excellent with vegetables, stir-fries, salad dressings etc.

Caramel-Coated Pears

4-5 medium ripe pears
4-5 wooded sticks
8 oz. caramels
6 oz. chocolate flavored candy coating
1/3 c. desired topping such as chopped nuts, chopped toasted, hulled pumpkin seeds, candy sprinkles, etc.

Wash and dry pears and remove stems. Insert sticks through top of pears. Melt caramels over low heat and dip pears, one at a time to cover pears about ¾ of the way up. Set pears on greased wax paper to cool. Melt chocolate coating over medium low heat, stirring often to avoid burning. Dip cooled pears in chocolate, but do not completely cover caramel. Dip pears in decorations to coat, leaving half of the chocolate uncovered. Chill pears in fridge to set chocolate. Wrap in cellophane or plastic wrap and keep chilled. Makes 4-5.

Italian Seasoning

½ c. dried basil
½ c. dried oregano
2 T. onion powder or 3 T. dried minced onion
2 T. garlic powder or 3 T. dried minced garlic
2 T. marjoram
1 T. dried rosemary
1 T. dried parsley
1 t. crushed red pepper

Use this blend in spaghetti sauce or other Italian dishes. Also, you can add to vinegar and oil with a little salt, if desired, to make a quick salad dressing.

Salad Herbs

½ c. dried parsley
¼ c. dried minced onion
1 T. dried thyme
1 T. celery seeds
2 t. dried oregano
1 t. dried marjoram
1 t. dill seeds

Combine all ingredients and store in a cool, dry, dark place. If you like the herbs can be combined in a blender and powdered, then used as an herb shake. Powdered herbs should be kept refrigerated to keep flavor longer. Makes about 1 cup.

To use: Add to vinegar and oil for a quick salad dressing or add to steamed, boiled and stir fried vegetables. Also good with dairy products. For a simple cheese ball add 1-2 t. of the herb blend along with a dash of pepper, a diced green onion and a tablespoon of mayo to 8 oz. of cream cheese for a great cheese ball. Chill before serving.

Creole Spice

1 t. each black, red and white pepper
½ t. thyme
¼ t. dry mustard
¼ t. mace
1 bay leaf, crumbled fine or powdered

Combine all ingredients and store in a cool dry place. Use sparingly, it is HOT!

Pizza Seasoning

3 T. dried basil
2 T. dried oregano
1 T. red pepper flakes
1 T. dried minced onion
1 T. fennel seeds
1 t. garlic powder

Combine all ingredients and store in a cool, dark, dry place.

To use: Add 1-2 t. per cup of tomato sauce to make pizza sauce. Also good sprinkled on bagels with sauce and cheese or added to any tomato or pepper dish. Also makes a great cheese ball. Add 1-2 t. of the seasoning with a little diced sweet red pepper, a diced green onion and a few slices of cooked, crumbled bacon or turkey bacon with 8-oz. cream cheese.

Poultry Seasoning

3 T. dried thyme
2 T. each dried marjoram and dried rosemary
1 T. each dried sage and dried savory
2 t. celery seeds
½ t. each ground allspice and dried oregano
¼ t. pepper

Whirl ingredients in a blender until powdered. Store cool and dry.

To use: Add to poultry dishes, stuffing, gravies, and in chicken soup.

Curry Powder

2 t. ground cumin
2 t. ground coriander
2 t. ground turmeric
1 t. nutmeg
1 t. salt
½ t. cinnamon
¼ t. cayenne pepper
¼ t. ground black pepper

Combine all ingredients and store in a cool, dry place.

Hot Cocoa Mix

2½ c. nonfat dry milk
1 c. cocoa
1 c. sugar
½ c. non-dairy powdered creamer
¼ t. salt
1 c. mini marshmallows (optional)

In large bowl, mix all ingredients well. Store in an airtight jar and use within 6 months. To use, add 5 T. to 8 ounces boiling water.

Variation: Flavor with cinnamon, instant coffee or even dried orange peel.

Coffee Liqueur

3¾ c. sugar
1 qt. water
1 qt. vodka
6 T. instant coffee
1 (2-inch) vanilla bean
2 t. glycerin

Bring sugar and water to boil. When sugar has dissolved remove from heat, stir in coffee powder and stir to dissolve. Cool completely. Add remaining ingredients and mature at least a month.

Variation: Add 2 (4-inch) cinnamon sticks for cinnamon coffee-flavored liqueur.

Herb Vinegars

You will need:

A clean jar or bottle with a tight-fitting lid
Fresh or dried herbs
Vinegar, any flavor but must be 5% acidity
Food grade cheesecloth or coffee filters
Decorative jars or bottles

Nice extras: Whole garlic cloves, hot peppers, fruit, edible flowers or herb sprigs

For herb vinegar you need 2 c. of vinegar for each cup of fresh herbs or each 1/3 c. of dried herbs. Place herbs in jar and pour over the vinegar. Screw on lid and store in a cool, dry place for 10 days or longer. You can then strain out the herbs and pour the vinegar through a filter- lined strainer. You can use the cheesecloth or coffee filters. Vinegar will be completely clear. Now just bottle your herb vinegar in a pretty bottle and seal. You can make your own decorative labels or even seal with paraffin. You can add garlic (6-8 cloves per quart) to your vinegar, before or after filtering for flavor. You can also add hot peppers to spice it up. An edible flower like chive blossoms can be added for appearance or just a sprig of the fresh herb. Lemon or orange peel in a thin strip adds flavor and looks nice as well as raspberries or blackberries.

Some good herbs for vinegar include: basil, dill, fennel, chives (blossoms), garlic chives (blossoms), marjoram, mint, rosemary, sage, tarragon, thyme and lavender. This, of course, is only a partial list and you can use other herbs that you like.

You can also make herb vinegar by placing herb sprigs and flowers in a pretty bottle then filling with vinegar. Seal and decorate bottle before giving as a gift.

To use paraffin to seal your bottle: Always melt paraffin over hot water, never over direct heat or in a microwave. Place a ribbon over the top of the corked bottle, hanging down a couple of inches on each side. Tie this piece down with another piece of ribbon around the neck of the bottle. Now dip the bottle top in the melted paraffin and allow to cool. You can trim off some of the ribbon, but leave enough to get hold of. The ribbon becomes a means of easily unsealing the vinegar. Just pull on the ribbon to remove the wax.

Make your own labels and add a recipe or use ideas if you like. For color retention, vinegar should be refrigerated. Use within a year of making.

Orange and Rosemary Jelly

1½ c. boiling water
2 T. dried rosemary leaves or ¼ c. fresh
½ t. coriander seed, lightly crushed
1 (6 oz. can) frozen orange juice concentrate
1 box powdered pectin
¼ c. lemon juice
1 T. white vinegar
1/8 t. non-iodized salt
3¼ c. sugar

Pour boiling water over seasonings and allow to steep 10 minutes. Strain and discard rosemary and coriander. Re-measure and add water if needed to get 1¼ cup. Combine water with all remaining ingredients, except sugar and bring to a full rolling boil. Stir in sugar and bring back to a full boil. Skim off any foam and ladle into hot, clean jelly jars. Process in a boiling water bath for 5 minutes. Makes about 4 jars.

Grape and Thyme Jelly

1¼ c. boiling water
1 T. dried thyme or 3 T. fresh
1 bay leaf, crumbled
4 whole cloves
1 (6 oz. can) frozen white grape juice concentrate
1 box powdered pectin
3 T. cider vinegar
1/8 t. non-iodized salt
3½ c. sugar

Pour boiling water over seasonings and allow to stand 10 minutes. Strain and discard solids. Re-measure and add water if needed to have 1¼ cup. Mix water with all remaining ingredients, except sugar, and bring to a boil. Add sugar and return to the boil. Boil 1 minute. Remove from heat and skim off any foam. Ladle into clean, hot jelly glasses and process in a boiling water bath 5 minutes. Makes about 4.

Wine Jelly

3 c. wine
4½ c. sugar
2 (3 oz. pouches) liquid pectin

Combine wine and sugar in saucepan and bring nearly to a boil, stirring often. Remove from heat and stir in pectin. Stir for 1 minute. Ladle jelly into hot, clean jelly jars and place in a boiling water bath. Process 5 minutes. Makes about 5 jars.

About the Author

Judi is a lecturer and cooking instructor. She worked for the Extension Service in Cuyahoga County in the horticulture department. She also was the home-ec answer lady. She currently teaches classes for both adults and children throughout the Greater Cleveland area and conducts cooking camps for children in the summer months.

She is also the author of two books on herbs, *The Charmed Garden: An Introduction to Herb Gardening* and *The Charmed Kitchen: A Guide to Cooking with Herbs and Spices.*

She learned to bake from her late father who had been a professional baker. She also has been trained in food safety and food preservation.

www.ingramcontent.com/pod-product-compliance
Lightning Source LLC
Chambersburg PA
CBHW070040080526
44586CB00013B/866